The
Four
Gospels

THE TARCHER CORNERSTONE EDITIONS

Tao Te Ching
by Lao Tzu, translated by Jonathan Star

The Essential Marcus Aurelius
newly translated and introduced
by by Jacob Needleman and John P. Piazza

Accept This Gift: Selections from A Course in Miracles
edited by Frances Vaughan, Ph.D., and Roger Walsh, M.D., Ph.D.
foreword by Marianne Williamson

The Kybalion
by Three Initiates

The Spiritual Emerson
Essential Works by Ralph Waldo Emerson
introduction by Jacob Needleman

The Four Gospels
The Contemporary English Version
foreword by Phyllis Tickle

The Hermetica: The Lost Wisdom of the Pharaohs
Timothy Freke and Peter Gandy

Rumi: In the Arms of the Beloved
translations by Jonathan Star

JEREMY P. TARCHER/PENGUIN
a member of Penguin Group (USA) Inc.
New York

The
Four
Gospels

THE CONTEMPORARY
ENGLISH VERSION

AMERICAN BIBLE SOCIETY

Foreword by Phyllis Tickle

JEREMY P. TARCHER/PENGUIN
Published by the Penguin Group
Penguin Group (USA) Inc., 375 Hudson Street, New York, New York 10014, USA • Penguin
Group (Canada), 90 Eglinton Avenue East, Suite 700, Toronto, Ontario M4P 2Y3, Canada
(a division of Pearson Canada Inc.) • Penguin Books Ltd, 80 Strand, London WC2R 0RL, England •
Penguin Ireland, 25 St Stephen's Green, Dublin 2, Ireland (a division of Penguin Books Ltd) • Penguin
Group (Australia), 250 Camberwell Road, Camberwell, Victoria 3124, Australia (a division of Pearson
Australia Group Pty Ltd) • Penguin Books India Pvt Ltd, 11 Community Centre, Panchsheel Park, New
Delhi—110 017, India • Penguin Group (NZ), 67 Apollo Drive, Rosedale, North Shore 0632, New Zealand
(a division of Pearson New Zealand Ltd) • Penguin Books (South Africa) (Pty) Ltd, 24 Sturdee Avenue,
Rosebank, Johannesburg 2196, South Africa

Penguin Books Ltd, Registered Offices: 80 Strand, London WC2R 0RL, England

The American Bible Society is glad to grant authors and publishers the right to use up to one thousand (1,000) verses
from the *Contemporary English Version* text in church, religious, and other publications without the need to seek and
receive written permission. However, the extent of the quotation must not comprise a complete book nor should it
amount to more than 50 percent of the work. The proper copyright notice must appear on the title or copyright
page.

When quotations from *CEV* are used in a nonsaleable media, such as church bulletins, orders of service, posters,
transparencies, or similar media, a complete copyright notice is not required, but the initials (*CEV*) must appear at
the end of each quotation.

Requests for quotations in excess of one thousand (1,000) verses in any publication must be directed to, and written
approval received from, the American Bible Society, 1865 Broadway, New York, NY 10023.

Most Tarcher/Penguin books are available at special quantity discounts for bulk purchase for sales promotions,
premiums, fund-raising, and educational needs. Special books or book excerpts also can be created to fit specific
needs. For details, write Penguin Group (USA) Inc. Special Markets, 375 Hudson Street, New York, NY 10014.

Library of Congress Cataloging-in-Publication Data

Bible. N. T. Gospels. English. Contemporary English. 2008.
The Four Gospels : the Contemporary English Version / American Bible Society ; foreword by Phyllis Tickle.
p.   cm.
ISBN 978-1-58542-677-5
I. American Bible Society.   II. Title.
BS2553.C66   2008   2008028592
226'.05208—dc22

Printed in the United States of America
1   3   5   7   9   10   8   6   4   2

While the author has made every effort to provide accurate telephone numbers and Internet addresses at the time
of publication, neither the publisher nor the author assumes any responsibility for errors, or for changes that occur
after publication. Further, the publisher does not have any control over and does not assume any responsibility for
author or third-party websites or their content.

Contents

Foreword

There's an old folk saying in my part of the world which holds that there are not many things in this life that are true. More a cautionary tale than a comforting bit of wisdom, this particular aphorism always seems to me to contain a challenge as well. It almost taunts one, in fact, with an imperative to sally forth and find out what *is* true. It doesn't take much movement in that direction, however, before one makes another discomforting discovery.

There may or may not be many things in this life that are true, according to whether one's life view is that of an optimist or a pessimist. The unsettling part is that we rarely, if ever, know the whole truth of the things that are true. We know, for example, that Columbus sailed west and landed somewhere on the coast of what is now the Americas. We all can agree that that voyage made a monumental difference in world affairs; but none of us can ever be entirely sure about who sailed with him, or where precisely they first landed, or even if Columbus was the first European sailor to make landfall in that spot, wherever it was.

There are some things we do know, and irrefutably so. We

know that we are here now and that our being here is intimately connected to Columbus's having been here first. We know that the figure of Columbus and the stories about him are some of the tools by which we teach ourselves and our children who we are and should be. And we know, of course, that so long as some of us are professional historians, or amateur historians, or even members of historical book clubs and societies, then some of us are going to be a lot more aggressively sure of ourselves and the details than are the rest of us.

All of this is by way of saying that one does not need to be a Christian to know beyond any shadow of doubt that something happened two thousand years ago. There was a man who, at the very least, became a movement; and that man and movement so dramatically changed the courses of human affairs as to cause even the world itself to date our time from his coming.

We are where we are and as we are because of a pivotal land-fall in Roman Judea. For that reason, it is our story as well as the Nazarene's which is caught in these pages. The language used here makes that even more abundantly clear; for nowhere is our story so pleasingly told or so carefully rendered as it is in the *Contemporary English Version* from which this volume is drawn. The truth, then, is what these pages and their stories are. What each of us may choose or not choose to believe about them is, of course, left for each of us to decide.

—PHYLLIS TICKLE
Compiler, *The Words of Jesus:
A Gospel of the Sayings of Our Lord*

The
Four
Gospels

I.

Matthew

From the very beginning, Matthew celebrates Jesus as the Messiah who fulfills the Jewish Scriptures. Some scholars have called Matthew "the most Jewish" of the Gospels. The teachings of Jesus are presented in five speeches. This way of organizing Jesus' teachings would have made Jewish readers think of Moses, because their tradition taught that Moses wrote the five books of the Law (Torah). This similarity suggests that the author of Matthew is presenting Jesus as "the new Moses." The book also constantly refers to the Jewish Scriptures, uses a Jewish literary style, and employs number symbolism common in some Jewish circles at that time. Scholars also call Matthew "the Gospel of the church" because of the book's focus on Jesus as the risen Lord, on the kingdom of heaven, and on the church itself. In fact, Matthew is the only Gospel to use the Greek word for "church." Matthew often shows Jesus standing "outside of time," presenting both Jesus' ministry in the context of history and his glory as the eternal, resurrected Lord.

Outline

The Ancestors of Jesus
(Luke 3.23-38)

1 Jesus Christ came from the family of King David and also from the family of Abraham. And this is a list of his ancestors. 2-6a From Abraham to King David, his ancestors were:

Abraham, Isaac, Jacob, Judah and his brothers (Judah's sons were Perez and Zerah, and their mother was Tamar), Hezron;

Ram, Amminadab, Nahshon, Salmon, Boaz (his mother was Rahab), Obed (his mother was Ruth), Jesse, and King David.

6b-11 From David to the time of the exile in Babylonia, the ancestors of Jesus were:

David, Solomon (his mother had been Uriah's wife), Rehoboam, Abijah, Asa, Jehoshaphat, Jehoram;

Uzziah, Jotham, Ahaz, Hezekiah, Manasseh, Amon, Josiah, and Jehoiachin and his brothers.

12-16 From the exile to the birth of Jesus, his ancestors were:

Jehoiachin, Shealtiel, Zerubbabel, Abiud, Eliakim, Azor, Zadok, Achim;

Eliud, Eleazar, Matthan, Jacob, and Joseph, the husband of Mary, the mother of Jesus, who is called the Messiah.

17 There were fourteen generations from Abraham to David. There were also fourteen from David to the exile in Babylonia and fourteen more to the birth of the Messiah.

The Birth of Jesus
(Luke 2.1-7)

[18]This is how Jesus Christ was born. A young woman named Mary was engaged to Joseph from King David's family. But before they were married, she learned that she was going to have a baby by God's Holy Spirit. [19]Joseph was a good man[a] and did not want to embarrass Mary in front of everyone. So he decided to quietly call off the wedding.

[20]While Joseph was thinking about this, an angel from the Lord appeared to him in a dream. The angel said, "Joseph, the baby that Mary will have is from the Holy Spirit. Go ahead and marry her. [21]Then after her baby is born, name him Jesus,[b] because he will save his people from their sins."

[22]So the Lord's promise came true, just as the prophet had said, [23]"A virgin will have a baby boy, and he will be called Immanuel," which means "God is with us."

[24]After Joseph woke up, he and Mary were soon married, just as the Lord's angel had told him to do. [25]But they did not sleep together before her baby was born. Then Joseph named him Jesus.

The Wise Men

2 When Jesus was born in the village of Bethlehem in Judea, Herod was king. During this time some wise men[c] from the east came to Jerusalem [2]and said, "Where is the child born to be king of the Jews? We saw his star in the east[d] and have come to worship him."

[3]When King Herod heard about this, he was worried, and so was everyone else in Jerusalem. [4]Herod brought together the chief priests and the teachers of the Law of Moses and asked them, "Where will the Messiah be born?"

[5]They told him, "He will be born in Bethlehem, just as the prophet wrote,

[6]"Bethlehem in the land
    of Judea,
you are very important
    among the towns of Judea.

---

a1.19 *good man:* Or "kind man," or "man who always did the right thing."   b1.21 *name him Jesus:* In Hebrew the name "Jesus" means "the Lord saves."   c2.1 *wise men:* People famous for studying the stars.   d2.2 *his star in the east:* Or "his star rise."

From your town
will come a leader,
who will be like a shepherd
for my people Israel.' "

[7]Herod secretly called in the wise men and asked them when they had first seen the star. [8]He told them, "Go to Bethlehem and search carefully for the child. As soon as you find him, let me know. I also want to go and worship him."

[9]The wise men listened to what the king said and then left. And the star they had seen in the east went on ahead of them until it stopped over the place where the child was. [10]They were thrilled and excited to see the star.

[11]When the men went into the house and saw the child with Mary, his mother, they knelt down and worshiped him. They took out their gifts of gold, frankincense, and myrrh[e] and gave them to him. [12]Later they were warned in a dream not to return to Herod, and they went back home by another road.

The Escape to Egypt

[13]After the wise men had gone, an angel from the Lord appeared to Joseph in a dream and said, "Get up! Hurry and take the child and his mother to Egypt! Stay there until I tell you to return, because Herod is looking for the child and wants to kill him."

[14]That night, Joseph got up and took his wife and the child to Egypt, [15]where they stayed until Herod died. So the Lord's promise came true, just as the prophet had said, "I called my son out of Egypt."

The Killing of the Children

[16]When Herod found out that the wise men from the east had tricked him, he was very angry. He gave orders for his men to kill all the boys who lived in or near Bethlehem and were two years old and younger. This was based on what he had learned from the wise men.

[17]So the Lord's promise came true, just as the prophet Jeremiah had said,

---

e2.11 frankincense, and myrrh: Frankincense was a valuable powder that was burned to make a sweet smell. Myrrh was a valuable sweet-smelling powder often used in perfume.

[18]"In Ramah a voice was heard
    crying and weeping loudly.
Rachel was mourning
    for her children,
and she refused
to be comforted,
    because they were dead."

The Return from Egypt

[19]After King Herod died, an angel from the Lord appeared in a dream to Joseph while he was still in Egypt. [20]The angel said, "Get up and take the child and his mother back to Israel. The people who wanted to kill him are now dead."

[21]Joseph got up and left with them for Israel. [22]But when he heard that Herod's son Archelaus was now ruler of Judea, he was afraid to go there. Then in a dream he was told to go to Galilee, [23]and they went to live there in the town of Nazareth. So the Lord's promise came true, just as the prophet had said, "He will be called a Nazarene."[f]

The Preaching of John the Baptist
(Mark 1.1-8; Luke 3.1-18; John 1.19-28)

3 Years later, John the Baptist started preaching in the desert of Judea. [2]He said, "Turn back to God! The kingdom of heaven[g] will soon be here."[h]
[3]John was the one the prophet Isaiah was talking about, when he said,
"In the desert someone
    is shouting,
'Get the road ready
    for the Lord!
Make a straight path
    for him.'"

[4]John wore clothes made of camel's hair. He had a leather strap around his waist and ate grasshoppers and wild honey.

---

f2.23 He will be called a Nazarene: The prophet who said this is not known.   g3.2 kingdom of heaven: In the Gospel of Matthew "kingdom of heaven" is used with the same meaning as "God's kingdom" in Mark and Luke.   h3.2 will soon be here: Or "is already here."

⁵From Jerusalem and all Judea and from the Jordan River Valley crowds of people went to John. ⁶They told how sorry they were for their sins, and he baptized them in the river.

⁷Many Pharisees and Sadducees also came to be baptized. But John said to them:

> You bunch of snakes! Who warned you to run from the coming judgment? ⁸Do something to show you have really given up your sins. ⁹And don't start telling yourselves that you belong to Abraham's family. I tell you that God can turn these stones into children for Abraham. ¹⁰An ax is ready to cut the trees down at their roots. Any tree that doesn't produce good fruit will be chopped down and thrown into a fire.
>
> ¹¹I baptize you with water so you will give up your sins.ⁱ But someone more powerful is going to come, and I am not good enough even to carry his sandals.ʲ He will baptize you with the Holy Spirit and with fire. ¹²His threshing fork is in his hand, and he is ready to separate the wheat from the husks.ᵏ He will store the wheat in a barn and burn the husks in a fire that never goes out.

The Baptism of Jesus
(Mark 1.9-11; Luke 3.21, 22)

¹³Jesus left Galilee and went to the Jordan River to be baptized by John. ¹⁴But John kept objecting and said, "I ought to be baptized by you. Why have you come to me?"

¹⁵Jesus answered, "For now this is how it should be, because we must do all God wants us to do." Then John agreed.

¹⁶So Jesus was baptized. And as soon as he came out of the water, the sky opened, and he saw the Spirit of God coming down on him like a dove. ¹⁷Then a voice from heaven said, "This is my own dear Son, and I am pleased with him."

---

i3.11 so you will give up your sins: Or "because you have given up your sins." j3.11 carry his sandals: This was one of the duties of a slave. k3.12 His threshing fork is in his hand, and he is ready to separate the wheat from the husks: After Jewish farmers had trampled out the grain, they used a large fork to pitch the grain and the husks into the air. Wind would blow away the light husks, and the grain would fall back to the ground, where it could be gathered up.

Jesus and the Devil
(Mark 1.12,13; Luke 4.1-13)

4 The Holy Spirit led Jesus into the desert, so that the devil could test him. [2]After Jesus had gone without eating[1] for 40 days and nights, he was very hungry. [3]Then the devil came to him and said, "If you are God's Son, tell these stones to turn into bread."

[4]Jesus answered, "The Scriptures say:

'No one can live only on food.
People need every word
    that God has spoken.' "

[5]Next, the devil took Jesus into the holy city to the highest part of the temple. [6] The devil said, "If you are God's Son, jump off. The Scriptures say:

'God will give his angels
    orders about you.
They will catch you
    in their arms,
and you won't hurt
    your feet on the stones.'"

[7]Jesus answered, "The Scriptures also say, 'Don't try to test the Lord your God!'"

[8]Finally, the devil took Jesus up on a very high mountain and showed him all the kingdoms on earth and their power. [9]The devil said to him, "I will give all this to you, if you will bow down and worship me."

[10]Jesus answered, "Go away Satan! The Scriptures say:

'Worship the Lord your God
    and serve only him.'"

[11]Then the devil left Jesus, and angels came to help him.

14.2 without eating: The Jewish people sometimes went without eating (also called "fasting") to show their love for God or to show sorrow for their sins.

Jesus Begins His Work
(Mark 1.14,15; Luke 4.14,15)

[12]When Jesus heard that John had been put in prison, he went to Galilee. [13]But instead of staying in Nazareth, Jesus moved to Capernaum. This town was beside Lake Galilee in the territory of Zebulun and Naphtali.[m] [14]So God's promise came true, just as the prophet Isaiah had said,

[15]"Listen, lands of Zebulun
and Naphtali,
lands along the road
to the sea
and across the Jordan.
Listen Galilee,
land of the Gentiles!
[16]Although your people
live in darkness,
they will see
a bright light.
Although they live
in the shadow of death,
a light will shine
on them."

[17]Then Jesus started preaching, "Turn back to God! The kingdom of heaven will soon be here."[n]

Jesus Chooses Four Fishermen
(Mark 1.16-20; Luke 5.1-11)

[18]While Jesus was walking along the shore of Lake Galilee, he saw two brothers. One was Simon, also known as Peter, and the other was Andrew. They were fishermen, and they were casting their net into the lake. [19]Jesus said to them, "Follow me! I will teach you how to bring in people instead of fish." [20]Right then the two brothers dropped their nets and went with him.

m4.13 *Zebulun and Naphtali:* In Old Testament times these tribes were in northern Palestine, and in New Testament times many Gentiles lived where these tribes had once been.   n4.17 *The kingdom of heaven will soon be here:* See the two notes at 3.2.

[21]Jesus walked on until he saw James and John, the sons of Zebedee. They were in a boat with their father, mending their nets. Jesus asked them to come with him. [22]At once they left the boat and their father and went with Jesus.

Jesus Teaches, Preaches, and Heals

(Luke 6.17-19)

[23]Jesus went all over Galilee, teaching in their synagogues and preaching the good news about God's kingdom. He also healed every kind of disease and sickness. [24]News about him spread all over Syria, and people with every kind of sickness or disease were brought to him. Some of them had a lot of demons in them, others were thought to be crazy,[o] and still others could not walk. But Jesus healed them all.

[25]Large crowds followed Jesus from Galilee and the region around the ten cities known as Decapolis.[p] They also came from Jerusalem, Judea, and from across the Jordan River.

The Sermon on the Mount

5 When Jesus saw the crowds, he went up on the side of a mountain and sat down.[q]

Blessings

(Luke 6.20-23)

Jesus' disciples gathered around him, [2]and he taught them:

[3]God blesses those people
who depend only on him.
They belong to the kingdom
of heaven![r]
[4]God blesses those people
who grieve.
They will find comfort!
[5]God blesses those people

o4.24 thought to be crazy: In ancient times people with epilepsy were thought to be crazy. p4.25 the ten cities known as Decapolis: A group of ten cities east of Samaria and Galilee, where the people followed the Greek way of life. q5.1 sat down: Teachers in the ancient world, including Jewish teachers, usually sat down when they taught. r5.3 They belong to the kingdom of heaven: Or "The kingdom of heaven belongs to them."

who are humble.
The earth will belong
   to them!
⁶God blesses those people
who want to obey himˢ
   more than to eat or drink.
They will be given
   what they want!
⁷God blesses those people
   who are merciful.
They will be treated
   with mercy!
⁸God blesses those people
whose hearts are pure.
   They will see him!
⁹God blesses those people
   who make peace.
They will be called
   his children!
¹⁰God blesses those people
who are treated badly
   for doing right.
They belong to the kingdom
   of heaven.ᵗ

¹¹God will bless you when people insult you, mistreat you, and tell all kinds of evil lies about you because of me. ¹²Be happy and excited! You will have a great reward in heaven. People did these same things to the prophets who lived long ago.

Salt and Light
(Mark 9.50; Luke 14.34, 35)

¹³You are the salt for everyone on earth. But if salt no longer tastes like salt, how can it make food salty? All it is good for is to be thrown out and walked on.

---

s5.6 *who want to obey him:* Or "who want to do right" or "who want everyone to be treated right."
t5.10 *They belong to the kingdom of heaven:* See the note at 5.3.

¹⁴You are the light for the whole world. A city built on top of a hill cannot be hidden, ¹⁵and no one lights a lamp and put it under a clay pot. Instead, it is placed on a lampstand, where it can give light to everyone in the house. ¹⁶Make your light shine, so others will see the good you do and will praise your Father in heaven.

The Law of Moses

¹⁷Don't suppose I came to do away with the Law and the Prophets.ᵘ I did not come to do away with them, but to give them their full meaning. ¹⁸Heaven and earth may disappear. But I promise you not even a period or comma will ever disappear from the Law. Everything written in it must happen.

¹⁹If you reject even the least important command in the Law and teach others to do the same, you will be the least important person in the kingdom of heaven. But if you obey and teach others its commands, you will have an important place in the kingdom. ²⁰You must obey God's commands better than the Pharisees and the teachers of the Law obey them. If you don't, I promise you will never get into the kingdom of heaven.

Anger

²¹You know our ancestors were told, "Do not murder" and "A murderer must be brought to trial." ²²But I promise you if you are angry with someone,ᵛ you will have to stand trial. If you call someone a fool, you will be taken to court. And if you say that someone is worthless, you will be in danger of the fires of hell.

²³So if you are about to place your gift on the altar and remember that someone is angry with you, ²⁴leave your gift there in front of the altar. Make peace with that person, then come back and offer your gift to God.

²⁵Before you are dragged into court, make friends with the person who has accused you of doing wrong. If you don't, you will be

---

u5.17 the Law and the Prophets: The Jewish Scriptures, that is, the Old Testament.   v5.22 someone: In verses 22-24 the Greek text has "brother," which may refer to people in general or to other followers.

handed over to the judge and then to the officer who will put you in jail. [26]I promise you will not get out until you have paid the last cent you owe.

Marriage

[27]You know the commandment which says, "Be faithful in marriage." [28]But I tell you if you look at another woman and want her, you are already unfaithful in your thoughts. [29]If your right eye causes you to sin, poke it out and throw it away. It is better to lose one part of your body, than for your whole body to end up in hell. [30]If your right hand causes you to sin, chop it off and throw it away! It is better to lose one part of your body, than for your whole body to be thrown into hell.

Divorce
(Matthew 19.9; Mark 10.11,12; Luke 16.18)

[31]You have been taught that a man who divorces his wife must write out divorce papers for her.[w] [32]But I tell you not to divorce your wife unless she has committed some terrible sexual sin.[x] If you divorce her, you will cause her to be unfaithful, just as any man who marries her is guilty of taking another man's wife.

Promises

[33]You know our ancestors were told, "Don't use the Lord's name to make a promise unless you are going to keep it." [34]But I tell you not to swear by anything when you make a promise! Heaven is God's throne, so don't swear by heaven. [35]The earth is God's footstool, so don't swear by the earth. Jerusalem is the city of the great king, so don't swear by it. [36]Don't swear by your own head. You can-

---

w5.31 write out divorce papers for her: Jewish men could divorce their wives, but the women could not divorce their husbands. The purpose of writing these papers was to make it harder for a man to divorce his wife. Before this law was made, all a man had to do was to send his wife away and say that she was no longer his wife.   x5.32 some terrible sexual sin: This probably refers to the laws about the wrong kinds of marriages that are forbidden in Leviticus 18.6-18 or to some serious sexual sin.

The Four Gospels

not make one hair white or black. [37]When you make a promise, say only "Yes" or "No." Anything else comes from the devil.

Revenge
(Luke 6.29, 30)

[38]You know you have been taught, "An eye for an eye and a tooth for a tooth." [39]But I tell you not to try to get even with a person who has done something to you. When someone slaps your right cheek,[y] turn and let that person slap your other cheek. [40]If someone sues you for your shirt, give up your coat as well. [41]If a soldier forces you to carry his pack one mile, carry it two miles.[z] [42]When people ask you for something, give it to them. When they want to borrow money, lend it to them.

Love
(Luke 6.27, 28, 32-36)

[43]You have heard people say, "Love your neighbors and hate your enemies." [44]But I tell you to love your enemies and pray for anyone who mistreats you. [45]Then you will be acting like your Father in heaven. He makes the sun rise on both good and bad people. And he sends rain for the ones who do right and for the ones who do wrong. [46]If you love only those people who love you, will God reward you for this? Even tax collectors[a] love their friends. [47]If you greet only your friends, what's so great about this? Don't even unbelievers do that? [48]But you must always act like your Father in heaven.

Giving

6 When you do good deeds, don't try to show off. If you do, you won't get a reward from your Father in heaven.

[2]When you give to the poor, don't blow a loud horn. That's what show-offs do in the synagogues and on the street corners, because they

y5.39 right cheek: A slap on the right cheek was a bad insult.   z5.41 two miles: A Roman soldier had the right to force a person to carry his pack as far as one mile.   a5.46 tax collectors: These were usually Jewish people who paid the Romans for the right to collect taxes. They were hated by other Jews who thought of them as traitors to their country and to their religion.

are always looking for praise. I can assure you that they already have their reward.

³When you give to the poor, don't let anyone know about it.[b] ⁴Then your gift will be given in secret. Your Father knows what is done in secret and will reward you.

Prayer
(Luke 11.2-4)

⁵When you pray, don't be like those show-offs who love to stand up and pray in the synagogues and on the street corners. They do this just to look good. I can assure you that they already have their reward.

⁶When you pray, go into a room alone and close the door. Pray to your Father in private. He knows what is done in private and will reward you.

⁷When you pray, don't talk on and on as people do who don't know God. They think God likes to hear long prayers. ⁸Don't be like them. Your Father knows what you need even before you ask.

⁹You should pray like this:

Our Father in heaven,
help us to honor
your name.
¹⁰Come and set up
your kingdom,
so that everyone on earth
will obey you,
as you are obeyed
in heaven.
¹¹Give us our food for today.[c]
¹²Forgive us for doing wrong,
as we forgive others.
¹³Keep us from being tempted[d]
and protect us from evil.[e]

---

b6.3 don't let anyone know about it: The Greek text has, "Don't let your left hand know what your right hand is doing."   c6.11 our food for today: Or "the food that we need" or "our food for the coming day."   d6.13 tempted: Or "tested."   e6.13 evil: Or "the evil one," that is, the devil. Some manuscripts add, "The kingdom, the power, and the glory are yours forever. Amen."

[14]If you forgive others for the wrongs they do to you, your Father in heaven will forgive you. [15]But if you don't forgive others, your Father will not forgive your sins.

Worshiping God by Going Without Eating

[16]When you go without eating,[f] don't try to look gloomy as those show-offs do when they go without eating. I can assure you that they already have their reward. [17]Instead, comb your hair and wash your face. [18]Then others won't know you are going without eating. But your Father sees what is done in private, and he will reward you.

Treasures in Heaven
(Luke 12.33, 34)

[19]Don't store up treasures on earth! Moths and rust can destroy them, and thieves can break in and steal them. [20]Instead, store up your treasures in heaven, where moths and rust cannot destroy them, and thieves cannot break in and steal them. [21]Your heart will always be where your treasure is.

Light
(Luke 11.34-36)

[22]Your eyes are a window for your body. When they are good, you have all the light you need. [23]But when your eyes are bad, everything is dark. If the light inside you is dark, you surely are in the dark.

Money
(Luke 16.13)

[24]You cannot be the slave of two masters! You will like one more than the other or be more loyal to one than the other. You cannot serve both God and money.

f6.16 without eating: See the note at 4.2.

Worry
(Luke 12.22-31)

[25]I tell you not to worry about your life. Don't worry about having something to eat, drink, or wear. Isn't life more than food or clothing? [26]Look at the birds in the sky! They don't plant or harvest. They don't even store grain in barns. Yet your Father in heaven takes care of them. Aren't you worth much more than birds?

[27]Can worry make you live longer?[g] [28]Why worry about clothes? Look how the wild flowers grow. They don't work hard to make their clothes. [29]But I tell you that Solomon with all his wealth[h] wasn't as well clothed as one of them. [30]God gives such beauty to everything that grows in the fields, even though it is here today and thrown into a fire tomorrow. God will surely do even more for you! Why do you have such little faith?

[31]Don't worry and ask yourselves, "Will we have anything to eat? Will we have anything to drink? Will we have any clothes to wear?" [32]Only people who don't know God are always worrying about such things. Your Father in heaven knows you need all of these. [33]But more than anything else, put God's work first and do what he wants. Then the other things will be yours as well.

[34]Don't worry about tomorrow. It will take care of itself. You have enough to worry about today.

Judging Others
(Luke 6.37, 38, 41, 42)

7 Don't condemn others, and God won't condemn you. [2]God will be as hard on you as you are on others! He will treat you exactly as you treat them.

[3]You can see the speck in your friend's eye, but you don't notice the log in your own eye. [4]How can you say, "My friend, let me take the speck out of your eye," when you don't see the log in your own eye? [5]You're nothing but show-offs! First, take the log out of

g6.27 live longer: Or "grow taller." h6.29 Solomon with all his wealth: The Jewish people thought that Solomon was the richest person who had ever lived.

your own eye; then you can see how to take the speck out of your friend's eye.

⁶Don't give to dogs what belongs to God. They will only turn and attack you. Don't throw pearls down in front of pigs. They will trample all over them.

Ask, Search, Knock
(Luke 11.9-13)

⁷Ask, and you will receive. Search, and you will find. Knock, and the door will be opened for you. ⁸Everyone who asks will receive. Everyone who searches will find. And the door will be opened for everyone who knocks. ⁹Would any of you give your hungry child a stone, if the child asked for some bread? ¹⁰Would you give your child a snake if the child asked for a fish? ¹¹As bad as you are, you still know how to give good gifts to your children. But your heavenly Father is even more ready to give good things to people who ask.

¹²Treat others as you want them to treat you. This is what the Law and the Prophets[i] are all about.

The Narrow Gate
(Luke 13.24)

¹³Go in through the narrow gate. The gate to destruction is wide, and the road that leads there is easy to follow. A lot of people go through that gate. ¹⁴But the gate to life is very narrow. The road that leads there is so hard to follow that only a few people find it.

A Tree and Its Fruit
(Luke 6.43-45)

¹⁵Watch out for false prophets! They dress up like sheep, but inside they are wolves who have come to attack you. ¹⁶You can tell what they are by what they do. No one picks grapes or figs from thornbushes. ¹⁷A good tree produces good fruit, and a bad tree produces bad fruit. ¹⁸A good tree cannot produce bad fruit, and a bad tree can-

i7.12 the Law and the Prophets: See the note at 5.17.

not produce good fruit. [19]Every tree producing bad fruit will be chopped down and burned. [20]You can tell who the false prophets are by their deeds.

A Warning
(Luke 13.26, 27)

[21]Not everyone who calls me their Lord will get into the kingdom of heaven. Only the ones who obey my Father in heaven will get in. [22]On the day of judgment many will call me their Lord. They will say, "We preached in your name, and in your name we forced out demons and worked many miracles." [23]But I will tell them, "I will have nothing to do with you! Get out of my sight, you evil people!"

Two Builders
(Luke 6.47-49)

[24]Anyone who hears and obeys these teachings of mine is like a wise person who built a house on solid rock. [25]Rain poured down, rivers flooded, and winds beat against that house. But it was built on solid rock, and so it did not fall.

[26]Anyone who hears my teachings and doesn't obey them is like a foolish person who built a house on sand. [27]Rain poured down, rivers flooded, and the winds blew and beat against that house. Finally, it fell with a crash.

[28]When Jesus finished speaking, the crowds were surprised at his teaching. [29]He taught them like someone with authority, and not like their teachers of the Law of Moses.

Jesus Heals a Man
(Mark 1.40-45; Luke 5.12-16)

8 As Jesus came down the mountain, he was followed by large crowds. [2]Suddenly a man with leprosy[j] came and knelt in front of Jesus. He said, "Lord, you have the power to make me well, if only you wanted to."

[3]Jesus put his hand on the man and said, "I want to! Now you are well."

j8.2 leprosy: In biblical times the word "leprosy" was used for many different kinds of skin diseases.

At once the man's leprosy disappeared. [4]Jesus told him, "Don't tell anyone about this, but go and show the priest that you are well. Then take a gift to the temple just as Moses commanded, and everyone will know that you have been healed."[k]

Jesus Heals an Army Officer's Servant
(Luke 7.1-10; John 4.43-54)

[5]When Jesus was going into the town of Capernaum, an army officer came up to him and said, [6]"Lord, my servant is at home in such terrible pain that he can't even move."

[7]"I will go and heal him," Jesus replied.

[8]But the officer said, "Lord, I'm not good enough for you to come into my house. Just give the order, and my servant will get well. [9]I have officers who give orders to me, and I have soldiers who take orders from me. I can say to one of them, 'Go!' and he goes. I can say to another, 'Come!' and he comes. I can say to my servant, 'Do this!' and he will do it."

[10]When Jesus heard this, he was so surprised that he turned and said to the crowd following him, "I tell you in all of Israel I've never found anyone with this much faith! [11]Many people will come from everywhere to enjoy the feast in the kingdom of heaven with Abraham, Isaac, and Jacob. [12]But the ones who should have been in the kingdom will be thrown out into the dark. They will cry and grit their teeth in pain."

[13]Then Jesus said to the officer, "You may go home now. Your faith has made it happen."

Right then his servant was healed.

Jesus Heals Many People
(Mark 1.29-34; Luke 4.38-41)

[14]Jesus went to the home of Peter, where he found that Peter's mother-in-law was sick in bed with fever. [15]He took her by the hand, and the fever left her. Then she got up and served Jesus a meal.

[16]That evening many people with demons in them were brought to Jesus.

k8.4 everyone will know that you have been healed: People with leprosy had to be examined by a priest and told that they were well (that is "clean") before they could once again live a normal life in the Jewish community. The gift that Moses commanded was the sacrifice of some lambs together with flour mixed with olive oil.

And with only a word he forced out the evil spirits and healed everyone who was sick. [17]So God's promise came true, just as the prophet Isaiah had said,

"He healed our diseases
and made us well."

Some Who Wanted to Go with Jesus
(Luke 9.57-62)

[18]When Jesus saw the crowd,[l] he went across Lake Galilee. [19]A teacher of the Law of Moses came up to him and said, "Teacher, I'll go anywhere with you!"

[20]Jesus replied, "Foxes have dens, and birds have nests. But the Son of Man doesn't have a place to call his own."

[21]Another disciple said to Jesus, "Lord, let me wait till I bury my father."

[22]Jesus answered, "Follow me, and let the dead bury their dead."[m]

A Storm
(Mark 4.35-41; Luke 8.22-25)

[23]After Jesus left in a boat with his disciples, [24]a terrible storm suddenly struck the lake, and waves started splashing into their boat.

Jesus was sound asleep, [25]so the disciples went over to him and woke him up. They said, "Lord, wake up! Save us before we drown!"

[26]But Jesus replied, "Why are you so afraid? You surely don't have much faith." Then he got up and ordered the wind and the waves to calm down. And everything was calm.

[27]The men in the boat were amazed and said, "Who is this? Even the wind and the waves obey him."

Two Men with Demons in Them
(Mark 5.1-20; Luke 8.26-39)

[28]After Jesus had crossed the lake, he came to shore near the town of Gadara[n] and started down the road. Two men with demons in them came to him from the tombs.[o] They were so fierce that no one could travel that way. [29]Sud-

l8.18 saw the crowd: Some manuscripts have "large crowd." Others have "large crowds."   m8.22 let the dead bury their dead: For the Jewish people a proper burial of their dead was a very important duty. But Jesus teaches that following him is even more important.   n8.28 Gadara: Some manuscripts have "Gergesa." Others have "Gerasa."   o8.28 tombs: It was thought that demons and evil spirits lived in tombs and in caves that were used for burying the dead.

denly they shouted, "Jesus, Son of God, what do you want with us? Have you come to punish us before our time?"

30Not far from there a large herd of pigs was feeding. 31So the demons begged Jesus, "If you force us out, please send us into those pigs!" 32Jesus told them to go, and they went out of the men and into the pigs. All at once the pigs rushed down the steep bank into the lake and drowned.

33The people taking care of the pigs ran to the town and told everything, especially what had happened to the two men. 34Everyone in town came out to meet Jesus. When they saw him, they begged him to leave their part of the country.

Jesus Heals a Man Who Could Not Walk

(Mark 2.1-12; Luke 5.17-26)

9 Jesus got into a boat and crossed back over to the town where he lived.[p]
2Some people soon brought to him a man lying on a mat because he could not walk. When Jesus saw how much faith they had, he said to the man, "My friend, don't worry! Your sins are forgiven."

3Some teachers of the Law of Moses said to themselves, "Jesus must think he is God!"

4But Jesus knew what was in their minds, and he said, "Why are you
thinking such evil things? 5Is it easier for me to tell this man his sins are for-
given or to tell him to get up and walk? 6But I will show you that the Son of Man has the right to forgive sins here on earth." So Jesus said to the man, "Get up! Pick up your mat and go on home." 7The man got up and went home.
8When the crowds saw this, they were afraid[q] and praised God for giving such authority to people.

Jesus Chooses Matthew

(Mark 2.13-17; Luke 5.27-32)

9As Jesus was leaving, he saw a tax collector[r] named Matthew sitting at the place for paying taxes. Jesus said to him, "Follow me." Matthew got up and went with him.

10Later, Jesus and his disciples were having dinner at Matthew's house.[s]

p9.1 where he lived: Capernaum (see 4.13). q9.8 afraid: Some manuscripts have "amazed." r9.9 tax collector: See the note at 5.46. s9.10 Matthew's house: Or "Jesus' house."

Many tax collectors and other sinners were also there. [11]Some Pharisees asked Jesus' disciples, "Why does your teacher eat with tax collectors and other sinners?"

[12]Jesus heard them and answered, "Healthy people don't need a doctor, but sick people do. [13]Go and learn what the Scriptures mean when they say, 'Instead of offering sacrifices to me, I want you to be merciful to others.' I didn't come to invite good people to be my followers. I came to invite sinners."

People Ask About Going Without Eating
(Mark 2.18-22; Luke 5.33-39)

[14]Some followers of John the Baptist came and asked Jesus, "Why do we and the Pharisees often go without eating,[t] while your disciples never do?"

[15]Jesus answered:

The friends of a bridegroom aren't sad while he is still with them. But the time will come when he will be taken from them. Then they will go without eating.

[16]No one uses a new piece of cloth to patch old clothes. The patch would shrink and tear a bigger hole.

[17]No one pours new wine into old wineskins. The wine would swell and burst the old skins.[u] Then the wine would be lost, and the skins would be ruined. New wine must be put into new wineskins. Both the skins and the wine will then be safe.

A Dying Girl and a Sick Woman
(Mark 5.21-43; Luke 8.40-56)

[18]While Jesus was still speaking, an official came and knelt in front of him. The man said, "My daughter has just now died! Please come and place your hand on her. Then she will live again."

[19]Jesus and his disciples got up and went with the man.

[20]A woman who had been bleeding for twelve years came up behind Jesus and barely touched his clothes. [21]She had said to herself, "If I can just touch his clothes, I will be healed."

---

t9.14 *without eating:* See the note at 4.2.   u9.17 *swell and burst the old skins:* While the juice from grapes was becoming wine, it would swell and stretch the skins in which it had been stored. If the skins were old and stiff, they would burst.

²²Jesus turned. He saw the woman and said, "Don't worry! You are now healed because of your faith." At that moment she was healed.

²³When Jesus went into the home of the official and saw the musicians and the crowd of mourners,ᵛ ²⁴he said, "Get out of here! The little girl isn't dead. She is just asleep." Everyone started laughing at Jesus. ²⁵But after the crowd had been sent out of the house, Jesus went to the girl's bedside. He took her by the hand and helped her up.

²⁶News about this spread all over that part of the country.

Jesus Heals Two Blind Men

²⁷As Jesus was leaving that place, two blind men began following him and shouting, "Son of David,ʷ have pity on us!"

²⁸After Jesus had gone indoors, the two blind men came up to him. He asked them, "Do you believe I can make you well?"

"Yes, Lord," they answered.

²⁹Jesus touched their eyes and said, "Because of your faith, you will be healed." ³⁰They were able to see, and Jesus strictly warned them not to tell anyone about him. ³¹But they left and talked about him to everyone in that part of the country.

Jesus Heals a Man Who Could Not Talk

³²As Jesus and his disciples were on their way, some people brought to him a man who could not talk because a demon was in him. ³³After Jesus had forced the demon out, the man started talking. The crowds were so amazed they began saying, "Nothing like this has ever happened in Israel!"

³⁴But the Pharisees said, "The leader of the demons gives him the power to force out demons."

Jesus Has Pity on People

³⁵Jesus went to every town and village. He taught in their synagogues and preached the good news about God's kingdom. Jesus also healed every

v9.23 the crowd of mourners: The Jewish people often hired mourners for funerals.   w9.27 Son of David: The Jewish people expected the Messiah to be from the family of King David, and for this reason the Messiah was often called the "Son of David."

kind of disease and sickness. ³⁶When he saw the crowds, he felt sorry for them. They were confused and helpless, like sheep without a shepherd. ³⁷He said to his disciples, "A large crop is in the fields, but there are only a few workers. ³⁸Ask the Lord in charge of the harvest to send out workers to bring it in."

Jesus Chooses His Twelve Apostles
(Mark 3.13-19; Luke 6.12-16)

10 Jesus called together his twelve disciples. He gave them the power to force out evil spirits and to heal every kind of disease and sickness. ²The first of the twelve apostles was Simon, better known as Peter. His brother Andrew was an apostle, and so were James and John, the two sons of Zebedee. ³Philip, Bartholomew, Thomas, Matthew the tax collector,ˣ James the son of Alphaeus, and Thaddaeus were also apostles. ⁴The others were Simon, known as the Eager One,ʸ and Judas Iscariot,ᶻ who later betrayed Jesus.

Instructions
for the Twelve Apostles
(Mark 6.7-13; Luke 9.1-6)

⁵Jesus sent out the twelve apostles with these instructions:

Stay away from the Gentiles and don't go to any Samaritan town. ⁶Go only to the people of Israel, because they are like a flock of lost sheep. ⁷As you go, announce that the kingdom of heaven will soon be here.ᵃ ⁸Heal the sick, raise the dead to life, heal people who have leprosy,ᵇ and force out demons. You received without paying, now give without being paid. ⁹Don't take along any gold, silver, or copper coins. ¹⁰And don't carryᶜ a traveling bag or an extra shirt or sandals or a walking stick.

Workers deserve their food. ¹¹So when you go to a town or a vil-

---

x10.3 *tax collector:* See the note at 5.46.   y10.4 *known as the Eager One:* The Greek text has "Cananaean," which probably comes from a Hebrew word meaning "zealous" (see Luke 6.15). "Zealot" was the name later given to the members of a Jewish group that resisted and fought against the Romans.   z10.4 *Iscariot:* This may mean "a man from Kerioth" (a place in Judea). But more probably it means "a man who was a liar" or "a man who was a betrayer."   a10.7 *will soon be here:* Or "is already here."   b10.8 *leprosy:* See the note at 8.2.   c10.9,10 *Don't take along . . . don't carry:* Or "Don't accept . . . don't accept."

lage, find someone able and willing to have you as their guest and stay with them until you leave. [12]When you go to a home, give it your blessing of peace. [13]If the home is deserving, let your blessing remain with them. But if the home doesn't accept you, take back your blessing of peace. [14]If someone won't welcome you or listen to your message, leave their home or town. And shake the dust from your feet at them.[d] [15]I promise you the day of judgment will be easier for the towns of Sodom and Gomorrah[e] than for that town.

Warning About Trouble
(Mark 13.9-13; Luke 21.12-17)

[16]I am sending you like lambs into a pack of wolves. So be as wise as snakes and as innocent as doves. [17]Watch out for people who will take you to court and have you beaten in their synagogues. [18]Because of me, you will be dragged before rulers and kings to tell them and the Gentiles about your faith. [19]But when someone arrests you, don't worry about what you will say or how you will say it. At that time you will be given the words to say. [20]But you will not really be the one speaking. The Spirit from your Father will tell you what to say.

[21]Brothers and sisters will betray one another and have each other put to death. Parents will betray their own children, and children will turn against their parents and have them killed. [22]Everyone will hate you because of me. But if you remain faithful until the end, you will be saved. [23]When people mistreat you in one town, hurry to another one. I promise you before you have gone to all the towns of Israel, the Son of Man will come.

[24]Students are not better than their teacher, and slaves are not better than their master. [25]It is enough for students to be like their teacher and for slaves to be like their master. If people call the head of the family Satan, what will they say about the rest of the family?

d10.14 shake the dust from your feet at them: This was a way of showing rejection (see Acts 13.51). e10.15 Sodom and Gomorrah: During the time of Abraham the Lord destroyed these towns because the people there were so evil.

The One to Fear
(Luke 12.2-7)

²⁶Don't be afraid of anyone! Everything that is hidden will be found out, and every secret will be known. ²⁷Whatever I say to you in the dark, you must tell in the light. And you must announce from the housetops whatever I have whispered to you. ²⁸Don't be afraid of people. They can kill you, but they cannot harm your soul. Instead, you should fear God who can destroy both your body and your soul in hell. ²⁹Aren't two sparrows sold for only a penny? But your Father knows when any one of them falls to the ground. ³⁰Even the hairs on your head are counted. ³¹So don't be afraid! You are worth much more than many sparrows.

Telling Others About Christ
(Luke 12.8,9)

³²If you tell others you belong to me, I will tell my Father in heaven you are my followers. ³³But if you reject me, I will tell my Father in heaven you don't belong to me.

Not Peace, but Trouble
(Luke 12.51-53; 14.26, 27)

³⁴Don't think I came to bring peace to the earth! I came to bring trouble, not peace. ³⁵I came to turn sons against their fathers, daughters against their mothers, and daughters-in-law against their mothers-in-law. ³⁶Your worst enemies will be in your own family.

³⁷If you love your father or mother or even your sons and daughters more than me, you are not fit to be my disciples. ³⁸And unless you are willing to take up your cross and follow me, you are not fit to be my disciples. ³⁹If you try to save your life, you will lose it. But if you give it up for me, you will surely find it.

Rewards
(Mark 9.41)

⁴⁰Anyone who welcomes you welcomes me. And anyone who welcomes me also welcomes the one who sent me. ⁴¹Anyone who welcomes a prophet, just because that person is a prophet, will be given the same reward as a prophet. Anyone who welcomes a good person, just because that person is good, will be given the same reward as a good person. ⁴²And anyone who gives one of my most humble followers a cup of cool water, just because that person is my follower, will be rewarded.

John the Baptist
(Luke 7.18-35)

11 After Jesus had finished instructing his twelve disciples, he left and began teaching and preaching in the towns.ᶠ

²John was in prison when he heard what Christ was doing. So John sent some of his followers ³to ask Jesus, "Are you the one we should be looking for? Or must we wait for someone else?"

⁴Jesus answered, "Go and tell John what you have heard and seen. ⁵The blind are now able to see, and the lame can walk. People with leprosyᵍ are being healed, and the deaf can hear. The dead are raised to life, and the poor are hearing the good news. ⁶God will bless everyone who doesn't reject me because of what I do."

⁷As John's followers were going away, Jesus spoke to the crowds about John:

What sort of person did you go out into the desert to see? Was he like tall grass blown about by the wind? ⁸What kind of man did you go out to see? Was he someone dressed in fine clothes? People who dress like that live in the king's palace. ⁹What did you really go out to see? Was he a prophet? He certainly was. I tell you that he was more than a prophet. ¹⁰In the Scriptures God says about him, "I am sending my messenger ahead to get things ready for you." ¹¹I tell you no

---

f11.1 the towns: The Greek text has "their towns," which may refer to the towns of Galilee or to the towns where Jesus' disciples had lived.   g11.5 leprosy: See the note at 8.2.

one ever born on this earth is greater than John the Baptist. But whoever is least in the kingdom of heaven is greater than John.

¹²From the time of John the Baptist until now, violent people have been trying to take over the kingdom of heaven by force. ¹³All the Books of the Prophets and the Law of Moses[h] told what was going to happen up to the time of John. ¹⁴And if you believe them, John is Elijah, the prophet you are waiting for. ¹⁵If you have ears, pay attention!

¹⁶You people are like children sitting in the market and shouting to each other,

¹⁷"We played the flute,
   but you would not dance!
   We sang a funeral song,
   but you would not mourn!"

¹⁸John the Baptist did not go around eating and drinking, and you said, "That man has a demon in him!" ¹⁹But the Son of Man goes around eating and drinking, and you say, "That man eats and drinks too much! He is even a friend of tax collectors[i] and sinners." Yet Wisdom is shown to be right by what it does.

The Unbelieving Towns
(Luke 10.13-15)

²⁰In the towns where Jesus had worked most of his miracles, the people refused to turn to God. So Jesus was upset with them and said:

²¹You people of Chorazin are in for trouble! You people of Bethsaida are in for trouble too! If the miracles that took place here had happened in Tyre and Sidon, the people there would have turned to God long ago. They would have dressed in sackcloth and put ashes on their heads.[j] ²²I tell you on the day of judgment the people of Tyre and Sidon will get off easier than you will.

²³People of Capernaum, do you think you will be honored in heaven? You will go down to hell! If the miracles that took place in your town had happened in Sodom, would still be standing. ²⁴So I

---

h11.13 the Books of the Prophets and the Law of Moses: The Jewish Scriptures, that is, the Old Testament.   i11.19 tax collectors: See the note at 5.46.   j11.21 sackcloth . . . ashes on their heads: This was one way that people showed how sorry they were for their sins.

tell you on the day of judgment the people of Sodom will get off easier than you.

Come to Me and Rest
(Luke 10.21, 22)

²⁵At that moment Jesus said:

My Father, Lord of heaven and earth, I am grateful that you hid all this from wise and educated people and showed it to ordinary people. ²⁶Yes, Father, this is what pleased you.

²⁷My Father has given me everything, and he is the only one who knows the Son. The only one who truly knows the Father is the Son. But the Son wants to tell others about the Father, so they can know him too.

²⁸If you are tired from carrying heavy burdens, come to me and I will give you rest. ²⁹Take the yoke*ᵏ* I give you. Put it on your shoulders and learn from me. I am gentle and humble, and you will find rest. ³⁰This yoke is easy to bear, and this burden is light.

A Question About the Sabbath
(Mark 2.23-28; Luke 6.1-5)

12 One Sabbath, Jesus and his disciples were walking through some wheat fields.*ˡ* His disciples were hungry and began picking and eating grains of wheat. ²Some Pharisees noticed this and said to Jesus, "Why are your disciples picking grain on the Sabbath? They are not supposed to do this!"

³Jesus answered:

You surely must have read what David did when he and his followers were hungry. ⁴He went into the house of God, and then they ate the sacred loaves of bread that only priests are supposed to eat. ⁵Haven't you read in the Law of Moses that the priests are allowed to work in the temple on the Sabbath? But no one says they are guilty of breaking the law of the Sabbath. ⁶I tell you there is something here greater than the temple. ⁷Don't you know what the Scriptures mean

---

k11.29 yoke: Yokes were put on the necks of animals, so that they could pull a plow or wagon. A yoke was a symbol of obedience and hard work.   l12.1 walking through some wheat fields: It was the custom to let hungry travelers pick grains of wheat.

when they say, "Instead of offering sacrifices to me, I want you to be merciful to others?" If you knew what this means, you would not condemn these innocent disciples of mine. [8]So the Son of Man is Lord over the Sabbath.

A Man with a Paralyzed Hand
(Mark 3.1-6; Luke 6.6-11)

[9]Jesus left and went into one of their synagogues, [10]where there was a man whose hand was paralyzed. Some Pharisees wanted to accuse Jesus of doing something wrong, so they asked him, "Is it right to heal someone on the Sabbath?"

[11]Jesus answered, "If one of your sheep fell into a ditch on the Sabbath, wouldn't you lift it out? [12]People are worth much more than sheep, and so it is right to do good on the Sabbath." [13]Then Jesus told the man, "Hold out your hand." The man did, and it became as healthy as the other one.

[14]The Pharisees left and started making plans to kill Jesus.

God's Chosen Servant

[15]When Jesus found out what was happening, he left there and large crowds followed him. He healed all of their sick, [16]but warned them not to tell anyone about him. [17]So God's promise came true, just as Isaiah the prophet had said,

[18]"Here is my chosen servant!
I love him,
    and he pleases me.
I will give him my Spirit,
and he will bring justice
    to the nations.
[19]He won't shout or yell
    or call out in the streets.
[20]He won't break off a bent reed
    or put out a dying flame,
but he will make sure
    that justice is done.
[21]All nations will place
    their hope in him."

Jesus and the Ruler of the Demons
(Mark 3.20-30; Luke 11.14-23; 12.10)

²²Some people brought to Jesus a man who was blind and could not talk because he had a demon in him. Jesus healed the man, and then he was able to talk and see. ²³The crowds were so amazed they asked, "Could Jesus be the Son of David?"ᵐ

²⁴When the Pharisees heard this, they said, "He forces out demons by the power of Beelzebul, the ruler of the demons!"

²⁵Jesus knew what they were thinking, so he said to them:

Any kingdom where people fight each other will end up ruined. And a town or family that fights will soon destroy itself. ²⁶So if Satan fights against himself, how can his kingdom last? ²⁷If I use the power of Beelzebul to force out demons, whose power do your own followers use to force them out? Your followers are the ones who will judge you. ²⁸But when I force out demons by the power of God's Spirit, it proves that God's kingdom has already come to you. ²⁹How can anyone break into a strong man's house and steal his things, unless he first ties up the strong man? Then he can take everything.

³⁰If you are not on my side, you are against me. If you don't gather in the harvest with me, you scatter it. ³¹⁻³²I tell you any sinful thing you do or say can be forgiven. Even if you speak against the Son of Man, you can be forgiven. But if you speak against the Holy Spirit, you can never be forgiven, either in this life or in the life to come.

A Tree and Its Fruit
(Luke 6.43-45)

³³A good tree produces good fruit, and a bad tree produces bad fruit. You can tell what a tree is like by the fruit it produces. ³⁴You are a bunch of evil snakes, so how can you say anything good? Your words show what is in your hearts. ³⁵Good people bring good things out of their hearts, but evil people bring evil things out of their hearts.

m12.23 Could Jesus be the Son of David: Or "Does Jesus think he is the Son of David?" See the note at 9.27.

[36]I promise you on the day of judgment, everyone will have to account for every careless word they have spoken. [37]On that day they will be told they are either innocent or guilty because of the things they have said.

A Sign from Heaven
(Mark 8.11,12; Luke 11.29-32)

[38]Some Pharisees and teachers of the Law of Moses said, "Teacher, we want you to show us a sign from heaven."

[39]But Jesus replied:

You want a sign because you are evil and won't believe! But the only sign you will get is the sign of the prophet Jonah. [40]He was in the stomach of a big fish for three days and nights, just as the Son of Man will be deep in the earth for three days and nights. [41]On the day of judgment the people of Nineveh[n] will stand there with you and condemn you. They turned to God when Jonah preached, and yet here is something far greater than Jonah. [42]The Queen of the South[o] will also stand there with you and condemn you. She traveled a long way to hear Solomon's wisdom, and yet here is something much greater than Solomon.

Return of an Evil Spirit
(Luke 11.24-26)

[43]When an evil spirit leaves a person, it travels through the desert, looking for a place to rest. But when the demon doesn't find a place, [44]it says, "I will go back to the home I left." When it gets there and finds the place empty, clean, and neat, [45]it goes off and finds seven other evil spirits even worse than itself. They all come and make their home there, and the person ends up in worse shape than before. That's how it will be with you evil people of today.

n12.41 Nineveh: During the time of Jonah this city was the capital of the Assyrian Empire, which was Israel's worst enemy. But Jonah was sent there to preach, so that the people would turn to the Lord and be saved.   o12.42 South: Sheba, probably a country in southern Arabia.

Jesus' Mother and Brothers
(Mark 3.31-35; Luke 8.19-21)

[46]While Jesus was still speaking to the crowds, his mother and brothers came and stood outside because they wanted to talk with him. [47]Someone told Jesus, "Your mother and brothers are standing outside and want to talk with you."[p]

[48]Jesus answered, "Who is my mother and who are my brothers?" [49]Then he pointed to his disciples and said, "These are my mother and my brothers! [50]Anyone who obeys my Father in heaven is my brother or sister or mother."

A Story About a Farmer
(Mark 4.1-9; Luke 8.4-8)

13 That same day Jesus left the house and went out beside Lake Galilee, where he sat down to teach.[q] [2]Such large crowds gathered around him that he had to sit in a boat, while the people stood on the shore. [3]Then he taught them many things by using stories. He said:

A farmer went out to scatter seed in a field. [4]While the farmer was scattering the seed, some of it fell along the road and was eaten by birds. [5]Other seeds fell on thin, rocky ground and quickly started growing because the soil wasn't very deep. [6]But when the sun came up, the plants were scorched and dried up, because they did not have deep roots. [7]Some other seeds fell where thornbushes grew up and choked the plants. [8]But a few seeds did fall on good ground where the plants produced 100 or 60 or 30 times as much as was scattered. [9]If you have ears, pay attention!

Why Jesus Used Stories
(Mark 4.10-12; Luke 8.9,10)

[10]Jesus' disciples came to him and asked, "Why do you use stories to speak to the people?"

[11]Jesus answered:

I have explained the secrets about the kingdom of heaven to you, but not to others. [12]Everyone who has something will be given

---

p12.47 *with you:* Some manuscripts do not have verse 47.   q13.1 *sat down to teach:* See the note at 5.1.

more. But people who don't have anything will lose even what little they have. [13]I use stories when I speak to them because when they look, they cannot see, and when they listen, they cannot hear or understand. [14]So God's promise came true, just as the prophet Isaiah had said,

"These people will listen
and listen,
but never understand.
They will look and look,
but never see.
[15]All of them have
stubborn minds!
They refuse to listen;
they cover their eyes.
They cannot see or hear
or understand.
If they could,
they would turn to me,
and I would heal them."

[16]But God has blessed you, because your eyes can see and your ears can hear! [17]Many prophets and good people were eager to see what you see and to hear what you hear. But I tell you they did not see or hear.

Jesus Explains the Story About the Farmer
(Mark 4.13-20; Luke 8.11-15)

[18]Now listen to the meaning of the story about the farmer:

[19]The seeds that fell along the road are the people who hear the message about the kingdom, but don't understand it. Then the evil one comes and snatches the message from their hearts. [20]The seeds that fell on rocky ground are the people who gladly hear the message and accept it at once. [21]But they don't have deep roots, and they don't last very long. As soon as life gets hard or the message gets them in trouble, they give up.

[22]The seeds that fell among the thornbushes are also people who hear the message. But they start worrying about the needs of this life

and are fooled by the desire to get rich. So the message gets choked out, and they never produce anything. ²³The seeds that fell on good ground are the people who hear and understand the message. They produce as much as 100 or 60 or 30 times what was planted.

Weeds Among the Wheat

²⁴Jesus then told them this story:

The kingdom of heaven is like what happened when a farmer scattered good seed in a field. ²⁵But while everyone was sleeping, an enemy came and scattered weed seeds in the field and then left.

²⁶When the plants came up and began to mature, the farmer's servants could see the weeds. ²⁷The servants came and asked, "Sir, didn't you scatter good seed in your field? Where did these weeds come from?"

²⁸"An enemy did this," he replied.

His servants then asked, "Do you want us to go out and pull up the weeds?"

²⁹"No!" he answered. "You might also pull up the wheat. ³⁰Leave the weeds alone until harvest time. Then I'll tell my workers to gather the weeds and tie them up and burn them. But I'll order them to store the wheat in my barn."

Stories about a Mustard Seed and Yeast
(Mark 4.30-32; Luke 13.18-21)

³¹Jesus told them another story:

The kingdom of heaven is like what happens when a farmer plants a mustard seed in a field. ³²Although it is the smallest of all seeds, it grows larger than any garden plant and becomes a tree. Birds even come and nest on its branches.

³³Jesus also said:

The kingdom of heaven is like what happens when a woman mixes a little yeast into three big batches of flour. Finally, all the dough rises.

The Reason for Teaching with Stories
(Mark 4.33, 34)

[34]Jesus used stories when he spoke to the people. In fact, he did not tell them anything without using stories. [35]So God's promise came true, just as the prophet[r] had said,

> "I will use stories
>   to speak my message
> and to explain things hidden
> since the creation
>   of the world."

Jesus Explains the Story About the Weeds

[36]After Jesus left the crowd and went inside,[s] his disciples came to him and said, "Explain to us the story about the weeds in the wheat field."

[37]Jesus answered:

The one who scattered the good seed is the Son of Man. [38]The field is the world, and the good seeds are the people who belong to the kingdom. The weeds are those who belong to the evil one, [39]and the one who scattered them is the devil. The harvest is the end of time, and angels are the ones who bring in the harvest.

[40]Weeds are gathered and burned. That's how it will be at the end of time. [41]The Son of Man will send out his angels, and they will gather from his kingdom everyone who does wrong or causes others to sin. [42]Then he will throw them into a flaming furnace, where people will cry and grit their teeth in pain. [43]But everyone who has done right will shine like the sun in their Father's kingdom. If you have ears, pay attention!

A Hidden Treasure

[44]The kingdom of heaven is like what happens when someone finds a treasure hidden in a field and buries it again. Such a person is happy and goes and sells everything in order to buy that field.

---

r13.35 the prophet: Some manuscripts have "the prophet Isaiah."   s13.36 went inside: Or "went home."

A Valuable Pearl

[45]The kingdom of heaven is like what happens when a shop owner is looking for fine pearls. [46]After finding a very valuable one, the owner goes and sells everything in order to buy that pearl.

A Fish Net

[47]The kingdom of heaven is like what happens when a net is thrown into a lake and catches all kinds of fish. [48]When the net is full, it is dragged to the shore, and the fishermen sit down to separate the fish. They keep the good ones, but throw the bad ones away. [49]That's how it will be at the end of time. Angels will come and separate the evil people from the ones who have done right. [50]Then those evil people will be thrown into a flaming furnace, where they will cry and grit their teeth in pain.

New and Old Treasures

[51]Jesus asked his disciples if they understood all these things. They said, "Yes, we do."

[52]So he told them, "Every student of the Scriptures who becomes a disciple in the kingdom of heaven is like someone who brings out new and old treasures from the storeroom."

The People of Nazareth Turn Against Jesus
(Mark 6.1-6; Luke 4.16-30)

[53]When Jesus had finished telling these stories, he left [54]and went to his hometown. He taught in their synagogue, and the people were so amazed that they asked, "Where does he get all this wisdom and the power to work these miracles? [55]Isn't he the son of the carpenter? Isn't Mary his mother, and aren't James, Joseph, Simon, and Judas his brothers? [56]Don't his sisters still live here in our town? How can he do all this?" [57]So the people were upset because of what he was doing.

But Jesus said, "Prophets are honored by everyone, except the people of their hometown and their own family." [58]And because the people did not have any faith, Jesus did not work many miracles there.

The Death of John the Baptist
(Mark 6.14-29; Luke 9.7-9)

14 About this time Herod the ruler[t] heard the news about Jesus [2]and told his officials, "This is John the Baptist! He has come back from death, and that's why he has the power to work these miracles."

[3-4]Herod had earlier arrested John and had him chained and put in prison. He did this because John had told him, "It isn't right for you to take Herodias, the wife of your brother Philip." [5]Herod wanted to kill John. But the people thought John was a prophet, and Herod was afraid of what they might do.

[6]When Herod's birthday came, the daughter of Herodias danced for the guests. She pleased Herod [7]so much he swore to give her whatever she wanted. [8]But the girl's mother told her to say, "Here on a serving plate I want the head of John the Baptist!"

[9]Herod was sorry for what he had said. But he did not want to break the promise he had made in front of his guests. So he ordered a guard [10]to go to the prison and cut off John's head. [11]It was taken on a serving plate to the girl, and she gave it to her mother. [12]John's followers took his body and buried it. Then they told Jesus what had happened.

Jesus Feeds Five Thousand
(Mark 6.30-44; Luke 9.10-17; John 6.1-14)

[13]After Jesus heard about John, he crossed Lake Galilee[u] to go to some place where he could be alone. But the crowds found out and followed him on foot from the towns. [14]When Jesus got out of the boat, he saw the large crowd. He felt sorry for them and healed everyone who was sick.

[15]That evening the disciples came to Jesus and said, "This place is like a desert, and it's already late. Let the crowds leave, so they can go to the villages and buy some food."

[16]Jesus replied, "They don't have to leave. Why don't you give them something to eat?"

[17]But they said, "We have only five small loaves of bread[v] and two fish." [18]Jesus asked his disciples to bring the food to him, [19]and he told the crowd

---

t14.1 Herod the ruler: Herod Antipas, the son of Herod the Great (see 2.1). u14.13 crossed Lake Galilee: To the east side. v14.17 small loaves of bread: These would have been flat and round or in the shape of a bun.

to sit down on the grass. Jesus took the five loaves and the two fish. He looked up toward heaven and blessed the food. Then he broke the bread and handed it to his disciples, and they gave it to the people.

²⁰After everyone had eaten all they wanted, Jesus' disciples picked up twelve large baskets of leftovers.

²¹There were about 5,000 men who ate, not counting the women and children.

Jesus Walks on the Water
(Mark 6.45-52; John 6.15-21)

²²At once, Jesus made his disciples get into a boat and start back across the lake.ʷ But he stayed until he had sent the crowds away. ²³Then he went up on a mountain where he could be alone and pray. Later in the evening, he was still there.

²⁴By this time the boat was a long way from the shore. It was going against the wind and was being tossed around by the waves. ²⁵A little while before morning, Jesus came walking on the water toward his disciples. ²⁶When they saw him, they thought he was a ghost. They were terrified and started screaming.

²⁷At once, Jesus said to them, "Don't worry! I am Jesus. Don't be afraid."

²⁸Peter replied, "Lord, if it really is you, tell me to come to you on the water."

²⁹"Come on!" Jesus said. Peter then got out of the boat and started walking on the water toward him.

³⁰But when Peter saw how strong the wind was, he was afraid and started sinking. "Save me, Lord!" he shouted.

³¹At once, Jesus reached out his hand. He helped Peter up and said, "You surely don't have much faith. Why do you doubt?"

³²When Jesus and Peter got into the boat, the wind died down. ³³The men in the boat worshiped Jesus and said, "You really are the Son of God!"

Jesus Heals Sick People in Gennesaret
(Mark 6.53-56)

³⁴Jesus and his disciples crossed the lake and came to shore near the town of Gennesaret. ³⁵The people found out he was there, and they sent word to

w14.22 *back across the lake:* To the west side.

everyone who lived in this part of the country. So they brought all the sick people to Jesus. ³⁶They begged him just to let them touch his clothes, and everyone who did was healed.

The Teaching of the Ancestors
(Mark 7.1-13)

15 About this time some Pharisees and teachers of the Law of Moses came from Jerusalem. They asked Jesus, ²"Why don't your disciples obey what our ancestors taught us to do? They don't even wash their hands^x before they eat."

³Jesus answered:

Why do you disobey God and follow your own teaching? ⁴Didn't God command you to respect your father and mother? Didn't he tell you to put to death all who curse their parents? ⁵But you let people get by without helping their parents when they should. You let them say that what they have been offered to God.^y ⁶Is this any way to show respect to your parents? You ignore God's commands in order to follow your own teaching. ⁷And you are nothing but show-offs! Isaiah the prophet was right when he wrote that God had said,

⁸"All of you praise me
   with your words,
but you never really
   think about me.
⁹It is useless for you
   to worship me,
when you teach rules
   made up by humans."

What Really Makes People Unclean
(Mark 7.14-23)

¹⁰Jesus called the crowd together and said, "Pay attention and try to understand what I mean. ¹¹The food you put into your mouth doesn't make you

x15.2 *wash their hands:* The Jewish people had strict laws about washing their hands before eating, especially if they had been out in public. y15.5 *has been offered to God:* According to Jewish custom, when people said something was offered to God, it belonged to him and could not be used for anyone else, not even for their own parents.

unclean and unfit to worship God. The bad words that come out of your mouth are what make you unclean."

[12]Then his disciples came over to him and asked, "Do you know you insulted the Pharisees by what you said?"

[13]Jesus answered, "Every plant that my Father in heaven did not plant will be pulled up by the roots. [14]Stay away from those Pharisees! They are like blind people leading other blind people, and all of them will fall into a ditch."

[15]Peter replied, "What did you mean when you talked about the things that make people unclean?"

[16]Jesus then said:

> Don't any of you know by now what I am talking about? [17]Don't you know that the food you put into your mouth goes into your stomach and then out of your body? [18]But the words that come out of your mouth come from your heart. And they are what make you unfit to worship God. [19]Out of your heart come evil thoughts, murder, unfaithfulness in marriage, vulgar deeds, stealing, telling lies, and insulting others. [20]These are what make you unclean. Eating without washing your hands will not make you unfit to worship God.

A Woman's Faith
(Mark 7.24-30)

[21]Jesus left and went to the territory near the towns of Tyre and Sidon. [22]Suddenly a Canaanite woman[z] from there came out shouting, "Lord and Son of David,[a] have pity on me! My daughter is full of demons." [23]Jesus did not say a word. But the woman kept following along and shouting, so his disciples came up and asked him to send her away.

[24]Jesus said, "I was sent only to the people of Israel! They are like a flock of lost sheep."

[25]The woman came closer. Then she knelt down and begged, "Please help me, Lord!"

[26]Jesus replied, "It isn't right to take food away from children and feed it to dogs."[b]

z15.22 Canaanite woman: This woman was not Jewish.   a15.22 Son of David: See the note at 9.27.
b15.26 feed it to dogs: Some Jewish people referred to Gentiles as dogs.

²⁷"Lord, this is true," the woman said, "but even puppies get the crumbs that fall from their owner's table."

²⁸Jesus answered, "Dear woman, you really do have a lot of faith, and you will be given what you want." At that moment her daughter was healed.

Jesus Heals Many People

²⁹From there, Jesus went along Lake Galilee. Then he climbed a hill and sat down. ³⁰Large crowds came and brought many people who were paralyzed or blind or lame or unable to talk. They placed them, and many others, in front of Jesus, and he healed them all. ³¹Everyone was amazed at what they saw and heard. People who had never spoken could now speak. The lame were healed, the paralyzed could walk, and the blind were able to see. Everyone was praising the God of Israel.

Jesus Feeds Four Thousand
(Mark 8.1-10)

³²Jesus called his disciples together and told them, "I feel sorry for these people. They have been with me for three days, and they don't have anything to eat. I don't want to send them away hungry. They might faint on their way home."

³³His disciples said, "This place is like a desert. Where can we find enough food to feed such a crowd?"

³⁴Jesus asked them how much food they had. They replied, "Seven small loaves of breadᶜ and a few little fish."

³⁵After Jesus had told the people to sit down, ³⁶he took the seven loaves of bread and the fish and gave thanks. He then broke them and handed them to his disciples, who passed them around to the crowds.

³⁷Everyone ate all they wanted, and the leftovers filled seven large baskets.

³⁸There were 4,000 men who ate, not counting the women and children.

³⁹After Jesus had sent the crowds away, he got into a boat and sailed across the lake. He came to shore near the town of Magadan.ᵈ

c15.34 small loaves of bread: See the note at 14.17.   d15.39 Magadan: The location is unknown.

A Demand for a Sign from Heaven
(Mark 8.11-13; Luke 12.54-56)

16 The Pharisees and Sadducees came to Jesus and tried to test him by asking for a sign from heaven. [2]He told them:

If the sky is red in the evening, you say the weather will be good. [3]But if the sky is red and gloomy in the morning, you say it is going to rain. You can tell what the weather will be like by looking at the sky. But you don't understand what is happening now.[e] [4]You want a sign because you are evil and won't believe! But the only sign you will be given is what happened to Jonah.[f]

Then Jesus left.

The Yeast of the Pharisees and Sadducees
(Mark 8.14-21)

[5]The disciples had forgotten to bring any bread when they crossed the lake.[g] [6]Jesus then warned them, "Watch out! Guard against the yeast of the Pharisees and Sadducees."

[7]The disciples talked this over and said to each other, "He must be saying this because we didn't bring along any bread."

[8]Jesus knew what they were thinking and said:

You surely don't have much faith! Why are you talking about not having any bread? [9]Don't you understand? Have you forgotten about the 5,000 people and all those baskets of leftovers from just five loaves of bread? [10]And what about the 4,000 people and all those baskets of leftovers from only seven loaves of bread? [11]Don't you know by now that I am not talking to you about bread? Watch out for the yeast of the Pharisees and Sadducees!

[12]Finally, the disciples understood that Jesus wasn't talking about the yeast used to make bread, but about the teaching of the Pharisees and Sadducees.

e16.2,3 If the sky is red . . . what is happening now: The words of Jesus in verses 2 and 3 are not in some manuscripts.   f16.4 what happened to Jonah: Jonah was in the stomach of a big fish for three days and nights (see 12.40).   g16.5 crossed the lake: To the east side.

Who Is Jesus?
(Mark 8.27-30; Luke 9.18-21)

¹³When Jesus and his disciples were near the town of Caesarea Philippi, he asked them, "What do people say about the Son of Man?"

¹⁴The disciples answered, "Some people say you are John the Baptist or maybe Elijah[h] or Jeremiah or some other prophet."

¹⁵Then Jesus asked, "But who do you say I am?"

¹⁶Simon Peter spoke up, "You are the Messiah, the Son of the living God."

¹⁷Jesus told him:

Simon, son of Jonah, you are blessed! You didn't discover this on your own. It was shown to you by my Father in heaven. ¹⁸So I will call you Peter, which means "a rock." On this rock I will build my church, and death itself will not have any power over it. ¹⁹I will give you the keys to the kingdom of heaven, and God in heaven will allow whatever you allow on earth. But he will not allow anything you don't allow.

²⁰Jesus told his disciples not to tell anyone he was the Messiah.

Jesus Speaks About His Suffering and Death
(Mark 8.31–9.1; Luke 9.22-27)

²¹From then on, Jesus began telling his disciples what would happen to him. He said, "I must go to Jerusalem. There the nation's leaders, the chief priests, and the teachers of the Law of Moses will make me suffer terribly. I will be killed, but three days later I will rise to life."

²²Peter took Jesus aside and told him to stop talking like that. He said, "God would never let this happen to you, Lord!"

²³Jesus turned to Peter and said, "Satan, get away from me! You're in my way because you think like everyone else and not like God."

²⁴Then Jesus said to his disciples:

If any of you want to be my followers, you must forget about yourself. You must take up your cross and follow me. ²⁵If you want to save your life,[i] you will destroy it. But if you give up your

---

h16.14 Elijah: Many of the Jewish people expected the prophet Elijah to come and prepare the way for the Messiah. i16.25 life: In verses 25 and 26 the same Greek word is translated "life," "yourself," and "soul."

life for me, you will find it. ²⁶What will you gain, if you own the whole world but destroy yourself? What would you give to get back your soul?

²⁷The Son of Man will soon come in the glory of his Father and with his angels to reward all people for what they have done. ²⁸I promise you some of those standing here will not die before they see the Son of Man coming with his kingdom.

The True Glory of Jesus
(Mark 9.2-13; Luke 9.28-36)

17 Six days later Jesus took Peter and the brothers James and John with him. They went up on a very high mountain where they could be alone. ²There in front of the disciples, Jesus was completely changed. His face was shining like the sun, and his clothes became white as light.

³All at once Moses and Elijah were there talking with Jesus. ⁴So Peter said to him, "Lord, it is good for us to be here! Let us make three shelters, one for you, one for Moses, and one for Elijah."

⁵While Peter was still speaking, the shadow of a bright cloud passed over them. From the cloud a voice said, "This is my own dear Son, and I am pleased with him. Listen to what he says!" ⁶When the disciples heard the voice, they were so afraid they fell flat on the ground. ⁷But Jesus came over and touched them. He said, "Get up and don't be afraid!" ⁸When they opened their eyes, they saw only Jesus.

⁹On their way down from the mountain, Jesus warned his disciples not to tell anyone what they had seen until after the Son of Man had been raised from death.

¹⁰The disciples asked Jesus, "Don't the teachers of the Law of Moses say Elijah must come before the Messiah does?"

¹¹Jesus told them, "Elijah certainly will come and get everything ready. ¹²In fact, he has already come. But the people did not recognize him and treated him just as they wanted to. They will soon make the Son of Man suffer in the same way." ¹³Then the disciples understood Jesus was talking to them about John the Baptist.

Jesus Heals a Boy
(Mark 9.14-29; Luke 9.37-43a)

[14]Jesus and his disciples returned to the crowd. A man knelt in front of him [15]and said, "Lord, have pity on my son! He has a bad case of epilepsy and often falls into a fire or into water. [16]I brought him to your disciples, but none of them could heal him."

[17]Jesus said, "You people are too stubborn to have any faith! How much longer must I be with you? Why do I have to put up with you? Bring the boy here." [18]Then Jesus spoke sternly to the demon. It went out of the boy, and right then he was healed.

[19]Later the disciples went to Jesus in private and asked him, "Why couldn't we force out the demon?"

[20-21]Jesus replied:

It is because you don't have enough faith! But I can promise you this. If you had faith no larger than a mustard seed, you could tell this mountain to move from here to there. And it would. Everything would be possible for you.[j]

Jesus Again Speaks About His Death
(Mark 9.30-32; Luke 9.43b-45)

[22]While Jesus and his disciples were going from place to place in Galilee, he told them, "The Son of Man will be handed over to people [23]who will kill him. But three days later he will rise to life." All of this made the disciples very sad.

Paying the Temple Tax

[24]When Jesus and the others arrived in Capernaum, the collectors for the temple tax came to Peter and asked, "Does your teacher pay the temple tax?"

[25]"Yes, he does," Peter answered.

After they had returned home, Jesus went up to Peter and asked him, "Simon, what do you think? Do the kings of this earth collect taxes and fees from their own people or from foreigners?"[k]

j17.20,21 *for you:* Some manuscripts add, "But the only way to force out that kind of demon is by praying and going without eating."   k17.25 *from their own people or from foreigners:* Or "from their children or from others."

²⁶Peter answered, "From foreigners."

Jesus replied, "Then their own people¹ don't have to pay. ²⁷But we don't want to cause trouble. So go cast a line into the lake and pull out the first fish you hook. Open its mouth, and you will find a coin. Use it to pay your taxes and mine."

Who Is the Greatest?
(Mark 9.33-37; Luke 9.46-48)

18 About this time the disciples came to Jesus and asked him who would be the greatest in the kingdom of heaven. ²Jesus called for a child to come over and stand near him. ³Then he said:

I promise you this. If you don't change and become like a child, you will never get into the kingdom of heaven. ⁴But if you are as humble as this child, you are the greatest in the kingdom of heaven. ⁵And when you welcome one of these children because of me, you welcome me.

Temptations to Sin
(Mark 9.42-48; Luke 17.1, 2)

⁶It will be terrible for people who cause even one of my little followers to sin. Those people would be better off thrown into the deepest part of the ocean with a heavy stone tied around their necks! ⁷The world is in for trouble because of the way it causes people to sin. There will always be something to cause people to sin, but anyone who does this will be in for trouble.

⁸If your hand or foot causes you to sin, chop it off and throw it away! You would be better off to go into life paralyzed or lame than to have two hands or two feet and be thrown into the fire that never goes out. ⁹If your eye causes you to sin, poke it out and get rid of it. You would be better off to go into life with only one eye than to have two eyes and be thrown into the fires of hell.

117.26 From foreigners . . . their own people: Or "From other people . . . their children."

The Lost Sheep
(Luke 15.3-7)

[10-11]Don't be cruel to any of these little ones! I promise you their angels are always with my Father in heaven.[m] [12]Let me ask you this. What would you do if you had 100 sheep and one of them wandered off? Wouldn't you leave the 99 on the hillside and go look for the one that had wandered away? [13]I am sure that finding it would make you happier than having the 99 that never wandered off. [14]That's how it is with your Father in heaven. He doesn't want any of these little ones to be lost.

When Someone Sins
(Luke 17.3)

[15]If one of my followers[n] sins against you, go and point out what was wrong. But do it in private, just between the two of you. If that person listens, you have won back a follower. [16]But if that one refuses to listen, take along one or two others. The Scriptures teach that every complaint must be proven true by two or more witnesses. [17]If the follower refuses to listen to them, report the matter to the church. Anyone who refuses to listen to the church must be treated like an unbeliever or a tax collector.[o]

Allowing and Not Allowing

[18]I promise you God in heaven will allow whatever you allow on earth, but God will not allow anything you don't allow. [19]I promise that when any two of you on earth agree about something you are praying for, my Father in heaven will do it for you. [20]Whenever two or three of you come together in my name,[p] I am there with you.

---

m18.10,11 in heaven: Some manuscripts add, "The Son of Man came to save people who are lost." n18.15 followers: The Greek text has "brother," which is used here and elsewhere in this chapter to refer to a follower of Christ. o18.17 tax collector: See the note at 5.46. p18.20 in my name: Or "as my followers."

An Official Who Refused to Forgive

[21]Peter came up to the Lord and asked, "How many times should I forgive someone[q] who does something wrong to me? Is seven times enough?"

[22]Jesus answered:

Not just 7 times, but 77 times![r] [23]This story will show you what the kingdom of heaven is like:

One day a king decided to call in his officials and ask them to give an account of what they owed him. [24]As he was doing this, one official was brought in who owed him 50,000,000 silver coins. [25]But he didn't have any money to pay what he owed. The king ordered him to be sold, along with his wife and children and all he owned, in order to pay the debt.

[26]The official got down on his knees and began begging, "Have pity on me, and I will pay you every cent I owe!" [27]The king felt sorry for him and let him go free. He even told the official that he did not have to pay back the money.

[28]But as this official was leaving, he happened to meet another official, who owed him 100 silver coins. So he grabbed the man by the throat. He started choking him and said, "Pay me what you owe!"

[29]The man got down on his knees and began begging, "Have pity on me, and I will pay you back." [30]But the first official refused to have pity. Instead, he went and had the other official put in jail until he could pay what he owed.

[31]When some other officials found out what had happened, they felt sorry for the man who had been put in jail. Then they told the king what had happened. [32]The king called the first official back in and said, "You're an evil man! When you begged for mercy, I said you did not have to pay back a cent. [33]Don't you think you should show pity to someone else, as I did to you?" [34]The king was so angry that he ordered the official to be tortured until he could pay back everything he owed. [35]That is how my Father in heaven will treat you, if you don't forgive each of my followers with all your heart.

q18.21 someone: Or "a follower." See the note at 18.15.　　r18.22 77 times: Or "70 times 7." The large number means that one follower should never stop forgiving another.

Teaching About Divorce
(Mark 10.1-12)

19 When Jesus finished teaching, he left Galilee and went to the part of Judea east of the Jordan River. [2]Large crowds followed him, and he healed their sick.

[3]Some Pharisees wanted to test Jesus. They came up to him and asked, "Is it right for a man to divorce his wife for just any reason?"

[4]Jesus answered, "Don't you know in the beginning the Creator made a man and a woman? [5]That's why a man leaves his father and mother and gets married. He becomes like one person with his wife. [6]Then they are no longer two people, but one. And no one should separate a couple God has joined together."

[7]The Pharisees asked Jesus, "Why did Moses say a man could write out divorce papers and send his wife away?"

[8]Jesus replied, "You are so heartless! That's why Moses allowed you to divorce your wife. But from the beginning God did not intend it to be that way. [9]I say if your wife has not committed some terrible sexual sin,[s] you must not divorce her to marry someone else. If you do, you are unfaithful."

[10]The disciples said, "If that's how it is between a man and a woman, it's better not to get married."

[11]Jesus told them, "Only those people who have been given the gift of staying single can accept this teaching. [12]Some people are unable to marry because of birth defects or because of what someone has done to their bodies. Others stay single in order to serve God better. Anyone who can accept this teaching should do so."

Jesus Blesses Little Children
(Mark 10.13-16; Luke 18.15-17)

[13]Some people brought their children to Jesus, so he could place his hands on them and pray for them. His disciples told the people to stop bothering him. [14]But Jesus said, "Let the children come to me, and don't try to stop them! People who are like these children belong to God's kingdom."[t] [15]After Jesus had placed his hands on the children, he left.

---

s19.9 *some terrible sexual sin:* See the note at 5.32.   t19.14 *People who are like these children belong to God's kingdom:* Or "God's kingdom belongs to people who are like these children."

A Rich Young Man
(Mark 10.17-31; Luke 18.18-30)

¹⁶A man came to Jesus and asked, "Teacher, what good thing must I do to have eternal life?"

¹⁷Jesus said to him, "Why do you ask me about what is good? Only God is good. If you want to have eternal life, you must obey his commandments."

¹⁸"Which ones?" the man asked.

Jesus answered, "Do not murder. Be faithful in marriage. Do not steal. Do not tell lies about others. ¹⁹Respect your father and mother. And love others as much as you love yourself." ²⁰The young man said, "I have obeyed all of these. What else must I do?"

²¹Jesus replied, "If you want to be perfect, go sell everything you own! Give the money to the poor, and you will have riches in heaven. Then come and be my follower." ²²When the young man heard this, he went away sad, because he was very rich.

²³Jesus said to his disciples, "I tell you, it's terribly hard for rich people to get into the kingdom of heaven! ²⁴In fact, it's easier for a camel to go through the eye of a needle than for a rich person to get into God's kingdom."

²⁵When the disciples heard this, they were greatly surprised and asked, "How can anyone ever be saved?"

²⁶Jesus looked straight at them and said, "There are some things people cannot do, but God can do anything."

²⁷Peter replied, "Remember, we have left everything to be your followers! What will we get?"

²⁸Jesus answered:

Yes, all of you have become my followers. And so in the future world, when the Son of Man sits on his glorious throne, I promise you will sit on twelve thrones to judge the twelve tribes of Israel. ²⁹All who have given up home or brothers and sisters or father and mother or children or land for me will be given 100 times as much. They will also have eternal life. ³⁰But many who are now first will be last, and many who are last will be first.

Workers in a Vineyard

20As Jesus was telling what the kingdom of heaven would be like, he said:

Early one morning a man went out to hire some workers for his vineyard. ²After he had agreed to pay them the usual amount for a day's work, he sent them off to his vineyard.

³About nine that morning, the man saw some other people standing in the market with nothing to do. ⁴He promised to pay them what was fair, if they would work in his vineyard. ⁵So they went.

At noon and again about three in the afternoon he returned to the market. And each time he made the same agreement with others who were loafing around with nothing to do.

⁶Finally, about five in the afternoon the man went back and found some others standing there. He asked them, "Why have you been standing here all day long doing nothing?"

⁷"Because no one has hired us," they answered. Then he told them to go work in his vineyard.

⁸That evening the owner of the vineyard told the man in charge of the workers to call them in and give them their money. He also told the man to begin with the ones who were hired last. ⁹When the workers arrived, the ones who had been hired at five in the afternoon were given a full day's pay.

¹⁰The workers who had been hired first thought they would be given more than the others. But when they were given the same, ¹¹they began complaining to the owner of the vineyard. ¹²They said, "The ones who were hired last worked for only one hour. But you paid them the same that you did us. And we worked in the hot sun all day long!"

¹³The owner answered one of them, "Friend, I didn't cheat you. I paid you exactly what we agreed on. ¹⁴Take your money now and go! What business is it of yours if I want to pay them the same that I paid you? ¹⁵Don't I have the right to do what I want with my own money? Why should you be jealous, if I want to be generous?"

¹⁶Jesus then said, "So it is. Everyone who is now last will be first, and everyone who is first will be last."

Jesus Again Tells About His Death
(Mark 10.32-34; Luke 18.31-34)

¹⁷As Jesus was on his way to Jerusalem, he took his twelve disciples aside and told them in private:

[18]We are now on our way to Jerusalem, where the Son of Man will be handed over to the chief priests and the teachers of the Law of Moses. They will sentence him to death, [19]and then they will hand him over to foreigners[u] who will make fun of him. They will beat him and nail him to a cross. But on the third day he will rise from death.

A Mother's Request
(Mark 10.35-45)

[20]The mother of James and John[v] came to Jesus with her two sons. She knelt down and started begging him to do something for her. [21]Jesus asked her what she wanted, and she said, "When you come into your kingdom, please let one of my sons sit at your right side and the other at your left."[w]

[22]Jesus answered, "Not one of you knows what you are asking. Are you able to drink from the cup[x] that I must soon drink from?"

James and John said, "Yes, we are!"

[23]Jesus replied, "You certainly will drink from my cup! But it isn't for me to say who will sit at my right side and at my left. This is for my Father to say."

[24]When the ten other disciples heard this, they were angry with the two brothers. [25]But Jesus called the disciples together and said:

You know foreign rulers like to order their people around. And their great leaders have full power over everyone they rule. [26]But don't act like them. If you want to be great, you must be the servant of all the others. [27]And if you want to be first, you must be the slave of the rest. [28]The Son of Man did not come to be a slave master, but a slave who will give his life to rescue[y] many people.

Jesus Heals Two Blind Men
(Mark 10.46-52; Luke 18.35-43)

[29]Jesus was followed by a large crowd as he and his disciples were leaving Jericho. [30]Two blind men were sitting beside the road. And when they heard that

---

u20.19 foreigners: The Romans, who ruled Judea at this time.   v20.20 mother of James and John: The Greek text has "mother of the sons of Zebedee" (see 26.37).   w20.21 right side . . . left: The most powerful people in a kingdom sat at the right and left side of the king.   x20.22 drink from the cup: In the Scriptures a cup is sometimes used as a symbol of suffering. To "drink from the cup" is to suffer.   y20.28 rescue: The Greek word often, though not always, means the payment of a price to free a slave or a prisoner.

Jesus was coming their way, they shouted, "Lord and Son of David,[z] have pity on us!"

[31]The crowd told them to be quiet, but they shouted even louder, "Lord and Son of David, have pity on us!"

[32]When Jesus heard them, he stopped and asked, "What do you want me to do for you?"

[33]They answered, "Lord, we want to see!"

[34]Jesus felt sorry for them and touched their eyes. At once they could see, and they became his followers.

Jesus Enters Jerusalem
(Mark 11.1-11; Luke 19.28-38; John 12.12-19)

21 When Jesus and his disciples came near Jerusalem, he went to Bethphage on the Mount of Olives and sent two of them on ahead. [2]He told them, "Go into the next village, where you will at once find a donkey and her colt. Untie the two donkeys and bring them to me. [3]If anyone asks why you are doing this, just say, 'The Lord[a] needs them.' He will at once let you have the donkeys."

[4]So God's promise came true, just as the prophet had said,

[5]"Announce to the people
   of Jerusalem:
'Your king is coming to you!
He is humble
   and rides on a donkey.
He comes on the colt
   of a donkey.'"

[6]The disciples left and did what Jesus had told them to do. [7]They brought the donkey and its colt and laid some clothes on their backs. Then Jesus got on.

[8]Many people spread clothes in the road, while others put down branches[b] which they had cut from trees. [9]Some people walked ahead of Jesus and others followed behind. They were all shouting,

"Hooray[c] for the Son of David![d]
God bless the one who comes

---

z20.30 Son of David: See the note at 9.27.   a21.3 The Lord: Or "The master of the donkeys."
b21.8 spread clothes . . . put down branches: This was one way that the Jewish people welcomed a
famous person.   c21.9 Hooray: This translates a word that can mean "please save us." But it is most
often used as a shout of praise to God.   d21.9 Son of David: See the note at 9.27.

in the name of the Lord.
Hooray for God
    in heaven above!"

¹⁰When Jesus came to Jerusalem, everyone in the city was excited and asked, "Who can this be?"

¹¹The crowds answered, "This is Jesus, the prophet from Nazareth in Galilee."

Jesus in the Temple
(Mark 11.15-19; Luke 19.45-48; John 2.13-22)

¹²Jesus went into the temple and chased out everyone who was selling or buying. He turned over the tables of the moneychangers and the benches of the ones who were selling doves. ¹³He told them, "The Scriptures say, 'My house should be called a place of worship.' But you have turned it into a place where robbers hide."

¹⁴Blind and lame people came to Jesus in the temple, and he healed them. ¹⁵But the chief priests and the teachers of the Law of Moses were angry when they saw his miracles and heard the children shouting praises to the Son of David.^e ¹⁶The men said to Jesus, "Don't you hear what those children are saying?"

"Yes, I do!" Jesus answered. "Don't you know that the Scriptures say, 'Children and infants will sing praises'?" ¹⁷Then Jesus left the city and went out to the village of Bethany, where he spent the night.

Jesus Puts a Curse on a Fig Tree
(Mark 11.12-14, 20-24)

¹⁸When Jesus got up the next morning, he was hungry. He started out for the city, ¹⁹and along the way he saw a fig tree. But when he came to it, he found only leaves and no figs. So he told the tree, "You will never again grow any fruit!" Right then the fig tree dried up.

²⁰The disciples were shocked when they saw how quickly the tree had dried up. ²¹But Jesus said to them, "If you have faith and don't doubt, I promise you can do what I did to this tree. And you will be able to do even more.

e21.15 Son of David: See the note at 9.27.

You can tell this mountain to get up and jump into the sea, and it will. ²²If you have faith when you pray, you will be given whatever you ask for."

A Question About Jesus' Authority
(Mark 11.27-33; Luke 20.1-8)

²³Jesus had gone into the temple and was teaching when the chief priests and the leaders of the people came up to him. They asked, "What right do you have to do these things? Who gave you this authority?"

²⁴Jesus answered, "I have just one question to ask you. If you answer it, I will tell you where I got the right to do these things. ²⁵Who gave John the right to baptize? Was it God in heaven or merely some human being?"

They thought it over and said to each other, "We can't say God gave John this right. Jesus will ask us why we didn't believe John. ²⁶On the other hand, these people think John was a prophet, and we are afraid of what they might do to us. That's why we can't say it was merely some human who gave John the right to baptize." ²⁷So they told Jesus, "We don't know."

Jesus said, "Then I won't tell you who gave me the right to do what I do."

A Story About Two Sons

²⁸Jesus said:

I will tell you a story about a man who had two sons. Then you can tell me what you think. The father went to the older son and said, "Go work in the vineyard today!" ²⁹His son told him he would not do it, but later he changed his mind and went. ³⁰The man then told his younger son to go work in the vineyard. The boy said he would, but he didn't go. ³¹Which one of the sons obeyed his father?

"The older one," the chief priests and leaders answered.

Then Jesus told them:

You can be sure tax collectors^f and prostitutes will get into the kingdom of God before you ever will! ³²When John the Baptist showed you how to do right, you would not believe him. But these evil people did believe. And even when you saw what they did, you still would not change your minds and believe.

---

f21.31 tax collectors: See the note at 5.46.

Renters of a Vineyard
(Mark 12.1-12; Luke 20.9-19)

[33]Jesus told the chief priests and leaders to listen to this story:

A land owner once planted a vineyard. He built a wall around it and dug a pit to crush the grapes in. He also built a lookout tower. Then he rented out his vineyard and left the country.

[34]When it was harvest time, the owner sent some servants to get his share of the grapes. [35]But the renters grabbed those servants. They beat up one, killed one, and stoned one of them to death. [36]He then sent more servants than he did the first time. But the renters treated them in the same way.

[37]Finally, the owner sent his own son to the renters, because he thought they would respect him. [38]But when they saw the man's son, they said, "Someday he will own the vineyard. Let's kill him! Then we can have it all for ourselves." [39]So they grabbed him, threw him out of the vineyard, and killed him.

[40]Jesus asked, "When the owner of that vineyard comes, what do you suppose he will do to those renters?"

[41]The chief priests and leaders answered, "He will kill them in some horrible way. Then he will rent out his vineyard to people who will give him his share of grapes at harvest time."

[42]Jesus replied, "You surely know that the Scriptures say,

'The stone the builders
    tossed aside
is now the most important
    stone of all.
This is something
the Lord has done,
    and it is amazing to us.'

[43]I tell you God's kingdom will be taken from you and given to people who will do what he demands. [44]Anyone who stumbles over this stone will be crushed, and anyone it falls on will be smashed to pieces."[g]

[45]When the chief priests and the Pharisees heard these stories, they knew Jesus was talking about them. [46]So they looked for a way to arrest Jesus. But they were afraid to, because the people thought he was a prophet.

g21.44 pieces: Verse 44 is not in some manuscripts.

The Great Banquet
(Luke 14.15-24)

22 Once again Jesus used stories to teach the people:
²The kingdom of heaven is like what happened when a king gave a wedding banquet for his son. ³The king sent some servants to tell the invited guests to come to the banquet, but the guests refused. ⁴He sent other servants to say to the guests, "The banquet is ready! My cattle and prize calves have all been prepared. Everything is ready. Come to the banquet!"

⁵But the guests did not pay any attention. Some of them left for their farms, and some went to their places of business. ⁶Others grabbed the servants, then beat them up and killed them.

⁷This made the king so furious that he sent an army to kill those murderers and burn down their city. ⁸Then he said to the servants, "It is time for the wedding banquet, and the invited guests don't deserve to come. ⁹Go out to the street corners and tell everyone you meet to come to the banquet." ¹⁰They went out on the streets and brought in everyone they could find, good and bad alike. And the banquet room was filled with guests.

¹¹When the king went in to meet the guests, he found that one of them wasn't wearing the right kind of clothes for the wedding. ¹²The king asked, "Friend, why didn't you wear proper clothes for the wedding?" But the guest had no excuse. ¹³So the king gave orders for this person to be tied hand and foot and to be thrown outside into the dark. That's where people will cry and grit their teeth in pain. ¹⁴Many are invited, but only a few are chosen.

Paying Taxes
(Mark 12.13-17; Luke 20.20-26)

¹⁵The Pharisees got together and planned how they could trick Jesus into saying something wrong. ¹⁶They sent some of their followers and some of Herod's followers[h] to say to him, "Teacher, we know that you are honest. You teach the truth about what God wants people to do. And you treat everyone with

---

h22.16 *Herod's followers:* People who were political followers of the family of Herod the Great (see 2.1) and his son Herod Antipas (see 14.1), and who wanted Herod to be king in Jerusalem.

the same respect, no matter who they are. [17]Tell us what you think! Should we pay taxes to the Emperor or not?"

[18]Jesus knew their evil thoughts and said, "Why are you trying to test me? You show-offs! [19]Let me see one of the coins used for paying taxes." They brought him a silver coin, [20]and he asked, "Whose picture and name are on it?"

[21]"The Emperor's," they answered.

Then Jesus told them, "Give the Emperor what belongs to him and give God what belongs to God." [22]His answer surprised them so much that they walked away.

Life in the Future World
(Mark 12.18-27; Luke 20.27-40)

[23]The Sadducees did not believe people would rise to life after death. So that same day some of the Sadducees came to Jesus and said:

[24]Teacher, Moses wrote that if a married man dies and has no children, his brother should marry the widow. Their first son would then be thought of as the son of the dead brother.

[25]Once there were seven brothers who lived here. The first one married, but died without having any children. So his wife was left to his brother. [26]The same thing happened to the second and third brothers and finally to all seven of them. [27]At last the woman died. [28]When God raises people from death, whose wife will this woman be? She had been married to all seven brothers.

[29]Jesus answered:

You are completely wrong! You don't know what the Scriptures teach. And you don't know anything about the power of God. [30]When God raises people to life, they won't marry. They will be like the angels in heaven. [31]And as for people being raised to life, God was speaking to you when he said, [32]"I am the God worshiped by Abraham, Isaac, and Jacob."[i] He isn't the God of the dead, but of the living.

[33]The crowds were surprised to hear what Jesus was teaching.

---

i22.32 I am the God worshiped by Abraham, Isaac, and Jacob: Jesus argues that if God is worshiped by these three, they must still be alive, because he is the God of the living.

The Most Important Commandment
(Mark 12.28-34; Luke 10.25-28)

³⁴After Jesus had made the Sadducees look foolish, the Pharisees heard about it and got together. ³⁵One of them was an expert in the Jewish Law. So he tried to test Jesus by asking, ³⁶"Teacher, what is the most important commandment in the Law?"

³⁷Jesus answered:

Love the Lord your God with all your heart, soul, and mind. ³⁸This is the first and most important commandment. ³⁹The second most important commandment is like this one. And it is, "Love others as much as you love yourself." ⁴⁰All the Law of Moses and the Books of the Prophetsʲ are based on these two commandments.

About David's Son
(Mark 12.35-37; Luke 20.41-44)

⁴¹While the Pharisees were still there, Jesus asked them, ⁴²"What do you think about the Messiah? Whose family will he come from?"

They answered, "He will be a son of King David."ᵏ

⁴³Jesus replied, "How then could the Spirit lead David to call the Messiah his Lord? David said,

⁴⁴'The Lord said to my Lord:

Sit at my right sideˡ

until I make your enemies

into a footstool for you.'

⁴⁵If David called the Messiah his Lord, how can the Messiah be a son of King David?" ⁴⁶No one was able to give Jesus an answer, and from that day on, no one dared ask him any more questions.

j22.40 the Law of Moses and the Books of the Prophets: The Jewish Scriptures, that is, the Old Testament. k22.42 son of King David: See the note at 9.27. l22.44 right side: The place of power and honor.

Jesus Condemns the Pharisees and the Teachers of the Law of Moses
(Mark 12.38-40; Luke 11.37-52; 20.45-47)

23 Jesus said to the crowds and to his disciples: [2]The Pharisees and the teachers of the Law are experts in the Law of Moses. [3]So obey everything they teach you, but don't do as they do. After all, they say one thing and do something else.

[4]They pile heavy burdens on people's shoulders and won't lift a finger to help. [5]Everything they do is just to show off in front of others. They even make a big show of wearing Scripture verses on their foreheads and arms, and they wear big tassels[m] for everyone to see. [6]They love the best seats at banquets and the front seats in the synagogues. [7]And when they are in the market, they like to have people greet them as their teachers.

[8]But none of you should be called a teacher. You have only one teacher, and all of you are like brothers and sisters. [9]Don't call anyone on earth your father. All of you have the same Father in heaven. [10]None of you should be called the leader. The Messiah is your only leader. [11]Whoever is the greatest should be the servant of the others. [12]If you put yourself above others, you will be put down. But if you humble yourself, you will be honored.

[13-14]You Pharisees and teachers of the Law of Moses are in for trouble! You're nothing but show-offs. You lock people out of the kingdom of heaven. You won't go in yourselves, and you keep others from going in.[n]

[15]You Pharisees and teachers of the Law of Moses are in for trouble! You're nothing but show-offs. You travel over land and sea to win one follower. And when you have done so, you make that person twice as fit for hell as you are.

[16]You are in for trouble! You are supposed to lead others, but you are blind. You teach that it doesn't matter if a person swears by the

---

m23.5 *wearing Scripture verses on their foreheads and arms . . . tassels:* As a sign of their love for God and his teachings, the Jewish people often wore Scripture verses in small leather boxes. But the Pharisees tried to show off by making the boxes bigger than necessary. The Jewish people were also taught to wear tassels on the four corners of their robes to show their love for God.   n23.13,14 *from going in:* Some manuscripts add, "You Pharisees and teachers are in for trouble! And you're nothing but show-offs! You cheat widows out of their homes and then pray long prayers just to show off. So you will be punished most of all."

temple. But you say it does matter if someone swears by the gold in the temple. ¹⁷You blind fools! Which is greater, the gold or the temple that makes the gold sacred?

¹⁸You also teach that it doesn't matter if a person swears by the altar. But you say it does matter if someone swears by the gift on the altar. ¹⁹Are you blind? Which is more important, the gift or the altar that makes the gift sacred? ²⁰Anyone who swears by the altar also swears by everything on it. ²¹And anyone who swears by the temple also swears by God, who lives there. ²²To swear by heaven is the same as swearing by God's throne and by the one who sits on that throne.

²³You Pharisees and teachers are show-offs, and you're in for trouble! You give God a tenth of the spices from your garden, such as mint, dill, and cumin. Yet you neglect the more important matters of the Law, such as justice, mercy, and faithfulness. These are the important things you should have done, though you should not have left the others undone either. ²⁴You blind leaders! You strain out a small fly but swallow a camel.

²⁵You Pharisees and teachers are show-offs, and you're in for trouble! You wash the outside of your cups and dishes, while inside there is nothing but greed and selfishness. ²⁶You blind Pharisee! First clean the inside of a cup, and then the outside will also be clean.

²⁷You Pharisees and teachers are in for trouble! You're nothing but show-offs. You're like tombs that have been whitewashed.° On the outside they are beautiful, but inside they are full of bones and filth. ²⁸That's what you are like. Outside you look good, but inside you are evil and only pretend to be good.

²⁹You Pharisees and teachers are nothing but show-offs, and you're in for trouble! You build monuments for the prophets and decorate the tombs of good people. ³⁰And you claim you would not have taken part with your ancestors in killing the prophets. ³¹But you prove you really are the relatives of the ones who killed the prophets. ³²So keep on doing everything they did. ³³You are nothing but snakes and the children of snakes! How can you escape going to hell?

³⁴I will send to you prophets and wise people and experts in the

---

o23.27 *whitewashed:* Tombs were whitewashed to keep anyone from accidentally touching them. A person who touched a dead body or a tomb was considered unclean and could not worship with the rest of the Jewish people.

Law of Moses. You will kill them or nail them to a cross or beat them in your synagogues or chase them from town to town. [35]That's why you will be held guilty for the murder of every good person, beginning with the good man Abel. This also includes Barachiah's son Zechariah,[p] the man you murdered between the temple and the altar. [36]I can promise that you people living today will be punished for all these things!

Jesus Loves Jerusalem
(Luke 13.34,35)

[37]Jerusalem, Jerusalem! Your people have killed the prophets and have stoned the messengers who were sent to you. I have often wanted to gather your people, as a hen gathers her chicks under her wings. But you wouldn't let me. [38]And now your temple will be deserted. [39]You won't see me again until you say,

"Blessed is the one who comes
in the name of the Lord."

The Temple Will Be Destroyed
(Mark 13.1,2; Luke 21.5,6)

24 After Jesus left the temple, his disciples came over and said, "Look at all these buildings!"
[2]Jesus replied, "Do you see these buildings? They will certainly be torn down! Not one stone will be left in place."

Warning About Trouble
(Mark 13.3-13; Luke 21.7-19)

[3]Later, as Jesus was sitting on the Mount of Olives, his disciples came to him in private and asked, "When will this happen? What will be the sign of your coming and of the end of the world?"

p23.35 Zechariah: Genesis is the first book in the Jewish Scriptures, and it tells that Abel was the first person to be murdered. Second Chronicles is the last book in the Jewish Scriptures, and the last murder that it tells about is that of Zechariah.

[4]Jesus answered:

Don't let anyone fool you. [5]Many will come and claim to be me. They will say they are the Messiah, and they will fool many people.

[6]You will soon hear about wars and threats of wars, but don't be afraid. These things will have to happen first, but that isn't the end. [7]Nations and kingdoms will go to war against each other. People will starve to death, and in some places there will be earthquakes. [8]But this is just the beginning of troubles.

[9]You will be arrested, punished, and even killed. Because of me, you will be hated by people of all nations. [10]Many will give up and will betray and hate each other. [11]Many false prophets will come and fool a lot of people. [12]Evil will spread and cause many people to stop loving others. [13]But if you keep on being faithful right to the end, you will be saved. [14]When the good news about the kingdom has been preached all over the world and told to all nations, the end will come.

The Horrible Thing
(Mark 13.14-23; Luke 21.20-24)

[15]Someday you will see that "Horrible Thing" in the holy place, just as the prophet Daniel said. Everyone who reads this must try to understand! [16]If you are living in Judea at that time, run to the mountains. [17]If you are on the roof[q] of your house, don't go inside to get anything. [18]If you are out in the field, don't go back for your coat. [19]It will be a terrible time for women who are expecting babies or nursing young children. [20]And pray that you won't have to escape in winter or on a Sabbath.[r] [21]This will be the worst time of suffering since the beginning of the world, and nothing this terrible will ever happen again. [22]If God doesn't make the time shorter, no one will be left alive. But because of God's chosen ones, he will make the time shorter.

[23]Someone may say, "Here is the Messiah!" or "There he is!" But don't believe it. [24]False messiahs and false prophets will come and

---

q24.17 *roof:* In Palestine the houses usually had a flat roof. Stairs on the outside led up to the roof, which was made of beams and boards covered with packed earth.   r24.20 *in winter or on a Sabbath:* In Palestine the winters are cold and rainy and make travel difficult. The Jewish people were not allowed to travel much more than half a mile on the Sabbath. For these reasons it was hard for them to escape from their enemies in the winter or on a Sabbath.

work great miracles and signs. They will even try to fool God's chosen ones. [25]But I have warned you ahead of time. [26]If you are told the Messiah is out in the desert, don't go there! And if you are told he is in some secret place, don't believe it! [27]The coming of the Son of Man will be like lightning that can be seen from east to west. [28]Where there is a corpse, there will always be vultures.[s]

When the Son of Man Appears
(Mark 13.24-27; Luke 21.25-28)

[29]Right after those days of suffering,
"The sun will become dark,
and the moon
    will no longer shine.
The stars will fall,
and the powers in the sky[t]
    will be shaken."

[30]Then a sign will appear in the sky. And there will be the Son of Man.[u] All nations on earth will weep when they see the Son of Man coming on the clouds of heaven with power and great glory. [31]At the sound of a loud trumpet, he will send his angels to bring his chosen ones together from all over the earth.

A Lesson from a Fig Tree
(Mark 13.28-31; Luke 21.29-33)

[32]Learn a lesson from a fig tree. When its branches sprout and start putting out leaves, you know summer is near. [33]So when you see all these things happening, you will know the time has almost come.[v] [34]I can promise you that some of the people of this generation will still be

---

s24.28 *Where there is a corpse, there will always be vultures:* This saying may mean that when anything important happens, people soon know about it. Or the saying may mean that whenever something bad happens, curious people gather around and stare. But the word translated "vulture" also means "eagle" and may refer to the Roman army, which had an eagle as its symbol.   t24.29 *the powers in the sky:* In ancient times people thought that the stars were spiritual powers.   u24.30 *And there will be the Son of Man:* Or "And it will be the Son of Man."   v24.33 *the time has almost come:* Or "he (that is, the Son of Man) will soon be here."

alive when all this happens. ³⁵The sky and the earth won't last forever, but my words will.

No One Knows the Day or Time
(Mark 13.32-37; Luke 17.26-30, 34-36)

³⁶No one knows the day or hour. The angels in heaven don't know, and the Son himself doesn't know.ʷ Only the Father knows. ³⁷When the Son of Man appears, things will be just as they were when Noah lived. ³⁸People were eating, drinking, and getting married right up to the day the flood came and Noah went into the big boat. ³⁹They didn't know anything was happening until the flood came and swept them all away. This is how it will be when the Son of Man appears.

⁴⁰Two men will be in the same field, but only one will be taken. The other will be left. ⁴¹Two women will be together grinding grain, but only one will be taken. The other will be left. ⁴²So be on your guard! You don't know when your Lord will come. ⁴³Homeowners never know when a thief is coming, and they are always on guard to keep one from breaking in. ⁴⁴Always be ready! You don't know when the Son of Man will come.

Faithful and Unfaithful Servants
(Luke 12.35-48)

⁴⁵Who are faithful and wise servants? Who are the ones the master will put in charge of giving the other servants their food supplies at the proper time? ⁴⁶Servants are fortunate if their master comes and finds them doing their job. ⁴⁷You may be sure a servant who is always faithful will be put in charge of everything the master owns. ⁴⁸But suppose one of the servants thinks the master won't return until late. ⁴⁹Suppose this evil servant starts beating the other servants and eats and drinks with people who are drunk. ⁵⁰If that happens, the master will surely come on a day and at a time when the servant least expects him. ⁵¹This servant will then be punished and thrown out with the ones who only pretended to serve their master. There they will cry and grit their teeth in pain.

w24.36 and the Son himself doesn't know: These words are not in some manuscripts.

A Story About Ten Young Women

25 The kingdom of heaven is like what happened one night when ten young women took their oil lamps and went to a wedding to meet the groom.[x] [2]Five of them were foolish and five were wise. [3]The foolish ones took their lamps, but no extra oil. [4]The ones who were wise took along extra oil for their lamps.

[5]The groom was late arriving, and the young women became drowsy and fell asleep. [6]Then in the middle of the night someone shouted, "Here's the groom! Come to meet him!"

[7]When the women got up and started getting their lamps ready, [8]the foolish ones said to the others, "Let us have some of your oil! Our lamps are going out."

[9]Those who were wise answered, "There's not enough oil for all of us! Go and buy some for yourselves."

[10]While the foolish ones were on their way to get some oil, the groom arrived. The five who were ready went into the wedding, and the doors were closed. [11]Later the others returned and shouted, "Sir, sir! Open the door for us!"

[12]But the groom replied, "I don't even know you!"

[13]So, my disciples, always be ready! You don't know the day or the time when all this will happen.

A Story about Three Servants
(Luke 19.11-27)

[14]The kingdom is also like what happened when a man went away and put his three servants in charge of all he owned. [15]The man knew what each servant could do. So he handed 5,000 coins to the first servant, 2,000 to the second, and 1,000 to the third. Then he left the country.

[16]As soon as the man had gone, the servant with the 5,000 coins used them to earn 5,000 more. [17]The servant who had 2,000 coins did the same with his money and earned 2,000 more. [18]But the ser-

---

x25.1 *to meet the groom:* Some manuscripts add "and the bride." It was the custom for the groom to go to the home of the bride's parents to get his bride. Young women and other guests would then go with them to the home of the groom's parents, where the wedding feast would take place.

vant with 1,000 coins dug a hole and hid his master's money in the ground.

19Some time later the master of those servants returned. He called them in and asked what they had done with his money. 20The servant who had been given 5,000 coins brought them in with the 5,000 that he had earned. He said, "Sir, you gave me 5,000 coins, and I have earned 5,000 more."

21"Wonderful!" his master replied. "You are a good and faithful servant. I left you in charge of only a little, but now I will put you in charge of much more. Come and share in my happiness!"

22Next, the servant who had been given 2,000 coins came in and said, "Sir, you gave me 2,000 coins, and I have earned 2,000 more."

23"Wonderful!" his master replied. "You are a good and faithful servant. I left you in charge of only a little, but now I will put you in charge of much more. Come and share in my happiness!"

24The servant who had been given 1,000 coins then came in and said, "Sir, I know that you are hard to work for. You harvest what you don't plant and gather crops where you haven't scattered seed. 25I was frightened and went out and hid your money in the ground. Here is every single coin!"

26The master of the servant told him, "You are lazy and good-for-nothing! You know I harvest what I don't plant and gather crops where I haven't scattered seed. 27You could have at least put my money in the bank, so I could have earned interest on it."

28Then the master said, "Now your money will be taken away and given to the servant with 10,000 coins! 29Everyone who has something will be given more, and they will have more than enough. But everything will be taken from those who don't have anything. 30You are a worthless servant, and you will be thrown out into the dark where people will cry and grit their teeth in pain."

The Final Judgment

31When the Son of Man comes in his glory with all his angels, he will sit on his royal throne. 32The people of all nations will be brought before him, and he will separate them, as shepherds separate their sheep from their goats.

33He will place the sheep on his right and the goats on his left.

³⁴Then the king will say to those on his right, "My father has blessed you! Come and receive the kingdom that was prepared for you before the world was created. ³⁵When I was hungry, you gave me something to eat, and when I was thirsty, you gave me something to drink. When I was a stranger, you welcomed me, ³⁶and when I was naked, you gave me clothes to wear. When I was sick, you took care of me, and when I was in jail, you visited me."

³⁷Then the ones who pleased the Lord will ask, "When did we give you something to eat or drink? ³⁸When did we welcome you as a stranger or give you clothes to wear ³⁹or visit you while you were sick or in jail?"

⁴⁰The king will answer, "Whenever you did it for any of my people, no matter how unimportant they seemed, you did it for me."

⁴¹Then the king will say to those on his left, "Get away from me! You are under God's curse. Go into the everlasting fire prepared for the devil and his angels! ⁴²I was hungry, but you did not give me anything to eat, and I was thirsty, but you did not give me anything to drink. ⁴³I was a stranger, but you did not welcome me, and I was naked, but you did not give me any clothes to wear. I was sick and in jail, but you did not take care of me."

⁴⁴Then the people will ask, "Lord, when did we fail to help you when you were hungry or thirsty or a stranger or naked or sick or in jail?"

⁴⁵The king will say to them, "Whenever you failed to help any of my people, no matter how unimportant they seemed, you failed to do it for me."

⁴⁶Then Jesus said, "Those people will be punished forever. But the ones who pleased God will have eternal life."

The Plot to Kill Jesus
(Mark 14.1, 2; Luke 22.1, 2; John 11.45-53)

26 When Jesus had finished teaching, he told his disciples, ²"You know two days from now will be Passover. This is when the Son of Man will be handed over to his enemies and nailed to a cross."

³At that time the chief priests and the nation's leaders were meeting at the home of Caiaphas the high priest. ⁴They planned how they could sneak

around and have Jesus arrested and put to death. [5]But they said, "We must not do it during Passover, because the people will riot."

At Bethany
(Mark 14.3-9; John 12.1-8)

[6]Jesus was in the town of Bethany, eating at the home of Simon, who had leprosy.[y] [7]A woman came in with a bottle of expensive perfume and poured it on Jesus' head. [8]But when his disciples saw this, they became angry and complained, "Why such a waste? [9]We could have sold this perfume for a lot of money and given it to the poor."

[10]Jesus knew what they were thinking, and he said:

Why are you bothering this woman? She has done a beautiful thing for me. [11]You will always have the poor with you, but you won't always have me. [12]She has poured perfume on my body to prepare it for burial.[z] [13]You may be sure that wherever the good news is told all over the world, people will remember what she has done. And they will tell others.

Judas and the Chief Priests
(Mark 14.10,11; Luke 22.3-6)

[14]Judas Iscariot[a] was one of the twelve disciples. He went to the chief priests [15]and asked, "How much will you give me if I help you arrest Jesus?" They paid Judas 30 silver coins, [16]and from then on he started looking for a good chance to betray Jesus.

Jesus Eats the Passover Meal with His Disciples
(Mark 14.12-21; Luke 22.7-13; John 13.21-30)

[17]On the first day of the Festival of Thin Bread, Jesus' disciples came to him and asked, "Where do you want us to prepare the Passover meal?"

[18]Jesus told them to go to a certain man in the city and tell him, "Our

---

y26.6 leprosy: See the note at 8.2.   z26.12 poured perfume on my body to prepare it for burial: The Jewish people taught that giving someone a proper burial was even more important than helping the poor.   a26.14 Iscariot: See the note at 10.4.

teacher says, 'My time has come! I want to eat the Passover meal with my disciples in your home.'" [19]They did as Jesus told them and prepared the meal.

[20-21]When Jesus was eating with his twelve disciples that evening, he said, "One of you will surely hand me over to my enemies."

[22]The disciples were very sad, and each one said to Jesus, "Lord, you can't mean me!"

[23]He answered, "One of you men who has eaten with me from this dish will betray me. [24]The Son of Man will die, as the Scriptures say. But it's going to be terrible for the one who betrays me! That man would be better off if he had never been born."

[25]Judas said, "Teacher, you surely don't mean me!"

"That's what you say!" Jesus replied. But later, Judas did betray him.

The Lord's Supper
(Mark 14.22-26; Luke 22.14-23; 1 Corinthians 11.23-25)

[26]During the meal Jesus took some bread in his hands. He blessed the bread and broke it. Then he gave it to his disciples and said, "Take this and eat it. This is my body."

[27]Jesus picked up a cup of wine and gave thanks to God. He then gave it to his disciples and said, "Take this and drink it. [28]This is my blood, and with it God makes his agreement with you. It will be poured out, so that many people will have their sins forgiven. [29]From now on I am not going to drink any wine, until I drink new wine with you in my Father's kingdom." [30]Then they sang a hymn and went out to the Mount of Olives.

Peter's Promise
(Mark 14.27-31; Luke 22.31-34; John 13.36-38)

[31]Jesus said to his disciples, "During this very night, all of you will reject me, as the Scriptures say,

'I will strike down
    the shepherd,
and the sheep
    will be scattered.'

[32]But after I am raised to life, I will go ahead of you to Galilee."

[33]Peter spoke up, "Even if all the others reject you, I never will!"

[34]Jesus replied, "I promise you before a rooster crows tonight, you will say

three times that you don't know me." [35]But Peter said, "Even if I have to die with you, I will never say I don't know you."

All the others said the same thing.

Jesus Prays
(Mark 14.32-42; Luke 22.39-46)

[36]Jesus went with his disciples to a place called Gethsemane. When they got there, he told them, "Sit here while I go over there and pray."

[37]Jesus took along Peter and the two brothers, James and John.[b] He was very sad and troubled, [38]and he said to them, "I am so sad that I feel as if I am dying. Stay here and keep awake with me."

[39]Jesus walked on a little way. Then he knelt with his face to the ground and prayed, "My Father, if it is possible, don't make me suffer by drinking from this cup.[c] But do what you want, and not what I want."

[40]He came back and found his disciples sleeping. So he said to Peter, "Can't any of you stay awake with me for just one hour? [41]Stay awake and pray that you won't be tested. You want to do what is right, but you are weak."

[42]Again Jesus went to pray and said, "My Father, if there is no other way, and I must suffer, I will still do what you want."

[43]Jesus came back and found them sleeping again. They simply could not keep their eyes open. [44]He left them and prayed the same prayer once more.

[45]Finally, Jesus returned to his disciples and said, "Are you still sleeping and resting?[d] The time has come for the Son of Man to be handed over to sinners. [46]Get up! Let's go. The one who will betray me is already here."

Jesus Is Arrested
(Mark 14.43-50; Luke 22.47-53; John 18.3-12)

[47]Jesus was still speaking, when Judas the betrayer came up. He was one of the twelve disciples, and a large mob armed with swords and clubs was with him. They had been sent by the chief priests and the nation's leaders. [48]Judas had told them ahead of time, "Arrest the man I greet with a kiss."[e]

b26.37 the two brothers, James and John: The Greek text has "the two sons of Zebedee" (see 27.56). c26.39 by drinking from this cup: In the Scriptures "to drink from a cup" sometimes means to suffer (see the note at 20.22). d26.45 Are you still sleeping and resting: Or "You may as well keep on sleeping and resting." e26.48 the man I greet with a kiss: It was the custom for people to greet each other with a kiss on the cheek.

[49]Judas walked right up to Jesus and said, "Hello, teacher." Then Judas kissed him.

[50]Jesus replied, "My friend, do what you came for."[f]

The men grabbed Jesus and arrested him. [51]One of Jesus' followers pulled out a sword. He struck the servant of the high priest and cut off his ear.

[52]But Jesus told him, "Put your sword away. Anyone who lives by fighting will die by fighting. [53]Don't you know that I could ask my Father, and he would at once send me more than twelve armies of angels? [54]But then, how could the words of the Scriptures come true, which say this must happen?"

[55]Jesus said to the mob, "Why do you come with swords and clubs to arrest me like a criminal? Day after day I sat and taught in the temple, and you didn't arrest me. [56]But all this happened, so that what the prophets wrote would come true."

All Jesus' disciples left him and ran away.

Jesus Is Questioned by the Council
(Mark 14.53-65; Luke 22.54, 55, 63-71; John 18.13, 14, 19-24)

[57]After Jesus had been arrested, he was led off to the house of Caiaphas the high priest. The nation's leaders and the teachers of the Law of Moses were meeting there. [58]But Peter followed along at a distance and came to the courtyard of the high priest's palace. He went in and sat down with the guards to see what was going to happen.

[59]The chief priests and the whole council wanted to put Jesus to death. So they tried to find some people who would tell lies about him in court.[g] [60]But they could not find any, even though many did come and tell lies. At last, two men came forward [61]and said, "This man claimed he could tear down God's temple and build it again in three days."

[62]The high priest stood up and asked Jesus, "Why don't you say something in your own defense? Don't you hear the charges they are making against you?" [63]But Jesus did not answer. So the high priest said, "With the living God looking on, you must tell the truth. Are you the Messiah, the Son of God?"[h]

f26.50 do what you came for: Or "why are you here?"   g26.59 some people who would tell lies about him in court: The Law of Moses taught that two witnesses were necessary before a person could be put to death (see verse 60).   h26.63 Son of God: One of the titles used for the kings of Israel.

[64]"That is what you say!" Jesus answered. "But I tell all of you,
'Soon you will see
    the Son of Man
sitting at the right side[i]
    of God All-Powerful
and coming on the clouds
    of heaven.'"

[65]The high priest then tore his robe and said, "This man claims to be God! We don't need any more witnesses! You have heard what he said. [66]What do you think?"

They answered, "He is guilty and deserves to die!" [67]Then they spit in his face and hit him with their fists. Others slapped him [68]and said, "You think you are the Messiah! So tell us who hit you!"

Peter Says He Doesn't Know Jesus
(Mark 14.66-72; Luke 22.56-62; John 18.15-18, 25-27)

[69]While Peter was sitting out in the courtyard, a servant girl came up to him and said, "You were with Jesus from Galilee."

[70]But in front of everyone Peter said, "That isn't so! I don't know what you are talking about!"

[71]When Peter had gone out to the gate, another servant girl saw him and said to some people there, "This man was with Jesus from Nazareth."

[72]Again Peter denied it, and this time he swore, "I don't even know that man!"

[73]A little while later some people standing there walked over to Peter and said, "We know you are one of them. We can tell it because you talk like someone from Galilee."

[74]Peter began to curse and swear, "I don't know that man!"

Right then a rooster crowed, [75]and Peter remembered that Jesus had said, "Before a rooster crows, you will say three times you don't know me." Then Peter went out and cried bitterly.

i26.64 right side: See the note at 22.44.

Jesus Is Taken to Pilate
(Mark 15.1; Luke 23.1, 2; John 18.28-32)

27 Early the next morning all the chief priests and the nation's leaders met and decided that Jesus should be put to death. [2]They tied him up and led him away to Pilate the governor.

The Death of Judas
(Acts 1.18,19)

[3]Judas had betrayed Jesus, but when he learned that Jesus had been sentenced to death, he was sorry for what he had done. He returned the 30 silver coins to the chief priests and leaders [4]and said, "I have sinned by betraying a man who has never done anything wrong."

"So what? That's your problem," they replied. [5]Judas threw the money into the temple and then went out and hanged himself.

[6]The chief priests picked up the money and said, "This money was paid to have a man killed. We can't put it in the temple treasury." [7]Then they had a meeting and decided to buy a field that belonged to someone who made clay pots. They wanted to use it as a graveyard for foreigners. [8]This is why people still call that place "Field of Blood." [9]So the words of the prophet Jeremiah came true,

"They took
   the thirty silver coins,
the price of a person
   among the people of Israel.
[10]They paid it
   for a potter's field,[j]
as the Lord
   had commanded me."

Pilate Questions Jesus
(Mark 15.2-5; Luke 23.3-5; John 18.33-38)

[11]Jesus was brought before Pilate the governor, who asked him, "Are you the king of the Jews?"

j27.10 a potter's field: Perhaps a field owned by someone who made clay pots. But it may have been a field where potters came to get clay or to make pots or to throw away their broken pieces of pottery.

"Those are your words!" Jesus answered. [12]And when the chief priests and leaders brought their charges against him, he did not say a thing.

[13]Pilate asked him, "Don't you hear what crimes they say you have done?" [14]But Jesus did not say anything, and the governor was greatly amazed.

The Death Sentence
(Mark 15.6-15; Luke 23.13-26; John 18.39–19.16)

[15]During Passover the governor always freed a prisoner chosen by the people. [16]At that time a well-known terrorist named Jesus Barabbas[k] was in jail. [17]So when the crowd came together, Pilate asked them, "Which prisoner do you want me to set free? Do you want Jesus Barabbas or Jesus who is called the Messiah?" [18]Pilate knew the leaders had brought Jesus to him because they were jealous.

[19]While Pilate was judging the case, his wife sent him a message. It said, "Don't have anything to do with that innocent man. I have had nightmares because of him."

[20]But the chief priests and the leaders convinced the crowds to ask for Barabbas to be set free and for Jesus to be killed. [21]Pilate asked the crowd again, "Which of these two men do you want me to set free?"

"Barabbas!" they shouted.

[22]Pilate asked them, "What am I to do with Jesus, who is called the Messiah?"

They all yelled, "Nail him to a cross!"

[23]Pilate answered, "But what crime has he done?"

"Nail him to a cross!" they yelled even louder.

[24]Pilate saw that there was nothing he could do and that the people were starting to riot. So he took some water and washed his hands[l] in front of them and said, "I won't have anything to do with killing this man. You are the ones doing it!"

[25]Everyone answered, "We and our own families will take the blame for his death!"

[26]Pilate set Barabbas free. Then he ordered his soldiers to beat Jesus with a whip and nail him to a cross.

---

k27.16 Jesus Barabbas: Here and in verse 17 many manuscripts have "Barabbas." l27.24 washed his hands: To show that he was innocent.

Soldiers Make Fun of Jesus
(Mark 15.16-21; John 19.2,3)

[27]The governor's soldiers led Jesus into the fortress[m] and brought together the rest of the troops. [28]They stripped off Jesus' clothes and put a scarlet robe[n] on him. [29]They made a crown out of thorn branches and placed it on his head, and they put a stick in his right hand. The soldiers knelt down and pretended to worship him. They made fun of him and shouted, "Hey, you king of the Jews!" [30]Then they spit on him. They took the stick from him and beat him on the head with it.

Jesus Is Nailed to a Cross
(Mark 15.22-32; Luke 23.27-43; John 19.17-27)

[31]When the soldiers had finished making fun of Jesus, they took off the robe. They put his own clothes back on him and led him off to be nailed to a cross. [32]On the way they met a man named Simon who was from Cyrene, and they forced him to carry Jesus' cross.

[33]They came to a place named Golgotha, which means "Place of a Skull."[o] [34]There they gave Jesus some wine mixed with a drug to ease the pain. But when Jesus tasted what it was, he refused to drink it.

[35]The soldiers nailed Jesus to a cross and gambled to see who would get his clothes. [36]Then they sat down to guard him. [37]Above his head they put a sign that told why he was nailed there. It read, "This is Jesus, the King of the Jews." [38]The soldiers also nailed two criminals on crosses, one to the right of Jesus and the other to his left.

[39]People who passed by said terrible things about Jesus. They shook their heads and [40]shouted, "So you're the one who claimed you could tear down the temple and build it again in three days! If you are God's Son, save yourself and come down from the cross!"

[41]The chief priests, the leaders, and the teachers of the Law of Moses also made fun of Jesus. They said, [42]"He saved others, but he can't save himself. If he is the king of Israel, he should come down from the cross! Then we will

m27.27 fortress: The place where the Roman governor stayed. It was probably at Herod's palace west of Jerusalem, though it may have been Fortress Antonia north of the temple, where the Roman troops were stationed. n27.28 scarlet robe: This was probably a Roman soldier's robe. o27.33 Place of a Skull: The place was probably given this name because it was near a large rock in the shape of a human skull.

believe him. [43]He trusted God, so let God save him, if he wants to. He even said he was God's Son." [44]The two criminals also said cruel things to Jesus.

The Death of Jesus
(Mark 15.33-41; Luke 23.44-49; John 19.28-30)

[45]At noon the sky turned dark and stayed that way until three o'clock. [46]Then about that time Jesus shouted, "Eli, Eli, lema sabachthani?"[p] which means, "My God, my God, why have you deserted me?"

[47]Some of the people standing there heard Jesus and said, "He's calling for Elijah."[q] [48]One of them at once ran and grabbed a sponge. He soaked it in wine, then put it on a stick and held it up to Jesus.

[49]Others said, "Wait! Let's see if Elijah will come[r] and save him." [50]Once again Jesus shouted, and then he died.

[51]At once the curtain in the temple[s] was torn in two from top to bottom. The earth shook, and rocks split apart. [52]Graves opened, and many of God's people were raised to life. [53]They left their graves, and after Jesus had risen to life, they went into the holy city, where they were seen by many people.

[54]The officer and the soldiers guarding Jesus felt the earthquake and saw everything else that happened. They were frightened and said, "This man really was God's Son!"

[55]Many women had come with Jesus from Galilee to be of help to him, and they were there, looking on at a distance. [56]Mary Magdalene, Mary the mother of James and Joseph, and the mother of James and John[t] were some of these women.

Jesus Is Buried
(Mark 15.42-47; Luke 23.50-56; John 19.38-42)

[57]That evening a rich disciple named Joseph from the town of Arimathea [58]went and asked for Jesus' body. Pilate gave orders for it to be given to Joseph, [59]who took the body and wrapped it in a clean linen cloth. [60]Then Joseph

p27.46 Eli . . . sabachthani: These words are in Hebrew. q27.47 Elijah: In Aramaic the name "Elijah" sounds like "Eli," which means "my God." r27.49 Elijah will come: See the note at 16.14. s27.51 curtain in the temple: There were two curtains in the temple. One was at the entrance, and the other separated the holy place from the most holy place that the Jewish people thought of as God's home on earth. The second curtain is probably the one that is meant. t27.56 of James and John: The Greek text has "of Zebedee's sons" (see 26.37).

put the body in his own tomb that had been cut into solid rock[u] and had never been used. He rolled a big stone against the entrance to the tomb and went away.

⁶¹All this time Mary Magdalene and the other Mary were sitting across from the tomb.

⁶²On the next day, which was a Sabbath, the chief priests and the Pharisees went together to Pilate. ⁶³They said, "Sir, we remember what this liar said while he was still alive. He claimed in three days he would come back from death. ⁶⁴So please order the tomb to be carefully guarded for three days. If you don't, his disciples may come and steal his body. They will tell the people he has been raised to life, and this last lie will be worse than the first one."[v]

⁶⁵Pilate said to them, "All right, take some of your soldiers and guard the tomb as well as you know how." ⁶⁶So they sealed it tight and placed soldiers there to guard it.

Jesus Is Alive
(Mark 16.1-8; Luke 24.1-12; John 20.1-10)

28 The Sabbath was over, and it was almost daybreak on Sunday when Mary Magdalene and the other Mary went to see the tomb. ²Suddenly a strong earthquake struck, and the Lord's angel came down from heaven. He rolled away the stone and sat on it. ³The angel looked as bright as lightning, and his clothes were white as snow. ⁴The guards shook from fear and fell down, as though they were dead.

⁵The angel said to the women, "Don't be afraid! I know you are looking for Jesus, who was nailed to a cross. ⁶He isn't here! God has raised him to life, just as Jesus said he would. Come, see the place where his body was lying. ⁷Now hurry! Tell his disciples he has been raised to life and is on his way to Galilee. Go there, and you will see him. This is what I came to tell you."

⁸The women were frightened and yet very happy, as they hurried from the tomb and ran to tell his disciples. ⁹Suddenly Jesus met them and greeted them. They went near him, held on to his feet, and worshiped him. ¹⁰Then Jesus said, "Don't be afraid! Tell my followers to go to Galilee. They will see me there."

u27.60 tomb . . . solid rock: Some of the Jewish people buried their dead in rooms carved into solid rock. A heavy stone was rolled against the entrance.   v27.64 the first one: Probably the belief that Jesus is the Messiah.

Report of the Guard

[11]While the women were on their way, some soldiers who had been guarding the tomb went into the city. They told the chief priests everything that had happened. [12]So the chief priests met with the leaders and decided to bribe the soldiers with a lot of money. [13]They said to the soldiers, "Tell everyone that Jesus' disciples came during the night and stole his body while you were asleep. [14]If the governor[w] hears about this, we will talk to him. You won't have anything to worry about." [15]The soldiers took the money and did what they were told. The people of Judea still tell each other this story.

What Jesus' Followers Must Do
(Mark 16.14-18; Luke 24.36-49;
John 20.19-23; Acts 1.6-8)

[16]Jesus' eleven disciples went to a mountain in Galilee, where Jesus had told them to meet him. [17]They saw him and worshiped him, but some of them doubted.

[18]Jesus came to them and said:

I have been given all authority in heaven and on earth! [19]Go to the people of all nations and make them my disciples. Baptize them in the name of the Father, the Son, and the Holy Spirit, [20]and teach them to do everything I have told you. I will be with you always, even until the end of the world.

w28.14 *governor:* Pontius Pilate.

II.

Mark

Mark is the earliest Gospel and most likely was written for a community of Gentiles in Rome around A.D. 70. It encourages readers to understand that suffering was a necessary part of Jesus' identity, and invites them to realize, as does the Roman army officer at the foot of the cross, that Jesus "really was the Son of God." Mark was written in a popular dramatic style. Though the author immediately lets the reader know who Jesus is, the story is told so that the reader can share the discovery with Jesus' disciples that Jesus is the Son of God. Mark often shows Jesus through the eyes of the disciple Peter. This Gospel does not have many long speeches, but instead tries to touch the hearts of those who hear it or read it with lively, simple, and direct writing.

Outline

The Preaching of John the Baptist
(Matthew 3.1-12; Luke 3.1-18; John 1.19-28)

1 This is the good news about Jesus Christ, the Son of God.[a] ²It began just as God had said in the book written by Isaiah the prophet,

"I am sending my messenger
to get the way ready
for you.
³In the desert
someone is shouting,
'Get the road ready
for the Lord!
Make a straight path
for him.'"

⁴So John the Baptist showed up in the desert and told everyone, "Turn back to God and be baptized! Then your sins will be forgiven."

⁵From all Judea and Jerusalem crowds of people went to John. They told how sorry they were for their sins, and he baptized them in the Jordan River.

⁶John wore clothes made of camel's hair. He had a leather strap around his waist and ate grasshoppers and wild honey.

⁷John also told the people, "Someone more powerful is going to come.

a1.1 the Son of God: These words are not in some manuscripts.

And I am not good enough even to stoop down and untie his sandals.[b] [8]I baptize you with water, but he will baptize you with the Holy Spirit!"

The Baptism of Jesus
(Matthew 3.13-17; Luke 3.21,22)

[9]About that time Jesus came from Nazareth in Galilee, and John baptized him in the Jordan River. [10]As soon as Jesus came out of the water, he saw the sky open and the Holy Spirit coming down to him like a dove. [11]A voice from heaven said, "You are my own dear Son, and I am pleased with you."

Jesus and Satan
(Matthew 4.1-11; Luke 4.1-13)

[12]At once God's Spirit made Jesus go into the desert. [13]He stayed there for 40 days while Satan tested him. Jesus was with the wild animals, but angels took care of him.

Jesus Begins His Work
(Matthew 4.12-17; Luke 4.14,15)

[14]After John was arrested, Jesus went to Galilee and told the good news that comes from God.[c] [15]He said, "The time has come! God's kingdom will soon be here.[d] Turn back to God and believe the good news!"

Jesus Chooses Four Fishermen
(Matthew 4.18-22; Luke 5.1-11)

[16]As Jesus was walking along the shore of Lake Galilee, he saw Simon and his brother Andrew. They were fishermen and were casting their nets into the lake. [17]Jesus said to them, "Follow me! I will teach you how to bring in people instead of fish." [18]Right then the two brothers dropped their nets and went with him.

[19]Jesus walked on and soon saw James and John, the sons of Zebedee. They were in a boat, mending their nets. [20]At once Jesus asked them to come with him. They left their father in the boat with the hired workers and went with him.

---

b1.7 *untie his sandals:* This was the duty of a slave.   c1.14 *that comes from God:* Or "that is about God."   d1.15 *will soon be here:* Or "is already here."

A Man with an Evil Spirit
(Luke 4.31-37)

²¹Jesus and his disciples went to the town of Capernaum. Then on the next Sabbath he went into the synagogue and started teaching. ²²Everyone was amazed at his teaching. He taught with authority, and not like the teachers of the Law of Moses. ²³Suddenly a man with an evil spirit[e] in him entered the synagogue and yelled, ²⁴"Jesus from Nazareth, what do you want with us? Have you come to destroy us? I know who you are! You are God's Holy One."

²⁵Jesus told the evil spirit, "Be quiet and come out of the man!" ²⁶The spirit shook him. Then it gave a loud shout and left.

²⁷Everyone was completely surprised and kept saying to each other, "What is this? It must be some new kind of powerful teaching! Even the evil spirits obey him." ²⁸News about Jesus quickly spread all over Galilee.

Jesus Heals Many People
(Matthew 8.14-17; Luke 4.38-41)

²⁹As soon as Jesus left the synagogue with James and John, they went home with Simon and Andrew. ³⁰When they got there, Jesus was told that Simon's mother-in-law was sick in bed with fever. ³¹Jesus went to her. He took hold of her hand and helped her up. The fever left her, and she served them a meal.

³²That evening after sunset,[f] all who were sick or had demons in them were brought to Jesus. ³³In fact, the whole town gathered around the door of the house. ³⁴Jesus healed all kinds of terrible diseases and forced out a lot of demons. But the demons knew who he was, and he did not let them speak.

³⁵Very early the next morning before daylight, Jesus got up and went to a place where he could be alone and pray. ³⁶Simon and the others started looking for him. ³⁷And when they found him, they said, "Everyone is looking for you!"

³⁸Jesus replied, "We must go to the nearby towns, so that I can tell the good news to those people. This is why I have come." ³⁹Then Jesus went to their synagogues everywhere in Galilee, where he preached and forced out demons.

e1.23 evil spirit: A Jewish person who had an evil spirit was considered "unclean" and was not allowed to eat or worship with other Jewish people.   f1.32 after sunset: The Sabbath was over, and a new day began at sunset.

Jesus Heals a Man
(Matthew 8.1-4; Luke 5.12-16)

⁴⁰A man with leprosy^g came to Jesus and knelt down.^h He begged, "You have the power to make me well, if only you wanted to."

⁴¹Jesus felt sorry forⁱ the man. So he put his hand on him and said, "I want to! Now you are well." ⁴²At once the man's leprosy disappeared, and he was well.

⁴³After Jesus strictly warned the man, he sent him on his way. ⁴⁴He said, "Don't tell anyone about this. Just go and show the priest that you are well. Then take a gift to the temple as Moses commanded, and everyone will know that you have been healed."^j

⁴⁵The man talked about it so much and told so many people, that Jesus could no longer go openly into a town. He had to stay away from the towns, but people still came to him from everywhere.

Jesus Heals a Man Who Could Not Walk
(Matthew 9.1-8; Luke 5.17-26)

2 Jesus went back to Capernaum, and a few days later people heard that he was at home.^k ²Then so many of them came to the house that there wasn't even standing room left in front of the door.

Jesus was still teaching ³when four people came up, carrying a man on a mat because he could not walk. ⁴But because of the crowd, they could not get him to Jesus. So they made a hole in the roof^l above him and let the man down in front of everyone.

⁵When Jesus saw how much faith they had, he said to the man, "My friend, your sins are forgiven."

⁶Some of the teachers of the Law of Moses were sitting there. They started wondering, ⁷"Why would he say such a thing? He must think he is God! Only God can forgive sins."

g1.40 leprosy: In biblical times the word "leprosy" was used for many different kinds of skin diseases. h1.40 and knelt down: These words are not in some manuscripts. i1.41 felt sorry for: Some manuscripts have "was angry with." j1.44 everyone will know that you have been healed: People with leprosy had to be examined by a priest and told that they were well (that is, "clean") before they could once again live a normal life in the Jewish community. The gift that Moses commanded was the sacrifice of some lambs together with flour mixed with olive oil. k2.1 at home: Or "in the house" (perhaps Simon Peter's home). l2.4 roof: In Palestine the houses usually had a flat roof. Stairs on the outside led up to the roof that was made of beams and boards covered with packed earth.

[8]At once, Jesus knew what they were thinking, and he said, "Why are you thinking such things? [9]Is it easier for me to tell this man his sins are forgiven or to tell him to get up and pick up his mat and go on home? [10]I will show you that the Son of Man has the right to forgive sins here on earth." So Jesus said to the man, [11]"Get up! Pick up your mat and go on home."

[12]The man got right up. He picked up his mat and went out while everyone watched in amazement. They praised God and said, "We have never seen anything like this!"

Jesus Chooses Levi
(Matthew 9.9-13; Luke 5.27-32)

[13]Once again, Jesus went to the shore of Lake Galilee. A large crowd gathered around him, and he taught them. [14]As he walked along, he saw Levi, the son of Alphaeus. Levi was sitting at the place for paying taxes, and Jesus said to him, "Follow me!" So he got up and went with Jesus.

[15]Later, Jesus and his disciples were having dinner at Levi's house.[m] Many tax collectors[n] and other sinners had become followers of Jesus, and they were also guests at the dinner.

[16]Some of the teachers of the Law of Moses were Pharisees, and they saw Jesus eating with sinners and tax collectors. So they asked his disciples, "Why does he eat with tax collectors and sinners?"

[17]Jesus heard them and answered, "Healthy people don't need a doctor, but sick people do. I didn't come to invite good people to be my followers. I came to invite sinners."

People Ask About Going Without Eating
(Matthew 9.14-17; Luke 5.33-39)

[18]The followers of John the Baptist and the Pharisees often went without eating.[o] Some people came and asked Jesus, "Why do the followers of John and those of the Pharisees often go without eating, while your disciples never do?"

[19]Jesus answered:

m2.15 Levi's house: Or "Jesus' house." n2.15 tax collectors: These were usually Jewish people who paid the Romans for the right to collect taxes. They were hated by other Jews who thought of them as traitors to their country and to their religion. o2.18 without eating: The Jewish people sometimes went without eating (also called "fasting") to show their love for God or to show sorrow for their sins.

The friends of a bridegroom don't go without eating while he is still with them. [20]But the time will come when he will be taken from them. Then they will go without eating.

[21]No one patches old clothes by sewing on a piece of new cloth. The new piece would shrink and tear a bigger hole.

[22]No one pours new wine into old wineskins. The wine would swell and burst the old skins.[p] Then the wine would be lost, and the skins would be ruined. New wine must be put into new wineskins.

A Question About the Sabbath

(Matthew 12.1-8; Luke 6.1-5)

[23]One Sabbath Jesus and his disciples were walking through some wheat fields. His disciples were picking grains of wheat as they went along.[q] [24]Some Pharisees asked Jesus, "Why are your disciples picking grain on the Sabbath? They are not supposed to do that!"

[25]Jesus answered, "Haven't you read what David did when he and his followers were hungry and in need? [26]It was during the time of Abiathar the high priest. David went into the house of God and ate the sacred loaves of bread that only priests are allowed to eat. He also gave some to his followers."

[27]Jesus finished by saying, "People were not made for the good of the Sabbath. The Sabbath was made for the good of people. [28]So the Son of Man is Lord over the Sabbath."

A Man with a Paralyzed Hand

(Matthew 12.9-14; Luke 6.6-11)

3 The next time Jesus went into the synagogue, a man with a paralyzed hand was there. [2]The Pharisees[r] wanted to accuse Jesus of doing something wrong, and they kept watching to see if Jesus would heal him on the Sabbath.

[3]Jesus told the man to stand up where everyone could see him. [4]Then he asked, "On the Sabbath should we do good deeds or evil deeds? Should we save someone's life or destroy it?" But no one said a word.

[5]Jesus was angry as he looked around at the people. Yet he felt sorry for

p2.22 swell and burst the old skins: While the juice from grapes was becoming wine, it would swell and stretch the skins in which it had been stored. If the skins were old and stiff, they would burst. q2.23 went along: It was the custom to let hungry travelers pick grains of wheat. r3.2 Pharisees: The Greek text has "they" (but see verse 6).

them because they were so stubborn. Then he told the man, "Stretch out your hand." He did, and his bad hand was healed.

⁶The Pharisees left. And at once they started making plans with Herod's followers⁵ to kill Jesus.

Large Crowds Come to Jesus

⁷Jesus led his disciples down to the shore of the lake. Large crowds followed him from Galilee, Judea, ⁸and Jerusalem. People came from Idumea, as well as other places east of the Jordan River. They also came from the region around the towns of Tyre and Sidon. All of these crowds came because they had heard what Jesus was doing. ⁹He even had to tell his disciples to get a boat ready to keep him from being crushed by the crowds.

¹⁰After Jesus had healed many people, the other sick people begged him to let them touch him. ¹¹And whenever any evil spirits saw Jesus, they would fall to the ground and shout, "You are the Son of God!" ¹²But Jesus warned the spirits not to tell who he was.

Jesus Chooses His Twelve Apostles
(Matthew 10.1-4; Luke 6.12-16)

¹³Jesus decided to ask some of his disciples to go up on a mountain with him, and they went. ¹⁴Then he chose twelve of them to be his apostles,ᵗ so they could be with him. He also wanted to send them out to preach ¹⁵and to force out demons. ¹⁶Simon was one of the twelve, and Jesus named him Peter. ¹⁷There were also James and John, the two sons of Zebedee. Jesus called them Boanerges, which means "Thunderbolts." ¹⁸Andrew, Philip, Bartholomew, Matthew, Thomas, James son of Alphaeus, and Thaddaeus were also apostles. The others were Simon, known as the Eager One,ᵘ ¹⁹and Judas Iscariot,ᵛ who later betrayed Jesus.

---

s3.6 *Herod's followers:* People who were political followers of the family of Herod the Great and his son Herod Antipas.   t3.14 *to be his apostles:* These words are not in some manuscripts.   u3.18 *known as the Eager One:* The Greek text has "Cananaean," which probably comes from a Hebrew word meaning "zealous" (see Luke 6.15). "Zealot" was the name later given to the members of a Jewish group that resisted and fought against the Romans.   v3.19 *Iscariot:* This may mean "a man from Kerioth" (a place in Judea). But more probably it means "a man who was a liar" or "a man who was a betrayer."

Jesus and the Ruler of Demons
(Matthew 12.22-32; Luke 11.14-23; 12.10)

20Jesus went back home,ʷ and once again such a large crowd gathered that there was no chance even to eat. 21When Jesus' family heard what he was doing, they thought he was crazy and went to get him under control.

22Some teachers of the Law of Moses came from Jerusalem and said, "This man is under the power of Beelzebul, the ruler of demons! He is even forcing out demons with the help of Beelzebul."

23Jesus told the people to gather around him. Then he spoke to them in riddles and said:

How can Satan force himself out? 24A nation whose people fight each other won't last very long. 25And a family that fights won't last long either. 26So if Satan fights against himself, that will be the end of him.

27How can anyone break into the house of a strong man and steal his things, unless he first ties up the strong man? Then he can take everything.

28I promise you that any of the sinful things you say or do can be forgiven, no matter how terrible those things are. 29But if you speak against the Holy Spirit, you can never be forgiven. That sin will be held against you forever.

30Jesus said this because the people were saying that he had an evil spirit in him.

Jesus' Mother and Brothers
(Matthew 12.46-50; Luke 8.19-21)

31Jesus' mother and brothers came and stood outside. Then they sent someone with a message for him to come out to them. 32The crowd sitting around Jesus told him, "Your mother and your brothers and sistersˣ are outside and want to see you."

33Jesus asked, "Who is my mother and who are my brothers?" 34Then he looked at the people sitting around him and said, "Here are my mother and my brothers. 35Anyone who obeys God is my brother or sister or mother."

---

w3.20 went back home: Or "entered a house" (perhaps the home of Simon Peter).   x3.32 and sisters: These words are not in some manuscripts.

A Story About a Farmer
(Matthew 13.1-9; Luke 8.4-8)

4 The next time Jesus taught beside Lake Galilee, a big crowd gathered. It was so large that he had to sit in a boat out on the lake, while the people stood on the shore. ²He used stories to teach them many things, and this is part of what he taught:

³Now listen! A farmer went out to scatter seed in a field. ⁴While the farmer was scattering the seed, some of it fell along the road and was eaten by birds. ⁵Other seeds fell on thin, rocky ground and quickly started growing because the soil wasn't very deep. ⁶But when the sun came up, the plants were scorched and dried up, because they did not have deep roots. ⁷Some other seeds fell where thornbushes grew up and choked out the plants. So they did not produce any grain. ⁸But a few seeds did fall on good ground where the plants grew and produced 30 or 60 or even 100 times as much as was scattered. ⁹Then Jesus said, "If you have ears, pay attention."

Why Jesus Used Stories
(Matthew 13.10-17; Luke 8.9,10)

¹⁰When Jesus was alone with the twelve apostles and some others, they asked him about these stories. ¹¹He answered:

I have explained the secret about God's kingdom to you, but for others I can use only stories. ¹²The reason is,

"These people will look
and look, but never see.
They will listen and listen,
but never understand.
If they did,
they would turn to God
and be forgiven."

Jesus Explains the Story About the Farmer
(Matthew 13.18-23; Luke 8.11-15)

¹³Jesus then told them:

If you don't understand this story, you won't understand any others. ¹⁴What the farmer is spreading is really the message about the kingdom. [15]The seeds that fell along the road are the people who hear the message. But Satan soon comes and snatches it away from them. [16]The seeds that fell on rocky ground are the people who gladly hear the message and accept it at once. [17]But they don't have roots, and they don't last very long. As soon as life gets hard or the message gets them in trouble, they give up.

[18]The seeds that fell among the thornbushes are also people who hear the message. [19]But they start worrying about the needs of this life. They are fooled by the desire to get rich and to have all kinds of other things. So the message gets choked out, and they never produce anything. [20]The seeds that fell on good ground are the people who hear and welcome the message. They produce 30 or 60 or even 100 times as much as was planted.

Light
(Luke 8.16-18)

[21]Jesus also said:

You don't light a lamp and put it under a clay pot or under a bed. Don't you put a lamp on a lampstand? [22]There is nothing hidden that will not be made public. There is no secret that will not be well known. [23]If you have ears, pay attention!

[24]Listen carefully to what you hear! The way you treat others will be the way you will be treated—and even worse. [25]Everyone who has something will be given more. But people who don't have anything will lose what little they have.

Another Story About Seeds

[26]Again Jesus said:

God's kingdom is like what happens when a farmer scatters seed in a field. [27]The farmer sleeps at night and is up and around during the day. Yet the seeds keep sprouting and growing, and he doesn't understand how. [28]It is the ground that makes the seeds sprout and grow into plants that produce grain. [29]Then when harvest season comes and the grain is ripe, the farmer cuts it with a sickle.[y]

---

y4.29 sickle: A knife with a long curved blade, used to cut grain and other crops.

A Mustard Seed
(Matthew 13.31, 32; Luke 13.18,19)

³⁰Finally, Jesus said:

What is God's kingdom like? What story can I use to explain it? ³¹It is like what happens when a mustard seed is planted in the ground. It is the smallest seed in all the world. ³²But once it is planted, it grows larger than any garden plant. It even puts out branches that are big enough for birds to nest in its shade.

The Reason for Teaching with Stories
(Matthew 13.34, 35)

³³Jesus used many other stories when he spoke to the people, and he taught them as much as they could understand. ³⁴He did not tell them anything without using stories. But when he was alone with his disciples, he explained everything to them.

A Storm
(Matthew 8.23-27; Luke 8.22-25)

³⁵That evening, Jesus said to his disciples, "Let's cross to the east side." ³⁶So they left the crowd, and his disciples started across the lake with him in the boat. Some other boats followed along. ³⁷Suddenly a storm struck the lake. Waves started splashing into the boat, and it was about to sink.

³⁸Jesus was in the back of the boat with his head on a pillow, and he was asleep. His disciples woke him and said, "Teacher, don't you care that we're about to drown?"

³⁹Jesus got up and ordered the wind and the waves to be quiet. The wind stopped, and everything was calm.

⁴⁰Jesus asked his disciples, "Why were you afraid? Don't you have any faith?"

⁴¹Now they were more afraid than ever and said to each other, "Who is this? Even the wind and the waves obey him!"

A Man with Evil Spirits
(Matthew 8.28-34; Luke 8.26-39)

5 Jesus and his disciples crossed Lake Galilee and came to shore near the town of Gerasa.[z] [2]When he was getting out of the boat, a man with an evil spirit quickly ran to him [3]from the graveyard[a] where he had been living. No one was able to tie the man up anymore, not even with a chain. [4]He had often been put in chains and leg irons, but he broke the chains and smashed the leg irons. No one could control him. [5]Night and day he was in the graveyard or on the hills, yelling and cutting himself with stones.

[6]When the man saw Jesus in the distance, he ran up to him and knelt down. [7]He shouted, "Jesus, Son of God in heaven, what do you want with me? Promise me in God's name that you won't torture me!" [8]The man said this because Jesus had already told the evil spirit to come out of him.

[9]Jesus asked, "What is your name?"

The man answered, "My name is Lots, because I have 'lots' of evil spirits." [10]He then begged Jesus not to send them away.

[11]Over on the hillside a large herd of pigs was feeding. [12]So the evil spirits begged Jesus, "Send us into those pigs! Let us go into them." [13]Jesus let them go, and they went out of the man and into the pigs. The whole herd of about 2,000 pigs rushed down the steep bank into the lake and drowned.

[14]The men taking care of the pigs ran to the town and the farms to spread the news. Then the people came out to see what had happened. [15]When they came to Jesus, they saw the man who had once been full of demons. He was sitting there with his clothes on and in his right mind, and they were terrified.

[16]Everyone who had seen what had happened told about the man and the pigs. [17]Then the people started begging Jesus to leave their part of the country.

[18]When Jesus was getting into the boat, the man begged to go with him. [19]But Jesus would not let him. Instead, he said, "Go home to your family and tell them how much the Lord has done for you and how good he has been to you."

[20]The man went away into the region near the ten cities known as Decapolis[b] and began telling everyone how much Jesus had done for him. Everyone who heard what had happened was amazed.

---

z5.1 Gerasa: Some manuscripts have "Gadara," and others have "Gergesa."   a5.3 graveyard: It was thought that demons and evil spirits lived in graveyards.   b5.20 the ten cities known as Decapolis: A group of ten cities east of Samaria and Galilee, where the people followed the Greek way of life.

A Dying Girl and a Sick Woman
(Matthew 9.18-26; Luke 8.40-56)

[21]Once again Jesus got into the boat and crossed Lake Galilee.[c] Then as he stood on the shore, a large crowd gathered around him. [22]The person in charge of the synagogue was also there. His name was Jairus, and when he saw Jesus, he went over to him. He knelt at Jesus' feet [23]and started begging him for help. He said, "My little daughter is about to die! Please come and touch her, so she will get well and live." [24]Jesus went with Jairus. Many people followed along and kept crowding around.

[25]In the crowd was a woman who had been bleeding for twelve years. [26]She had gone to many doctors, and they had not done anything except cause her a lot of pain. She had paid them all the money she had. But instead of getting better, she only got worse.

[27]The woman had heard about Jesus, so she came up behind him in the crowd and barely touched his clothes. [28]She had said to herself, "If I can just touch his clothes, I will be healed." [29]As soon as she touched them, her bleeding stopped, and she knew she was healed.

[30]At that moment Jesus felt power go out from him. He turned to the crowd and asked, "Who touched my clothes?"

[31]His disciples said to him, "Look at all these people crowding around you! How can you ask who touched you?" [32]But Jesus turned to see who had touched him.

[33]The woman knew what had happened to her. So she came trembling with fear and knelt down in front of Jesus. Then she told him the whole story.

[34]Jesus said to the woman, "You are now well because of your faith. May God give you peace! You are healed, and you will no longer be in pain."

[35]While Jesus was still speaking, some people came from Jairus' home and said, "Your daughter has died! Why bother the teacher anymore?"

[36]Jesus heard[d] what they said, and he said to Jairus, "Don't worry. Just have faith!"

[37]Jesus did not let anyone go with him except Peter and the two brothers, James and John. [38]They went home with Jairus and saw the people crying and making a lot of noise.[e] [39]Then Jesus went inside and said to them,

---

c5.21 *crossed Lake Galilee:* To the west side.   d5.36 *heard:* Or "ignored."   e5.38 *crying and making a lot of noise:* The Jewish people often hired mourners for funerals.

"Why are you crying and carrying on like this? The child isn't dead. She is just asleep." [40]But the people laughed at him.

After Jesus had sent them all out of the house, he took the girl's father and mother and his three disciples and went to where she was. [41-42]He took the twelve-year-old girl by the hand and said, "Talitha, koum!"[f] which means, "Little girl, get up!" The girl got right up and started walking around.

Everyone was greatly surprised. [43]But Jesus ordered them not to tell anyone what had happened. Then he said, "Give her something to eat."

The People of Nazareth Turn Against Jesus
(Matthew 13.53-58; Luke 4.16-30)

6 Jesus left and returned to his hometown[g] with his disciples. [2]The next Sabbath he taught in the synagogue. Many of the people who heard him were amazed and asked, "How can he do all this? Where did he get such wisdom and the power to work these miracles? [3]Isn't he the carpenter,[h] the son of Mary? Aren't James, Joseph, Judas, and Simon his brothers? Don't his sisters still live here in our town?" The people were upset because of what he was doing.

[4]But Jesus said, "Prophets are honored by everyone, except the people of their hometown and their relatives and their own family." [5]Jesus could not work any miracles there, except to heal a few sick people by placing his hands on them. [6]He was surprised that the people did not have any faith.

Instructions for the Twelve Apostles
(Matthew 10.5-15; Luke 9.1-6)

Jesus taught in all the neighboring villages. [7]Then he called together his twelve apostles and sent them out two by two with power over evil spirits. [8]He told them, "You may take along a walking stick. But don't carry food or a traveling bag or any money. [9]It's all right to wear sandals, but don't take along a change of clothes. [10]When you are welcomed into a home, stay there until you leave that town. [11]If any place won't welcome you or listen to your message, leave and shake the dust from your feet[i] as a warning to them."

f5.41,42 Talitha, koum: These words are in Aramaic, a language spoken in Palestine during the time of Jesus. g6.1 hometown: Nazareth. h6.3 carpenter: The Greek word may also mean someone who builds or works with stone or brick. i6.11 shake the dust from your feet: This was a way of showing rejection.

[12]The apostles left and started telling everyone to turn to God. [13]They forced out many demons and healed a lot of sick people by putting olive oil[j] on them.

The Death of John the Baptist
(Matthew 14.1-12; Luke 9.7-9)

[14]Jesus became so well-known that Herod the ruler[k] heard about him. Some people thought he was John the Baptist, who had come back to life with the power to work miracles. [15]Others thought he was Elijah[l] or some other prophet who had lived long ago. [16]But when Herod heard about Jesus, he said, "This must be John! I had his head cut off, and now he has come back to life."

[17-18]Herod had earlier married Herodias, the wife of his brother Philip. But John had told him, "It isn't right for you to take your brother's wife!" So, in order to please Herodias, Herod arrested John and put him in prison.

[19]Herodias had a grudge against John and wanted to kill him. But she could not do it [20]because Herod was afraid of John and protected him. He knew that John was a good and holy man. Even though Herod was confused by what John said,[m] he was glad to listen to him. And he often did.

[21]Finally, Herodias got her chance when Herod gave a great birthday celebration for himself and invited his officials, his army officers, and the leaders of Galilee. [22]The daughter of Herodias[n] came in and danced for Herod and his guests. She pleased them so much that Herod said, "Ask for anything, and it's yours! [23]I swear that I will give you as much as half of my kingdom, if you want it."

[24]The girl left and asked her mother, "What do you think I should ask for?"

Her mother answered, "The head of John the Baptist!"

[25]The girl hurried back and told Herod, "Here and now on a serving plate I want the head of John the Baptist!"

[26]Herod was very sorry for what he had said. But he did not want to break the promise he had made in front of his guests. [27]At once he ordered a guard to cut off John's head there in prison. [28]The guard put the head on a serving plate and took it to the girl. Then she gave it to her mother.

j6.13 olive oil: The Jewish people used olive oil as a way of healing people. Sometimes olive oil is a symbol for healing by means of a miracle (see James 5.14). k6.14 Herod the ruler: Herod Antipas, the son of Herod the Great. l6.15 Elijah: Many of the Jewish people expected the prophet Elijah to come and prepare the way for the Messiah. m6.20 was confused by what John said: Some manuscripts have "did many things because of what John said." n6.22 Herodias: Some manuscripts have "Herod."

[29]When John's followers learned that he had been killed, they took his body and put it in a tomb.

Jesus Feeds Five Thousand

(Matthew 14.13-21; Luke 9.10-17; John 6.1-14)

[30]After the apostles returned to Jesus,[o] they told him everything they had done and taught. [31]But so many people were coming and going that Jesus and the apostles did not even have a chance to eat. Then Jesus said, "Let's go to a place[p] where we can be alone and get some rest." [32]They left in a boat for a place where they could be alone. [33]But many people saw them leave and figured out where they were going. So people from every town ran on ahead and got there first.

[34]When Jesus got out of the boat, he saw the large crowd that was like sheep without a shepherd. He felt sorry for the people and started teaching them many things.

[35]That evening the disciples came to Jesus and said, "This place is like a desert, and it's already late. [36]Let the crowds leave, so they can go to the farms and villages near here and buy something to eat."

[37]Jesus replied, "You give them something to eat."

But they asked him, "Don't you know it would take almost a year's wages[q] to buy all of these people something to eat?"

[38]Then Jesus said, "How much bread do you have? Go and see!"

They found out and answered, "We have five small loaves of bread[r] and two fish." [39]Jesus told his disciples to tell the people to sit down on the green grass. [40]They sat down in groups of 100 and groups of 50.

[41]Jesus took the five loaves and the two fish. He looked up toward heaven and blessed the food. Then he broke the bread and handed it to his disciples to give to the people. He also divided the two fish, so everyone could have some.

[42]After everyone had eaten all they wanted, [43]Jesus' disciples picked up twelve large baskets of leftover bread and fish.

[44]There were 5,000 men who ate the food.

o6.30 the apostles returned to Jesus: From the mission on which he had sent them (see 6.7,12,13). p6.31 a place: This was probably northeast of Lake Galilee (see verse 45). q6.37 almost a year's wages: The Greek text has "200 silver coins." Each coin was the average day's wage for a worker. r6.38 small loaves of bread: These would have been flat and round or in the shape of a bun.

Jesus Walks on the Water
(Matthew 14.22-33; John 6.15-21)

⁴⁵At once, Jesus made his disciples get into the boat and start back across to Bethsaida. But he stayed until he had sent the crowds away. ⁴⁶Then he told them goodbye and went up on the side of a mountain to pray.

⁴⁷Later in the evening he was still there by himself, and the boat was somewhere in the middle of the lake. ⁴⁸He could see that the disciples were struggling hard, because they were rowing against the wind. Not long before morning, Jesus came toward them. He was walking on the water and was about to pass the boat.

⁴⁹When the disciples saw Jesus walking on the water, they thought he was a ghost, and they started screaming. ⁵⁰All of them saw him and were terrified. But at this same time he said, "Don't worry! I am Jesus. Don't be afraid." ⁵¹He then got into the boat with them, and the wind died down. The disciples were completely confused. ⁵²Their minds were closed, and they could not understand the true meaning of the loaves of bread.

Jesus Heals Sick People in Gennesaret
(Matthew 14.34-36)

⁵³Jesus and his disciples crossed the lake and brought the boat to shore near the town of Gennesaret. ⁵⁴As soon as they got out of the boat, the people recognized Jesus. ⁵⁵So they ran all over that part of the country to bring their sick people to him on mats. They brought them each time they heard where he was. ⁵⁶In every village or farm or marketplace where Jesus went, the people brought their sick to him. They begged him to let them just touch his clothes, and everyone who did was healed.

The Teaching of the Ancestors
(Matthew 15.1-9)

7 Some Pharisees and several teachers of the Law of Moses from Jerusalem came and gathered around Jesus. ²They noticed that some of his disciples ate without first washing their hands.ˢ

---

s7.2 without first washing their hands: The Jewish people had strict laws about washing their hands before eating, especially if they had been out in public.

³The Pharisees and many others obey the teachings of their ancestors. They always wash their hands in the proper way[t] before eating. ⁴None of them will eat anything they buy in the market until it is washed. They also follow a lot of other teachings, such as washing cups, pitchers, and bowls.[u]

⁵The Pharisees and teachers asked Jesus, "Why don't your disciples obey what our ancestors taught us to do? Why do they eat without washing their hands?"

⁶Jesus replied:

You are nothing but show-offs! The prophet Isaiah was right when he wrote that God had said,

"All of you praise me
    with your words,
but you never really
    think about me.
⁷It is useless for you
    to worship me,
when you teach rules
    made up by humans."

⁸You disobey God's commands in order to obey what humans have taught. ⁹You are good at rejecting God's commands so that you can follow your own teachings! ¹⁰Didn't Moses command you to respect your father and mother? Didn't he tell you to put to death all who curse their parents? ¹¹But you let people get by without helping their parents when they should. You let them say that what they own has been offered to God.[v] ¹²You won't let those people help their parents. ¹³And you ignore God's commands in order to follow your own teaching. You do a lot of other things just as bad.

What Really Makes People Unclean
(Matthew 15.10-20)

¹⁴Jesus called the crowd together again and said, "Pay attention and try to understand what I mean. ¹⁵⁻¹⁶The food that you put into your mouth doesn't

t7.3 in the proper way: The Greek text has "with the fist," but the exact meaning is not clear. It could mean "to the wrist" or "to the elbow." u7.4 bowls: Some manuscripts add "and sleeping mats." v7.11 has been offered to God: According to Jewish custom, when anything was offered to God, it could not be used for anyone else, not even for a person's parents.

make you unclean and unfit to worship God. The bad words that come out of your mouth are what make you unclean."[w]

[17]After Jesus and his disciples had left the crowd and gone into the house, they asked him what these sayings meant. [18]He answered, "Don't you know what I am talking about by now? You surely know that the food you put into your mouth cannot make you unclean. [19]It doesn't go into your heart, but into your stomach, and then out of your body." By saying this, Jesus meant that all foods were fit to eat.

[20]Then Jesus said:

What comes from your heart is what makes you unclean. [21]Out of your heart come evil thoughts, vulgar deeds, stealing, murder, [22]unfaithfulness in marriage, greed, meanness, deceit, indecency, envy, insults, pride, and foolishness. [23]All of these come from your heart, and they are what make you unfit to worship God.

A Woman's Faith
(Matthew 15.21-28)

[24]Jesus left and went to the region near the town of Tyre, where he stayed in someone's home. He did not want people to know he was there, but they found out anyway. [25]A woman whose daughter had an evil spirit in her heard where Jesus was. And at once she came and knelt down at his feet. [26]The woman was Greek and had been born in the part of Syria known as Phoenicia. She begged Jesus to force the demon out of her daughter. [27]But Jesus said, "The children must first be fed! It isn't right to take away their food and feed it to dogs."[x]

[28]The woman replied, "Lord, even puppies eat the crumbs that children drop from the table."

[29]Jesus answered, "That's true! You may go now. The demon has left your daughter." [30]When the woman got back home, she found her child lying on the bed. The demon had gone.

Jesus Heals a Man Who Was Deaf and Could Hardly Talk

[31]Jesus left the region around Tyre and went by way of Sidon toward Lake Galilee. He went through the land near the ten cities known as Decapolis.[y]

w7.15,16 unclean: Some manuscripts add, "If you have ears, pay attention."   x7.27 feed it to dogs: Some Jewish people referred to Gentiles as dogs.   y7.31 the ten cities known as Decapolis: See the note at 5.20.

[32]Some people brought to him a man who was deaf and could hardly talk. They begged Jesus just to touch him.

[33]After Jesus had taken him aside from the crowd, he stuck his fingers in the man's ears. Then he spit and put it on the man's tongue. [34]Jesus looked up toward heaven, and with a groan he said, "Effatha!"[z] which means "Open up!" [35]At once the man could hear, and he had no more trouble talking clearly.

[36]Jesus told the people not to say anything about what he had done. But the more he told them, the more they talked about it. [37]They were completely amazed and said, "Everything he does is good! He even heals people who cannot hear or talk."

Jesus Feeds Four Thousand
(Matthew 15.32-39)

8 One day another large crowd gathered around Jesus. They had not brought along anything to eat. So Jesus called his disciples together and said, [2]"I feel sorry for these people. They have been with me for three days, and they don't have anything to eat. [3]Some of them live a long way from here. If I send them away hungry, they might faint on their way home."

[4]The disciples said, "This place is like a desert. Where can we find enough food to feed such a crowd?"

[5]Jesus asked them how much food they had. They replied, "Seven small loaves of bread."[a]

[6]After Jesus told the crowd to sit down, he took the seven loaves and gave thanks. He then broke the loaves and handed them to his disciples, who passed them out to the crowd. [7]They also had a few little fish, and after Jesus had blessed these, he told the disciples to pass them around.

[8-9]The crowd of about 4,000 people ate all they wanted, and the leftovers filled seven large baskets.

As soon as Jesus had sent the people away, [10]he got into the boat with the disciples and crossed to the territory near Dalmanutha.[b]

z7.34 Effatha: This word is in Aramaic, a language spoken in Palestine during the time of Jesus. a8.5 small loaves of bread: See the note at 6.38.   b8.10 Dalmanutha: The place is unknown.

A Sign from Heaven
(Matthew 16.1-4)

[11]The Pharisees came out and started an argument with Jesus. They wanted to test him by asking for a sign from heaven. [12]Jesus groaned and said, "Why are you always looking for a sign? I can promise you that you will not be given one!" [13]Then he left them. He again got into a boat and crossed over to the other side of the lake.

The Yeast of the Pharisees and of Herod
(Matthew 16.5-12)

[14]The disciples had forgotten to bring any bread, and they had only one loaf with them in the boat. [15]Jesus warned them, "Watch out! Guard against the yeast of the Pharisees and of Herod."[c]

[16]The disciples talked this over and said to each other, "He must be saying this because we don't have any bread."

[17]Jesus knew what they were thinking and asked, "Why are you talking about not having any bread? Don't you understand? Are your minds still closed? [18]Are your eyes blind and your ears deaf? Don't you remember [19]how many baskets of leftovers you picked up when I fed those 5,000 people with only five small loaves of bread?"

"Yes," the disciples answered. "There were twelve baskets."

[20]Jesus then asked, "And how many baskets of leftovers did you pick up when I broke seven small loaves of bread for those 4,000 people?"

"Seven," they answered.

[21]"Don't you know what I am talking about by now?" Jesus asked.

Jesus Heals a Blind Man at Bethsaida

[22]As Jesus and his disciples were going into Bethsaida, some people brought a blind man to him and begged him to touch the man. [23]Jesus took him by the hand and led him out of the village, where he spit into the man's eyes. He placed his hands on the blind man and asked him if he could see anything. [24]The man looked up and said, "I see people, but they look like trees walking around."

c8.15 Herod: Herod Antipas, the son of Herod the Great.

²⁵Once again Jesus placed his hands on the man's eyes, and this time the man stared. His eyes were healed, and he saw everything clearly. ²⁶Jesus said to him, "You may return home now, but don't go into the village."

Who Is Jesus?
(Matthew 16.13-20; Luke 9.18-21)

²⁷Jesus and his disciples went to the villages near the town of Caesarea Philippi. As they were walking along, he asked them, "What do people say about me?"

²⁸The disciples answered, "Some say you are John the Baptist or maybe Elijah.[d] Others say you are one of the prophets."

²⁹Then Jesus asked, "But who do you say I am?"

"You are the Messiah!" Peter replied.

³⁰Jesus warned the disciples not to tell anyone about him.

Jesus Speaks About His Suffering and Death
(Matthew 16.21-28; Luke 9.22-27)

³¹Jesus began telling his disciples what would happen to him. He said, "The nation's leaders, the chief priests, and the teachers of the Law of Moses will make the Son of Man suffer terribly. He will be rejected and killed, but three days later he will rise to life." ³²Then Jesus explained clearly what he meant.

Peter took Jesus aside and told him to stop talking like that. ³³But when Jesus turned and saw the disciples, he corrected Peter. He said to him, "Satan, get away from me! You are thinking like everyone else and not like God."

³⁴Jesus then told the crowd and the disciples to come closer, and he said:

If any of you want to be my followers, you must forget about yourself. You must take up your cross and follow me. ³⁵If you want to save your life,[e] you will destroy it. But if you give up your life for me and for the good news, you will save it. ³⁶What will you gain, if you own the whole world but destroy yourself? ³⁷What could you give to get back your soul?

³⁸Don't be ashamed of me and my message among these unfaithful and sinful people! If you are, the Son of Man will be ashamed of you when he comes in the glory of his Father with the holy angels.

---

d8.28 Elijah: See the note at 6.15.   e8.35 life: In verses 35-37 the same Greek word is translated "life," "yourself," and "soul."

9 I can assure you that some of the people standing here will not die before they see God's kingdom come with power.

The True Glory of Jesus
(Matthew 17.1-13; Luke 9.28-36)

[2]Six days later Jesus took Peter, James, and John with him. They went up on a high mountain, where they could be alone. There in front of the disciples, Jesus was completely changed. [3]And his clothes became much whiter than any bleach on earth could make them. [4]Then Elijah and Moses appeared and were talking with Jesus.

[5]Peter said to Jesus, "Teacher, it is good for us to be here! Let us make three shelters, one for you, one for Moses, and one for Elijah." [6]But Peter and the others were terribly frightened, and he did not know what he was talking about.

[7]The shadow of a cloud passed over and covered them. From the cloud a voice said, "This is my Son, and I love him. Listen to what he says!" [8]At once the disciples looked around, but they saw only Jesus.

[9]As Jesus and his disciples were coming down the mountain, he told them not to say a word about what they had seen, until the Son of Man had been raised from death. [10]So they kept it to themselves. But they wondered what he meant by the words "raised from death."

[11]The disciples asked Jesus, "Don't the teachers of the Law of Moses say that Elijah must come before the Messiah does?"

[12]Jesus answered:

Elijah certainly will come[f] to get everything ready. But don't the Scriptures also say that the Son of Man must suffer terribly and be rejected? [13]I can assure you that Elijah has already come. And people treated him just as they wanted to, as the Scriptures say they would.

Jesus Heals a Boy
(Matthew 17.14-20; Luke 9.37-43a)

[14]When Jesus and his three disciples came back down, they saw a large crowd around the other disciples. The teachers of the Law of Moses were arguing with them.

[15]The crowd was really surprised to see Jesus, and everyone hurried over to greet him.

f9.12 *Elijah certainly will come:* See the note at 6.15.

[16]Jesus asked, "What are you arguing about?"

[17]Someone from the crowd answered, "Teacher, I brought my son to you. A demon keeps him from talking. [18]Whenever the demon attacks my son, it throws him to the ground and makes him foam at the mouth and grit his teeth in pain. Then he becomes stiff. I asked your disciples to force out the demon, but they couldn't do it."

[19]Jesus said, "You people don't have any faith! How much longer must I be with you? Why do I have to put up with you? Bring the boy to me."

[20]They brought the boy, and as soon as the demon saw Jesus, it made the boy shake all over. He fell down and began rolling on the ground and foaming at the mouth.

[21]Jesus asked the boy's father, "How long has he been like this?"

The man answered, "Ever since he was a child. [22]The demon has often tried to kill him by throwing him into a fire or into water. Please have pity and help us if you can!"

[23]Jesus replied, "Why do you say 'if you can'? Anything is possible for someone who has faith!"

[24]At once the boy's father shouted, "I do have faith! Please help me to have even more."

[25]When Jesus saw that a crowd was gathering fast, he spoke sternly to the evil spirit that had kept the boy from speaking or hearing. He said, "I order you to come out of the boy! Don't ever bother him again."

[26]The spirit screamed and made the boy shake all over. Then it went out of him. The boy looked dead, and almost everyone said he was. [27]But Jesus took hold of his hand and helped him stand up.

[28]After Jesus and the disciples had gone back home and were alone, they asked him, "Why couldn't we force out that demon?"

[29]Jesus answered, "Only prayer can force out this kind of demon."

Jesus Again Speaks About His Death
(Matthew 17.22, 23; Luke 9.43b-45)

[30]Jesus left with his disciples and started through Galilee. He did not want anyone to know about it, [31]because he was teaching the disciples that the Son of Man would be handed over to people who would kill him. But three days later he would rise to life. [32]The disciples did not understand what Jesus meant, and they were afraid to ask.

Who Is the Greatest?
(Matthew 18.1-5; Luke 9.46-48)

[33]Jesus and his disciples went to his home in Capernaum. After they were inside the house, Jesus asked them, "What were you arguing about along the way?" [34]They had been arguing about which one of them was the greatest, and so they did not answer.

[35]After Jesus sat down and told the twelve disciples to gather around him, he said, "If you want the place of honor, you must become a slave and serve others!"

[36]Then Jesus asked a child to stand near him. He put his arm around the child and said, [37]"When you welcome even a child because of me, you welcome me. And when you welcome me, you welcome the one who sent me."

For or Against Jesus
(Luke 9.49,50)

[38]John said, "Teacher, we saw a man using your name to force demons out of people. But he wasn't one of us, and we told him to stop."

[39]Jesus said to his disciples:

Don't stop him! No one who works miracles in my name will soon turn and say something bad about me. [40]Anyone who isn't against us is for us. [41]And anyone who gives you a cup of water in my name, just because you belong to me, will surely be rewarded.

Temptations to Sin
(Matthew 18.6-9; Luke 17.1,2)

[42]It will be terrible for people who cause even one of my little followers to sin. Those people would be better off thrown into the ocean with a heavy stone tied around their necks. [43-44]So if your hand causes you to sin, cut it off! You would be better off to go into life paralyzed than to have two hands and be thrown into the fires of hell that never go out.[g] [45-46]If your foot causes you to sin, chop it off! You would be better off to go into life lame than to have two feet and be thrown into hell.[h] [47]If

g9.43,44 *never go out:* Some manuscripts add, "The worms there never die, and the fire never stops burning." h9.45,46 *thrown into hell:* Some manuscripts add, "The worms there never die, and the fire never stops burning."

your eye causes you to sin, get rid of it. You would be better off to go into God's kingdom with only one eye than to have two eyes and be thrown into hell. [48]The worms there never die, and the fire never stops burning.

[49]Everyone must be salted with fire.[i]

[50]Salt is good. But if it no longer tastes like salt, how can it be made salty again? Have salt among you and live at peace with each other.[j]

Teaching About Divorce
(Matthew 19.1-12; Luke 16.18)

10 After Jesus left, he went to Judea and then on to the other side of the Jordan River. Once again large crowds came to him, and as usual, he taught them.

[2]Some Pharisees wanted to test Jesus. So they came up to him and asked if it was right for a man to divorce his wife. [3]Jesus asked them, "What does the Law of Moses say about this?"

[4]They answered, "Moses allows a man to write out divorce papers and send his wife away."

[5]Jesus replied, "Moses gave you this law because you are so heartless. [6]But in the beginning God made a man and a woman. [7]That's why a man leaves his father and mother and gets married. [8]He becomes like one person with his wife. Then they are no longer two people, but one. [9]And no one should separate a couple that God has joined together."

[10]When Jesus and his disciples were back in the house, they asked him about what he had said. [11]He told them, "A man who divorces his wife and marries someone else is unfaithful to his wife. [12]A woman who divorces her husband[k] and marries again is also unfaithful."

---

i9.49 salted with fire: Some manuscripts add "and every sacrifice will be seasoned with salt." The verse may mean that Christ's followers must suffer because of their faith.   j9.50 Have salt among you and live at peace with each other: This may mean that when Christ's followers have to suffer because of their faith, they must still try to live at peace with each other.   k10.12 A woman who divorces her husband: Roman law let a woman divorce her husband, but Jewish law did not let a woman do this.

Jesus Blesses Little Children
(Matthew 19.13-15; Luke 18.15-17)

¹³Some people brought their children to Jesus so he could bless them by placing his hands on them. But his disciples told the people to stop bothering him.

¹⁴When Jesus saw this, he became angry and said, "Let the children come to me! Don't try to stop them. People who are like these little children belong to the kingdom of God.¹ ¹⁵I promise you that you cannot get into God's kingdom, unless you accept it the way a child does." ¹⁶Then Jesus took the children in his arms and blessed them by placing his hands on them.

A Rich Man
(Matthew 19.16-30; Luke 18.18-30)

¹⁷As Jesus was walking down a road, a man ran up to him. He knelt down, and asked, "Good teacher, what can I do to have eternal life?"

¹⁸Jesus replied, "Why do you call me good? Only God is good. ¹⁹You know the commandments. 'Do not murder. Be faithful in marriage. Do not steal. Do not tell lies about others. Do not cheat. Respect your father and mother.'"

²⁰The man answered, "Teacher, I have obeyed all these commandments since I was a young man."

²¹Jesus looked closely at the man. He liked him and said, "There's one thing you still need to do. Go sell everything you own. Give the money to the poor, and you will have riches in heaven. Then come with me."

²²When the man heard Jesus say this, he went away gloomy and sad because he was very rich.

²³Jesus looked around and said to his disciples, "It's hard for rich people to get into God's kingdom!" ²⁴The disciples were shocked to hear this. So Jesus told them again, "It's terribly hard^m to get into God's kingdom! ²⁵In fact, it's easier for a camel to go through the eye of a needle than for a rich person to get into God's kingdom."

²⁶Jesus' disciples were even more amazed. They asked each other, "How can anyone ever be saved?"

²⁷Jesus looked at them and said, "There are some things that people cannot do, but God can do anything."

---

l10.14 *People who are like these little children belong to the kingdom of God:* Or "The kingdom of God belongs to people who are like these little children."   m10.24 *hard:* Some manuscripts add "for people who trust in their wealth." Others add "for the rich."

[28]Peter replied, "Remember, we left everything to be your followers!" [29]Jesus told him:

You can be sure that anyone who gives up home or brothers or sisters or mother or father or children or land for me and for the good news [30]will be rewarded. In this world they will be given 100 times as many houses and brothers and sisters and mothers and children and pieces of land, though they will also be mistreated. And in the world to come, they will have eternal life. [31]But many who are now first will be last, and many who are now last will be first.

Jesus Again Tells About His Death
(Matthew 20.17-19; Luke 18.31-34)

[32]The disciples were confused as Jesus led them toward Jerusalem, and his other followers were afraid. Once again, Jesus took the twelve disciples aside and told them what was going to happen to him. He said:

[33]We are now on our way to Jerusalem where the Son of Man will be handed over to the chief priests and the teachers of the Law of Moses. They will sentence him to death and hand him over to foreigners,[n] [34]who will make fun of him and spit on him. They will beat him and kill him. But three days later he will rise to life.

The Request of James and John
(Matthew 20.20-28)

[35]James and John, the sons of Zebedee, came up to Jesus and asked, "Teacher, will you do us a favor?"

[36]Jesus asked them what they wanted, [37]and they answered, "When you come into your glory, please let one of us sit at your right side and the other at your left."[o]

[38]Jesus told them, "You don't really know what you're asking! Are you able to drink from the cup[p] that I must soon drink from or be baptized as I must be baptized?"[q]

n10.33 foreigners: The Romans who ruled Judea at this time.   o10.37 right side . . . left: The most powerful people in a kingdom sat at the right and left side of the king.   p10.38 drink from the cup: In the Scriptures a "cup" is sometimes used as a symbol of suffering. To "drink from the cup" would be to suffer.   q10.38 as I must be baptized: Baptism is used with the same meaning that "cup" has in this verse.

³⁹"Yes, we are!" James and John answered.

Then Jesus replied, "You certainly will drink from the cup from which I must drink. And you will be baptized just as I must! ⁴⁰But it isn't for me to say who will sit at my right side and at my left. This is for God to decide."

⁴¹When the ten other disciples heard this, they were angry with James and John. ⁴²But Jesus called the disciples together and said:

> You know that those foreigners who call themselves kings like to order their people around. And their great leaders have full power over the people they rule. ⁴³But don't act like them. If you want to be great, you must be the servant of all the others. ⁴⁴And if you want to be first, you must be everyone's slave. ⁴⁵The Son of Man did not come to be a slave master, but a slave who will give his life to rescue[r] many people.

Jesus Heals Blind Bartimaeus
(Matthew 20.29-34; Luke 18.35-43)

⁴⁶Jesus and his disciples went to Jericho. And as they were leaving, they were followed by a large crowd. A blind beggar by the name of Bartimaeus son of Timaeus was sitting beside the road. ⁴⁷When he heard that it was Jesus from Nazareth, he shouted, "Jesus, Son of David,[s] have pity on me!" ⁴⁸Many people told the man to stop, but he shouted even louder, "Son of David, have pity on me!"

⁴⁹Jesus stopped and said, "Call him over!"

They called out to the blind man and said, "Don't be afraid! Come on! He is calling for you." ⁵⁰The man threw off his coat as he jumped up and ran to Jesus.

⁵¹Jesus asked, "What do you want me to do for you?"

The blind man answered, "Master,[t] I want to see!"

⁵²Jesus told him, "You may go. Your eyes are healed because of your faith." At once the man could see, and he went down the road with Jesus.

---

r10.45 *rescue:* The Greek word often, though not always, means the payment of a price to free a slave or a prisoner.   s10.47 *Son of David:* The Jewish people expected the Messiah to be from the family of King David, and for this reason the Messiah was often called the "Son of David." t10.51 *Master:* A Hebrew word that may also mean "Teacher."

Jesus Enters Jerusalem
(Matthew 21.1-11; Luke 19.28-40; John 12.12-19)

11 Jesus and his disciples reached Bethphage and Bethany near the Mount of Olives. When they were getting close to Jerusalem, Jesus sent two of them on ahead. [2]He told them, "Go into the next village. As soon as you enter it, you will find a young donkey that has never been ridden. Untie the donkey and bring it here. [3]If anyone asks why you are doing this, say, 'The Lord[u] needs it and will soon bring it back.'"

[4]The disciples left and found the donkey tied near a door that faced the street. While they were untying it, [5]some of the people standing there asked, "Why are you untying the donkey?" [6]They told them what Jesus had said, and the people let them take it.

[7]The disciples led the donkey to Jesus. They put some of their clothes on its back, and Jesus got on. [8]Many people spread clothes on the road, while others spread branches they had cut from the fields.[v]

[9]In front of Jesus and behind him, people went along shouting,

"Hooray![w]
God bless the one who comes
    in the name of the Lord!
[10]God bless the coming kingdom
    of our ancestor David.
Hooray for God
    in heaven above!"

[11]After Jesus had gone to Jerusalem, he went into the temple and looked around at everything. But since it was already late in the day, he went back to Bethany with the twelve disciples.

Jesus Puts a Curse on a Fig Tree
(Matthew 21.18,19)

[12]When Jesus and his disciples left Bethany the next morning, he was hungry. [13]From a distance Jesus saw a fig tree covered with leaves, and he went to

---

u11.3 *The Lord:* Or "The master of the donkey."   v11.8 *spread . . . branches from the fields:* This was one way that the Jewish people welcomed a famous person.   w11.9 *Hooray:* This translates a word that can mean "please save us." But it is most often used as a shout of praise to God.

see if there were any figs on the tree. But there were none, because it wasn't the season for figs. ¹⁴So Jesus said to the tree, "Never again will anyone eat fruit from this tree!" The disciples heard him say this.

Jesus in the Temple
(Matthew 21.12-17; Luke 19.45-48; John 2.13-22)

¹⁵After Jesus and his disciples reached Jerusalem, he went into the temple and began chasing out everyone who was selling and buying. He turned over the tables of the moneychangers and the benches of those who were selling doves. ¹⁶Jesus would not let anyone carry things through the temple. ¹⁷Then he taught the people and said, "The Scriptures say, 'My house should be called a place of worship for all nations.' But you have made it a place where robbers hide!"

¹⁸The chief priests and the teachers of the Law of Moses heard what Jesus said, and they started looking for a way to kill him. They were afraid of him, because the crowds were completely amazed at his teaching.

¹⁹That evening, Jesus and the disciples went outside the city.

A Lesson from the Fig Tree
(Matthew 21.20-22)

²⁰As the disciples walked past the fig tree the next morning, they noticed that it was completely dried up, roots and all. ²¹Peter remembered what Jesus had said to the tree. Then Peter said, "Teacher, look! The tree you put a curse on has dried up."

²²Jesus told his disciples:

Have faith in God! ²³If you have faith in God and don't doubt, you can tell this mountain to get up and jump into the sea, and it will. ²⁴Everything you ask for in prayer will be yours, if you only have faith.

²⁵⁻²⁶Whenever you stand up to pray, you must forgive what others have done to you. Then your Father in heaven will forgive your sins.ˣ

x11.25,26 *your sins:* Some manuscripts add, "But if you do not forgive others, God will not forgive you."

A Question About Jesus' Authority
(Matthew 21.23-27; Luke 20.1-8)

²⁷Jesus and his disciples returned to Jerusalem. And as he was walking through the temple, the chief priests, the nation's leaders, and the teachers of the Law of Moses came over to him. ²⁸They asked, "What right do you have to do these things? Who gave you this authority?"

²⁹Jesus answered, "I have just one question to ask you. If you answer it, I will tell you where I got the right to do these things. ³⁰Who gave John the right to baptize? Was it God in heaven or merely some human being?"

³¹They thought it over and said to each other, "We can't say that God gave John this right. Jesus will ask us why we didn't believe John. ³²On the other hand, these people think that John was a prophet. So we can't say it was merely some human who gave John the right to baptize."

They were afraid of the crowd ³³and told Jesus, "We don't know."

Jesus replied, "Then I won't tell you who gave me the right to do what I do."

Renters of a Vineyard
(Matthew 21.33-46; Luke 20.9-19)

12 Jesus then told them this story:

A farmer once planted a vineyard. He built a wall around it and dug a pit to crush the grapes in. He also built a lookout tower. Then he rented out his vineyard and left the country.

²When it was harvest time, he sent a servant to get his share of the grapes. ³The renters grabbed the servant, beat him up, and sent him away without a thing.

⁴The owner sent another servant, but the renters beat him on the head and insulted him terribly. ⁵Then the man sent another servant, and they killed him. He kept sending servant after servant. They beat some of them and killed some.

⁶The owner had a son he loved very much. Finally, he sent his son to the renters because he thought they would respect him. ⁷But they said to themselves, "Someday he will own this vineyard. Let's kill him! That way we can have it all for ourselves." ⁸So they grabbed the owner's son, killed him, and threw his body out of the vineyard.

⁹Jesus asked, "What do you think the owner of the vineyard will do? He

will come and kill those renters and let someone else have his vineyard. [10]You surely know that the Scriptures say,

'The stone the builders
    tossed aside
is now the most important
    stone of all.
[11]This is something
the Lord has done,
    and it is amazing to us.'"

[12]The leaders knew that Jesus was really talking about them, and they wanted to arrest him. But because they were afraid of the crowd, they let him alone and left.

Paying Taxes
(Matthew 22.15-22; Luke 20.20-26)

[13]The Pharisees got together with Herod's followers.[y] Then they sent some men to trick Jesus into saying something wrong. [14]They went to him and said, "Teacher, we know that you are honest. You treat everyone with the same respect, no matter who they are. And you teach the truth about what God wants people to do. Tell us, should we pay taxes to the Emperor or not?"

[15]Jesus knew what they were up to, and he said, "Why are you trying to test me? Show me a coin!"

[16]They brought him a silver coin, and he asked, "Whose picture and name are on it?"

"The Emperor's," they answered.

[17]Then Jesus told them, "Give the Emperor what belongs to him and give God what belongs to God." The men were amazed at Jesus.

Life in the Future World
(Matthew 22.23-33; Luke 20.27-40)

[18]The Sadducees did not believe that people would rise to life after death. So some of them came to Jesus and said:

y12.13 Herod's followers: People who were political followers of the family of Herod the Great and his son Herod Antipas.

¹⁹Teacher, Moses wrote that if a married man dies and has no children, his brother should marry the widow. Their first son would then be thought of as the son of the dead brother. ²⁰There were once seven brothers. The first one married, but died without having any children. ²¹The second brother married his brother's widow, and he also died without having children. The same thing happened to the third brother, ²²and finally to all seven brothers. At last the woman died. ²³When God raises people from death, whose wife will this woman be? After all, she had been married to all seven brothers.

²⁴Jesus answered:

You are completely wrong! You don't know what the Scriptures teach. And you don't know anything about the power of God. ²⁵When God raises people to life, they won't marry. They will be like the angels in heaven. ²⁶You surely know about people being raised to life. You know that in the story about Moses and the burning bush, God said, "I am the God worshiped by Abraham, Isaac, and Jacob."ᶻ ²⁷He isn't the God of the dead, but of the living. You Sadducees are all wrong.

The Most Important Commandment
(Matthew 22.34-40; Luke 10.25-28)

²⁸One of the teachers of the Law of Moses came up while Jesus and the Sadducees were arguing. When he heard Jesus give a good answer, he asked him, "What is the most important commandment?"

²⁹Jesus answered, "The most important one says: 'People of Israel, you have only one Lord and God. ³⁰You must love him with all your heart, soul, mind, and strength.' ³¹The second most important commandment says: 'Love others as much as you love yourself.' No other commandment is more important than these."

³²The man replied, "Teacher, you are certainly right to say there is only one God. ³³It is also true that we must love God with all our heart, mind, and strength, and that we must love others as much as we love ourselves. These commandments are more important than all the sacrifices and offerings that we could possibly make."

---

z12.26 *I am the God worshiped by Abraham, Isaac, and Jacob:* Jesus argues that if God is worshiped by these three, they must still be alive, because he is the God of the living.

³⁴When Jesus saw that the man had given a sensible answer, he told him, "You are not far from God's kingdom." After this, no one dared ask Jesus any more questions.

About David's Son
(Matthew 22.41-46; Luke 20.41-44)

³⁵As Jesus was teaching in the temple, he said, "How can the teachers of the Law of Moses say the Messiah will come from the family of King David? ³⁶The Holy Spirit led David to say,

'The Lord said to my Lord:
  Sit at my right side[a]
until I make your enemies
  into a footstool for you.'

³⁷If David called the Messiah his Lord, how can the Messiah be his son?"[b] The large crowd enjoyed listening to Jesus teach.

Jesus Condemns the Pharisees and the Teachers of the Law of Moses
(Matthew 23.1-36; Luke 20.45-47)

³⁸As Jesus was teaching, he said:

Guard against the teachers of the Law of Moses! They love to walk around in long robes and be greeted in the market. ³⁹They like the front seats in the synagogues and the best seats at banquets. ⁴⁰But they cheat widows out of their homes and pray long prayers just to show off. They will be punished most of all.

A Widow's Offering
(Luke 21.1-4)

⁴¹Jesus was sitting in the temple near the offering box and watching people put in their gifts. He noticed that many rich people were giving a lot of money. ⁴²Finally, a poor widow came up and put in two coins worth only a few pennies. ⁴³Jesus told his disciples to gather around him. Then he said:

I tell you that this poor widow has put in more than all the oth-

a12.36 *right side:* The place of power and honor. b12.37 *David . . . his son:* See the note at 10.47.

ers. [44]Everyone else gave what they didn't need. But she is very poor and gave everything she had. Now she doesn't have a cent to live on.

The Temple Will Be Destroyed
(Matthew 24.1,2; Luke 21.5,6)

13 As Jesus was leaving the temple, one of his disciples said to him, "Teacher, look at these beautiful stones and wonderful buildings!"

[2]Jesus replied, "Do you see these huge buildings? They will certainly be torn down! Not one stone will be left in place."

Warning About Trouble
(Matthew 24.3-14; Luke 21.7-19)

[3]Later, as Jesus was sitting on the Mount of Olives across from the temple, Peter, James, John, and Andrew came to him in private. [4]They asked, "When will these things happen? What will be the sign that they are about to take place?"

[5]Jesus answered:

Watch out and don't let anyone fool you! [6]Many will come and claim to be me. They will use my name and fool many people.

[7]When you hear about wars and threats of wars, don't be afraid. These things will have to happen first, but that isn't the end. [8]Nations and kingdoms will go to war against each other. There will be earthquakes in many places, and people will starve to death. But this is just the beginning of troubles.

[9]Be on your guard! You will be taken to courts and beaten with whips in their synagogues. And because of me, you will have to stand before rulers and kings to tell about your faith. [10]But before the end comes, the good news must be preached to all nations.

[11]When you are arrested, don't worry about what you will say. You will be given the right words when the time comes. But you will not really be the ones speaking. Your words will come from the Holy Spirit.

[12]Brothers and sisters will betray each other and have each other put to death. Parents will betray their own children, and children will turn against their parents and have them killed. [13]Everyone will hate you because of me. But if you keep on being faithful right to the end, you will be saved.

The Horrible Thing
(Matthew 24.15-21; Luke 21.20-24)

¹⁴Someday you will see that "Horrible Thing" where it should not be.ᶜ Everyone who reads this must try to understand! If you are living in Judea at that time, run to the mountains. ¹⁵If you are on the roofᵈ of your house, don't go inside to get anything. ¹⁶If you are out in the field, don't go back for your coat. ¹⁷It will be an awful time for women who are expecting babies or nursing young children. ¹⁸Pray that it won't happen in winter.ᵉ ¹⁹This will be the worst time of suffering since God created the world, and nothing this terrible will ever happen again. ²⁰If the Lord doesn't make the time shorter, no one will be left alive. But because of his chosen and special ones, he will make the time shorter.

²¹If someone should say, "Here is the Messiah!" or "There he is!" don't believe it. ²²False messiahs and false prophets will come and work miracles and signs. They will even try to fool God's chosen ones. ²³But be on your guard! That's why I am telling you these things now.

When the Son of Man Appears
(Matthew 24.29-31; Luke 21.25-28)

²⁴In those days, right after this time of suffering,

"The sun will become dark,
and the moon
    will no longer shine.
²⁵The stars will fall,
and the powers in the skyᶠ
    will be shaken."

²⁶Then the Son of Man will be seen coming in the clouds with great power and glory. ²⁷He will send his angels to gather his chosen ones from all over the earth.

---

c13.14 *where it should not be:* Probably the holy place in the temple.   d13.15 *roof:* See the note at 2.4.   e13.18 *in winter:* In Palestine the winters are cold and rainy and make travel difficult. f13.25 *the powers in the sky:* In ancient times people thought that the stars were spiritual powers.

A Lesson from a Fig Tree
(Matthew 24.32-35; Luke 21.29-33)

²⁸Learn a lesson from a fig tree. When its branches sprout and start putting out leaves, you know summer is near. ²⁹So when you see all these things happening, you will know that the time has almost come.ᵍ ³⁰You can be sure that some of the people of this generation will still be alive when all this happens. ³¹The sky and the earth will not last forever, but my words will.

No One Knows the Day or Time
(Matthew 24.36-44)

³²No one knows the day or the time. The angels in heaven don't know, and the Son himself doesn't know. Only the Father knows. ³³So watch out and be ready! You don't know when the time will come. ³⁴It is like what happens when a man goes away for a while and places his servants in charge of everything. He tells each of them what to do, and he orders the guard to keep alert. ³⁵So be alert! You don't know when the master of the house will come back. It could be in the evening or at midnight or before dawn or in the morning. ³⁶But if he comes suddenly, don't let him find you asleep. ³⁷I tell everyone just what I have told you. Be alert!

A Plot to Kill Jesus
(Matthew 26.1-5; Luke 22.1,2; John 11.45-53)

14 It was now two days before Passover and the Festival of Thin Bread. The chief priests and the teachers of the Law of Moses were planning how they could sneak around and have Jesus arrested and put to death. ²They were saying, "We must not do it during the festival, because the people will riot."

At Bethany
(Matthew 26.6-13; John 12.1-8)

³Jesus was eating in Bethany at the home of Simon, who once had leprosy,ʰ when a woman came in with a very expensive bottle of sweet-smelling

---

g13.29 *the time has almost come:* Or "he (that is, the Son of Man) will soon be here."   h14.3 *leprosy:* In biblical times the word "leprosy" was used for many different skin diseases.

perfume.[i] After breaking it open, she poured the perfume on Jesus' head. [4]This made some of the guests angry, and they complained, "Why such a waste? [5]We could have sold this perfume for more than 300 silver coins and given the money to the poor!" So they started saying cruel things to the woman.

[6]But Jesus said:

Leave her alone! Why are you bothering her? She has done a beautiful thing for me. [7]You will always have the poor with you. And whenever you want to, you can give to them. But you won't always have me here with you. [8]She has done all she could by pouring perfume on my body to prepare it for burial. [9]You may be sure that wherever the good news is told all over the world, people will remember what she has done. And they will tell others.

Judas and the Chief Priests
(Matthew 26.14-16; Luke 22.3-6)

[10]Judas Iscariot[j] was one of the twelve disciples. He went to the chief priests and offered to help them arrest Jesus. [11]They were glad to hear this, and they promised to pay him. So Judas started looking for a good chance to betray Jesus.

Jesus Eats with His Disciples
(Matthew 26.17-25; Luke 22.7-14, 21-23; John 13.21-30)

[12]It was the first day of the Festival of Thin Bread, and the Passover lambs were being killed. Jesus' disciples asked him, "Where do you want us to prepare the Passover meal?"

[13]Jesus said to two of the disciples, "Go into the city, where you will meet a man carrying a jar of water.[k] Follow him, [14]and when he goes into a house, say to the owner, 'Our teacher wants to know if you have a room where he can eat the Passover meal with his disciples.' [15]The owner will take you upstairs and show you a large room furnished and ready for you to use. Prepare the meal there."

[16]The two disciples went into the city and found everything just as Jesus had told them. So they prepared the Passover meal.

---

i14.3 sweet-smelling perfume: The Greek text has "perfume made of pure spikenard," a plant used to make perfume. j14.10 Iscariot: See the note at 3.19. k14.13 a man carrying a jar of water: A male slave carrying water could mean that the family was rich.

[17-18]While Jesus and the twelve disciples were eating together that evening, he said, "The one who will betray me is now eating with me."

[19]This made the disciples sad, and one after another they said to Jesus, "You surely don't mean me!"

[20]He answered, "It is one of you twelve men who is eating from this dish with me. [21]The Son of Man will die, just as the Scriptures say. But it is going to be terrible for the one who betrays me. That man would be better off if he had never been born."

The Lord's Supper
(Matthew 26.26-30; Luke 22.14-23; 1 Corinthians 11.23-25)

[22]During the meal Jesus took some bread in his hands. He blessed the bread and broke it. Then he gave it to his disciples and said, "Take this. It is my body."

[23]Jesus picked up a cup of wine and gave thanks to God. He gave it to his disciples, and they all drank some. [24]Then he said, "This is my blood, which is poured out for many people, and with it God makes his agreement. [25]From now on I will not drink any wine, until I drink new wine in God's kingdom." [26]Then they sang a hymn and went out to the Mount of Olives.

Peter's Promise
(Matthew 26.31-35; Luke 22.31-34; John 13.36-38)

[27]Jesus said to his disciples, "All of you will reject me, as the Scriptures say,

'I will strike down
   the shepherd,
and the sheep
   will be scattered.'

[28]But after I am raised to life, I will go ahead of you to Galilee."

[29]Peter spoke up, "Even if all the others reject you, I never will!"

[30]Jesus replied, "This very night before a rooster crows twice, you will say three times that you don't know me."

[31]But Peter was so sure of himself that he said, "Even if I have to die with you, I will never say I don't know you!"

All the others said the same thing.

Jesus Prays

(Matthew 26.36-46; Luke 22.39-46)

[32]Jesus went with his disciples to a place called Gethsemane, and he told them, "Sit here while I pray."

[33]Jesus took along Peter, James, and John. He was sad and troubled and [34]told them, "I am so sad that I feel as if I am dying. Stay here and keep awake with me."

[35-36]Jesus walked on a little way. Then he knelt down on the ground and prayed, "Father,[l] if it is possible, don't let this happen to me! Father, you can do anything. Don't make me suffer by drinking from this cup.[m] But do what you want, and not what I want."

[37]When Jesus came back and found the disciples sleeping, he said to Simon Peter, "Are you asleep? Can't you stay awake for just one hour? [38]Stay awake and pray that you won't be tested. You want to do what is right, but you are weak."

[39]Jesus went back and prayed the same prayer. [40]But when he returned to the disciples, he found them sleeping again. They simply could not keep their eyes open, and they did not know what to say.

[41]When Jesus returned to the disciples the third time, he said, "Are you still sleeping and resting?[n] Enough of this! The time has come for the Son of Man to be handed over to sinners. [42]Get up! Let's go. The one who will betray me is already here."

Jesus Is Arrested

(Matthew 26.47-56; Luke 22.47-53; John 18.3-12)

[43]Jesus was still speaking, when Judas the betrayer came up. He was one of the twelve disciples, and a mob of men armed with swords and clubs were with him. They had been sent by the chief priests, the nation's leaders, and the teachers of the Law of Moses. [44]Judas had told them ahead of time, "Arrest the man I greet with a kiss.[o] Tie him up tight and lead him away."

[45]Judas walked right up to Jesus and said, "Teacher!" Then Judas kissed him, [46]and the men grabbed Jesus and arrested him.

---

l14.35,36 Father: The Greek text has "Abba," which is an Aramaic word meaning "father." m14.35,36 by drinking from this cup: See the note at 10.38. n14.41 Are you still sleeping and resting: Or "You may as well keep on sleeping and resting." o14.44 greet with a kiss: It was the custom for people to greet each other with a kiss on the cheek.

⁴⁷Someone standing there pulled out a sword. He struck the servant of the high priest and cut off his ear.

⁴⁸Jesus said to the mob, "Why do you come with swords and clubs to arrest me like a criminal? ⁴⁹Day after day I was with you and taught in the temple, and you didn't arrest me. But what the Scriptures say must come true."

⁵⁰All of Jesus' disciples ran off and left him. ⁵¹One of them was a young man who was wearing only a linen cloth. And when the men grabbed him, ⁵²he left the cloth behind and ran away naked.

Jesus Is Questioned by the Council
(Matthew 26.57-68; Luke 22.54, 55, 63-71; John 18.13, 14, 19-24)

⁵³Jesus was led off to the high priest. Then the chief priests, the nation's leaders, and the teachers of the Law of Moses all met together. ⁵⁴Peter had followed at a distance, and when he reached the courtyard of the high priest's house, he sat down with the guards to warm himself beside a fire.

⁵⁵The chief priests and the whole council tried to find someone to accuse Jesus of a crime, so they could put him to death. But they could not find anyone to accuse him. ⁵⁶Many people did tell lies against Jesus, but they did not agree on what they said. ⁵⁷Finally, some men stood up and lied about him. They said, ⁵⁸"We heard him say he would tear down this temple that we built. He also claimed that in three days he would build another one without any help." ⁵⁹But even then they did not agree on what they said.

⁶⁰The high priest stood up in the council and asked Jesus, "Why don't you say something in your own defense? Don't you hear the charges they are making against you?" ⁶¹But Jesus kept quiet and did not say a word. The high priest asked him another question, "Are you the Messiah, the Son of the glorious God?"^p

⁶²"Yes, I am!" Jesus answered.

"Soon you will see
the Son of Man
sitting at the right side^q
of God All-Powerful,
and coming with the clouds
of heaven."

p14.61 Son of the glorious God: "Son of God" was one of the titles used for the kings of Israel.
q14.62 right side: See the note at 12.36.

⁶³At once the high priest ripped his robe apart and shouted, "Why do we need more witnesses? ⁶⁴You heard him claim to be God! What is your decision?" They all agreed he should be put to death.

⁶⁵Some of the people started spitting on Jesus. They blindfolded him, hit him with their fists, and said, "Tell us who hit you!" Then the guards took charge of Jesus and beat him.

Peter Says He Doesn't Know Jesus
(Matthew 26.69-75; Luke 22.56-62; John 18.15-18, 25-27)

⁶⁶While Peter was still in the courtyard, a servant girl of the high priest came up ⁶⁷and saw Peter warming himself by the fire. She stared at him and said, "You were with Jesus from Nazareth!"

⁶⁸Peter replied, "That isn't true! I don't know what you're talking about. I don't have any idea what you mean." He went out to the gate, and a rooster crowed.ʳ

⁶⁹The servant girl saw Peter again and said to the people standing there, "This man is one of them!"

⁷⁰"No, I'm not!" Peter replied.

A little while later some of the people said to Peter, "You certainly are one of them. You're a Galilean!"

⁷¹This time Peter began to curse and swear, "I don't even know the man you're talking about!"

⁷²At once the rooster crowed a second time. Then Peter remembered that Jesus had told him, "Before a rooster crows twice, you will say three times that you don't know me." So Peter started crying.

Pilate Questions Jesus
(Matthew 27.1, 2, 11-14; Luke 23.1-5; John 18.28-38)

15 Early the next morning the chief priests, the nation's leaders, and the teachers of the Law of Moses met together with the whole Jewish council. They tied up Jesus and led him off to Pilate.

²He asked Jesus, "Are you the king of the Jews?"

"Those are your words," Jesus answered.

³The chief priests brought many charges against Jesus. ⁴Then Pilate ques-

---

r14.68 a rooster crowed: These words are not in some manuscripts.

tioned him again, "Don't you have anything to say? Don't you hear what crimes they say you have done?" [5]But Jesus did not answer, and Pilate was amazed.

The Death Sentence
(Matthew 27.15-26; Luke 23.13-25; John 18.39–19.16)

[6]During Passover, Pilate always freed one prisoner chosen by the people. [7]And at that time there was a prisoner named Barabbas. He and some others had been arrested for murder during a riot. [8]The crowd now came and asked Pilate to set a prisoner free, just as he usually did.

[9]Pilate asked them, "Do you want me to free the king of the Jews?" [10]Pilate knew that the chief priests had brought Jesus to him because they were jealous.

[11]But the chief priests told the crowd to ask Pilate to free Barabbas.

[12]Then Pilate asked the crowd, "What do you want me to do with this man you say is[s] the king of the Jews?"

[13]They yelled, "Nail him to a cross!"

[14]Pilate asked, "But what crime has he done?"

"Nail him to a cross!" they yelled even louder.

[15]Pilate wanted to please the crowd, so he set Barabbas free. Then he ordered his soldiers to beat Jesus with a whip and nail him to a cross.

Soldiers Make Fun of Jesus
(Matthew 27.27-30; John 19.2,3)

[16]The soldiers led Jesus inside the courtyard of the fortress[t] and called together the rest of the troops. [17]They put a purple robe[u] on him, and on his head they placed a crown they had made out of thorn branches. [18]They made fun of Jesus and shouted, "Hey, you king of the Jews!" [19]Then they beat him on the head with a stick. They spit on him and knelt down and pretended to worship him.

[20]When the soldiers had finished making fun of Jesus, they took off the purple robe. They put his own clothes back on him and led him off to be

---

s15.12 this man you say is: These words are not in some manuscripts. t15.16 fortress: The place where the Roman governor stayed. It was probably at Herod's palace west of Jerusalem, though it may have been Fortress Antonia, north of the temple, where the Roman troops were stationed. u15.17 purple robe: This was probably a Roman soldier's robe.

nailed to a cross. [21]Simon from Cyrene happened to be coming in from a farm, and they forced him to carry Jesus' cross. Simon was the father of Alexander and Rufus.

Jesus Is Nailed to a Cross
(Matthew 27.31-44; Luke 23.27-43; John 19.17-27)

[22]The soldiers took Jesus to Golgotha, which means "Place of a Skull."[v] [23]There they gave him some wine mixed with a drug to ease the pain, but he refused to drink it.

[24]They nailed Jesus to a cross and gambled to see who would get his clothes. [25]It was about nine o'clock in the morning when they nailed him to the cross. [26]On it was a sign that told why he was nailed there. It read, "This is the King of the Jews." [27-28]The soldiers also nailed two criminals on crosses, one to the right of Jesus and the other to his left.[w]

[29]People who passed by said terrible things about Jesus. They shook their heads and shouted, "Ha! So you're the one who claimed you could tear down the temple and build it again in three days. [30]Save yourself and come down from the cross!"

[31]The chief priests and the teachers of the Law of Moses also made fun of Jesus. They said to each other, "He saved others, but he can't save himself. [32]If he is the Messiah, the king of Israel, let him come down from the cross! Then we will see and believe." The two criminals also said cruel things to Jesus.

The Death of Jesus
(Matthew 27.45-56; Luke 23.44-49; John 19.28-30)

[33]About noon the sky turned dark and stayed that way until around three o'clock. [34]Then about that time Jesus shouted, "Eloi, Eloi, lema sabachthani?"[x] which means, "My God, my God, why have you deserted me?"

[35]Some of the people standing there heard Jesus and said, "He is calling for Elijah."[y] [36]One of them ran and grabbed a sponge. After he had soaked it

v15.22 Place of a Skull: The place was probably given this name because it was near a large rock in the shape of a human skull.   w15.27-28 left: Some manuscripts add, "So the Scriptures came true which say, 'He was accused of being a criminal.'"   x15.34 Eloi . . . sabachthani: These words are in Aramaic, a language spoken in Palestine during the time of Jesus.   y15.35 Elijah: The name "Elijah" sounds something like "Eloi," which means "my God."

in wine, he put it on a stick and held it up to Jesus. He said, "Let's wait and see if Elijah will come[z] and take him down!" [37]Jesus shouted and then died.

[38]At once the curtain in the temple[a] tore in two from top to bottom.

[39]A Roman army officer was standing in front of Jesus. When the officer saw how Jesus died, he said, "This man really was the Son of God!"

[40-41]Some women were looking on from a distance. They and many others had come with Jesus to Jerusalem. But even before this they had been his followers and had helped him while he was in Galilee. Mary Magdalene and Mary the mother of the younger James and of Joseph were two of these women. Salome was also one of them.

Jesus Is Buried
(Matthew 27.57-61; Luke 23.50-56; John 19.38-42)

[42]It was now the evening before the Sabbath, and the Jewish people were getting ready for that sacred day. [43]A man named Joseph from Arimathea was brave enough to ask Pilate for the body of Jesus. Joseph was a highly respected member of the Jewish council, and he was also waiting for God's kingdom to come.

[44]Pilate was surprised to hear that Jesus was already dead, and he called in the army officer to find out if Jesus had been dead very long. [45]After the officer told him, Pilate let Joseph have Jesus' body.

[46]Joseph bought a linen cloth and took the body down from the cross. He had it wrapped in the cloth, and he put it in a tomb that had been cut into solid rock. Then he rolled a big stone against the entrance to the tomb.

[47]Mary Magdalene and Mary the mother of Joseph were watching and saw where the body was placed.

Jesus Is Alive
(Matthew 28.1-8; Luke 24.1-12; John 20.1-10)

16 After the Sabbath, Mary Magdalene, Salome, and Mary the mother of James bought some spices to put on Jesus' body. [2]Very early on Sunday morning, just as the sun was coming up, they went to the tomb. [3]On their

z15.36 see if Elijah will come: See the note at 6.15.   a15.38 curtain in the temple: There were two curtains in the temple. One was at the entrance, and the other separated the holy place from the most holy place that the Jewish people thought of as God's home on earth. The second curtain is probably the one which is meant.

way, they were asking one another, "Who will roll the stone away from the entrance for us?" [4]But when they looked, they saw that the stone had already been rolled away. And it was a huge stone!

[5]The women went into the tomb, and on the right side they saw a young man in a white robe sitting there. They were alarmed.

[6]The man said, "Don't be alarmed! You are looking for Jesus from Nazareth, who was nailed to a cross. God has raised him to life, and he isn't here. You can see the place where they put his body. [7]Now go and tell his disciples, and especially Peter, that he will go ahead of you to Galilee. You will see him there, just as he told you."

[8]When the women ran from the tomb, they were confused and shaking all over. They were too afraid to tell anyone what had happened.

ONE OLD ENDING TO MARK'S GOSPEL[b]

Jesus Appears to Mary Magdalene
(Matthew 28.9,10; John 20.11-18)

[9]Very early on the first day of the week, after Jesus had risen to life, he appeared to Mary Magdalene. Earlier he had forced seven demons out of her. [10]She left and told his friends, who were crying and mourning. [11]Even though they heard that Jesus was alive and that Mary had seen him, they still would not believe it.

Jesus Appears to Two Disciples
(Luke 24.13-35)

[12]Later, Jesus appeared in another form to two disciples, as they were on their way out of the city. [13]But when these disciples told what had happened, the others would not believe either.

What Jesus' Followers Must Do
(Matthew 28.16-20; Luke 24.36-49; John 20.19-23; Acts 1.6-8)

[14]Afterwards, Jesus appeared to his eleven disciples as they were eating. He scolded them because they were too stubborn to believe the ones who had seen him after he had been raised to life. [15]Then he told them:

b16.9 One Old Ending to Mark's Gospel: Verses 9-20 are not in some manuscripts.

Go and preach the good news to everyone in the world. ¹⁶Anyone who believes me and is baptized will be saved. But anyone who refuses to believe me will be condemned. ¹⁷Everyone who believes me will be able to do wonderful things. By using my name they will force out demons, and they will speak new languages. ¹⁸They will handle snakes and will drink poison and not be hurt. They will also heal sick people by placing their hands on them.

Jesus Returns to Heaven
(Luke 24.50-53; Acts 1.9-11)

¹⁹After the Lord Jesus had said these things to the disciples, he was taken back up to heaven where he sat down at the right side[c] of God. ²⁰Then the disciples left and preached everywhere. The Lord was with them, and the miracles they worked proved that their message was true.

ANOTHER OLD ENDING
TO MARK'S GOSPEL[d]

⁹⁻¹⁰The women quickly told Peter and his friends what had happened. Later, Jesus sent the disciples to the east and to the west with his sacred and everlasting message of how people can be saved forever.

c16.19 right side: See the note at 12.36.   d16.9,10 Another Old Ending to Mark's Gospel: Some manuscripts and early translations have both this shorter ending and the longer one (verses 9-20).

III.

Luke

Luke and Acts were composed as one history. Luke—the story of Jesus' life, ministry, death, and resurrection—is completed by Acts, which shows how Jesus' disciples spread the good news of Jesus Christ throughout the Roman Empire in the first century. Written in the eloquent and compelling literary style popular among history writers at that time, this Gospel shows Jesus' ministry as the fulfillment of God's promise and saving love to his people. The book is rich in historical details. It also contains a number of stories about Jesus as well as parables (stories) Jesus taught that are not contained in the other Gospels. Scholars have pointed out that Luke "takes the long view," demonstrating how the events and timing of Jesus' ministry fit perfectly into God's plan for his creation.

Outline

1 Many people have tried to tell the story of what God has done among us. [2]They wrote what we had been told by the ones who were there in the beginning and saw what happened. [3]So I made a careful study[a] of everything and then decided to write and tell you exactly what took place. Honorable Theophilus, [4]I have done this to let you know the truth about what you have heard.

An Angel Tells About the Birth of John

[5]When Herod was king of Judea, there was a priest by the name of Zechariah from the priestly group of Abijah. His wife Elizabeth was from the family of Aaron.[b] [6]Both of them were good people and pleased the Lord God by obeying all that he had commanded. [7]But they did not have children. Elizabeth could not have any, and both Zechariah and Elizabeth were already old.

[8]One day Zechariah's group of priests were on duty, and he was serving God as a priest. [9]According to the custom of the priests, he had been chosen to go into the Lord's temple that day and to burn incense,[c] [10]while the people stood outside praying.

[11]All at once an angel from the Lord appeared to Zechariah at the right side of the altar. [12]Zechariah was confused and afraid when he saw the angel.

a1.3 a careful study: Or "a study from the beginning." b1.5 Aaron: The brother of Moses and the first priest. c1.9 burn incense: This was done twice a day, once in the morning and again in the late afternoon.

[13]But the angel told him:

Don't be afraid, Zechariah! God has heard your prayers. Your wife Elizabeth will have a son, and you must name him John. [14]His birth will make you very happy, and many people will be glad. [15]Your son will be a great servant of the Lord. He must never drink wine or beer, and the power of the Holy Spirit will be with him from the time he is born.

[16]John will lead many people in Israel to turn back to the Lord their God. [17]He will go ahead of the Lord with the same power and spirit that Elijah[d] had. And because of John, parents will be more thoughtful of their children. And people who now disobey God will begin to think as they ought to. This is how John will get people ready for the Lord.

[18]Zechariah said to the angel, "How will I know this is going to happen? My wife and I are both very old."

[19]The angel answered, "I am Gabriel, God's servant, and I was sent to tell you this good news. [20]You have not believed what I have said. So you will not be able to say a thing until all this happens. But everything will take place when it is supposed to."

[21]The crowd was waiting for Zechariah and kept wondering why he was staying in the temple so long. [22]When he did come out, he could not speak, and they knew he had seen a vision. He motioned to them with his hands, but did not say a thing.

[23]When Zechariah's time of service in the temple was over, he went home. [24]Soon after this, his wife was expecting a baby, and for five months she did not leave the house. She said to herself, [25]"What the Lord has done for me will keep people from looking down on me."[e]

An Angel Tells About the Birth of Jesus

[26]One month later God sent the angel Gabriel to the town of Nazareth in Galilee [27]with a message for a virgin named Mary. She was engaged to Joseph from the family of King David. [28]The angel greeted Mary and said, "You are truly blessed! The Lord is with you."

[29]Mary was confused by the angel's words and wondered what they meant.

---

d1.17 Elijah: The prophet Elijah was known for his power to work miracles.   e1.25 keep people from looking down on me: When a married woman could not have children, it was thought that the Lord was punishing her.

[30]Then the angel told Mary, "Don't be afraid! God is pleased with you, [31]and you will have a son. His name will be Jesus. [32]He will be great and will be called the Son of God Most High. The Lord God will make him king, as his ancestor David was. [33]He will rule the people of Israel forever, and his kingdom will never end."

[34]Mary asked the angel, "How can this happen? I am not even married!"

[35]The angel answered, "The Holy Spirit will come down to you, and God's power will come over you. So your child will be called the holy Son of God. [36]Your relative Elizabeth is also going to have a son, even though she is old. No one thought she could ever have a baby, but in three months she will have a son. [37]Nothing is impossible for God!"

[38]Mary said, "I am the Lord's servant! Let it happen as you have said." And the angel left her.

Mary Visits Elizabeth

[39]A short time later Mary hurried to a town in the hill country of Judea. [40]She went into Zechariah's home, where she greeted Elizabeth. [41]When Elizabeth heard Mary's greeting, her baby moved within her.

The Holy Spirit came upon Elizabeth. [42]Then in a loud voice she said to Mary:

> God has blessed you more than any other woman! He has also blessed the child you will have. [43]Why should the mother of my Lord come to me? [44]As soon as I heard your greeting, my baby became happy and moved within me. [45]The Lord has blessed you because you believed that he will keep his promise.

Mary's Song of Praise

[46]Mary said:
>   With all my heart
>   I praise the Lord,
>   [47]and I am glad
>   because of God my Savior.
>   [48]God cares for me,
>   his humble servant.
>   From now on,
>   all people will say
>   God has blessed me.

⁴⁹God All-Powerful has done
great things for me,
   and his name is holy.
⁵⁰He always shows mercy
to everyone
   who worships him.
⁵¹The Lord has used
   his powerful arm
to scatter those
   who are proud.
⁵² God drags strong rulers
   from their thrones
and puts humble people
   in places of power.
⁵³God gives the hungry
   good things to eat,
and sends the rich away
   with nothing.
⁵⁴God helps his servant Israel
and is always merciful
   to his people.
⁵⁵The Lord made this promise
   to our ancestors,
to Abraham and his family
   forever!

⁵⁶Mary stayed with Elizabeth about three months. Then she went back home.

The Birth of John the Baptist

⁵⁷When Elizabeth's son was born, ⁵⁸her neighbors and relatives heard how kind the Lord had been to her, and they too were glad.

⁵⁹Eight days later they did for the child what the Law of Moses commands.ᶠ They were going to name him Zechariah, after his father. ⁶⁰But Elizabeth said, "No! His name is John."

f1.59 what the Law of Moses commands: This refers to circumcision. It is the cutting off of skin from the private part of Jewish boys eight days after birth to show that they belong to the Lord.

⁶¹The people argued, "No one in your family has ever been named John." ⁶²So they motioned to Zechariah to find out what he wanted to name his son.

⁶³Zechariah asked for a writing tablet. Then he wrote, "His name is John." Everyone was amazed. ⁶⁴At once, Zechariah started speaking and praising God.

⁶⁵All the neighbors were frightened because of what had happened, and everywhere in the hill country people kept talking about these things. ⁶⁶Everyone who heard about this wondered what this child would grow up to be. They knew the Lord was with him.

Zechariah Praises the Lord

⁶⁷The Holy Spirit came upon Zechariah, and he began to speak:

⁶⁸Praise the Lord,
   the God of Israel!
He has come
   to save his people.
⁶⁹Our God has given us
   a mighty Savior[g]
from the family
   of David his servant.
⁷⁰Long ago the Lord promised
by the words
   of his holy prophets
⁷¹to save us from our enemies
and from everyone
   who hates us.
⁷²God said he would be kind
to our people and keep
   his sacred promise.
⁷³He told our ancestor Abraham
⁷⁴that he would rescue us
   from our enemies.
Then we could serve him
   without fear,

g1.69 *a mighty Savior:* The Greek text has "a horn of salvation." In the Scriptures animal horns are often a symbol of great strength.

⁷⁵by being holy and good
   as long as we live.

⁷⁶You, my son, will be called
   the prophet of God Most High.
You will go ahead of the Lord
to get everything ready
   for him.
⁷⁷You will tell his people
   that they can be saved
when their sins
   are forgiven.
⁷⁸God's love and kindness
   will shine upon us
like the sun that rises
   in the sky.^h
⁷⁹On us who live
in the dark shadow
   of death
this light will shine
to guide us
   into a life of peace.

⁸⁰As John grew up, God's Spirit gave him great power. John lived in the desert until the time he was sent to the people of Israel.

The Birth of Jesus
(Matthew 1.18-25)

2 About that time Emperor Augustus gave orders for the names of all the people to be listed in record books.ⁱ ²These first records were made when Quirinius was governor of Syria.^j

³Everyone had to go to their own hometown to be listed. ⁴So Joseph had to leave Nazareth in Galilee and go to Bethlehem in Judea. Long ago Bethle-

h1.78 like the sun that rises in the sky: Or "like the Messiah coming from heaven."   i2.1 names . . . listed in record books: This was done so that everyone could be made to pay taxes to the Emperor. j2.2 Quirinius was governor of Syria: It is known that Quirinius made a record of the people in A.D. 6 or 7. But the exact date of the record taking that Luke mentions is not known.

hem had been King David's hometown, and Joseph went there because he was from David's family.

⁵Mary was engaged to Joseph and traveled with him to Bethlehem. She was soon going to have a baby, ⁶and while they were there, ⁷she gave birth to her first-born[k] son. She dressed him in baby clothes[l] and laid him on a bed of hay, because there was no room for them in the inn.

The Shepherds

⁸That night in the fields near Bethlehem some shepherds were guarding their sheep. ⁹All at once an angel came down to them from the Lord, and the brightness of the Lord's glory flashed around them. The shepherds were frightened. ¹⁰But the angel said, "Don't be afraid! I have good news for you, which will make everyone happy. ¹¹This very day in King David's hometown a Savior was born for you. He is Christ the Lord. ¹²You will know who he is, because you will find him dressed in baby clothes and lying on a bed of hay."

¹³Suddenly many other angels came down from heaven and joined in praising God. They said:

¹⁴"Praise God in heaven!

Peace on earth to everyone
who pleases God."

¹⁵After the angels had left and gone back to heaven, the shepherds said to each other, "Let's go to Bethlehem and see what the Lord has told us about." ¹⁶They hurried off and found Mary and Joseph, and they saw the baby lying on a bed of hay.

¹⁷When the shepherds saw Jesus, they told his parents what the angel had said about him. ¹⁸Everyone listened and was surprised. ¹⁹But Mary kept thinking about all this and wondering what it meant.

²⁰As the shepherds returned to their sheep, they were praising God and saying wonderful things about him. Everything they had seen and heard was just as the angel had said.

²¹Eight days later Jesus' parents did for him what the Law of Moses commands.[m] And they named him Jesus, just as the angel had told Mary when he promised she would have a baby.

k2.7 first-born: The Jewish people said that the first-born son in each of their families belonged to the Lord.   l2.7 dressed him in baby clothes: The Greek text has "wrapped him in wide strips of cloth," which was how young babies were dressed.   m2.21 what the Law of Moses commands: See the note at 1.59.

Simeon Praises the Lord

[22]The time came for Mary and Joseph to do what the Law of Moses says a mother is supposed to do after her baby is born.[n]

They took Jesus to the temple in Jerusalem and presented him to the Lord, [23]just as the Law of the Lord says, "Each first-born[o] baby boy belongs to the Lord." [24]The Law of the Lord also says parents have to offer a sacrifice, giving at least a pair of doves or two young pigeons. So that is what Mary and Joseph did.

[25]At this time a man named Simeon was living in Jerusalem. Simeon was a good man. He loved God and was waiting for him to save the people of Israel. God's Spirit came to him [26]and told him that he would not die until he had seen Christ the Lord.

[27]When Mary and Joseph brought Jesus to the temple to do what the Law of Moses says should be done for a new baby, the Spirit told Simeon to go into the temple. [28]Simeon took the baby Jesus in his arms and praised God,

[29]"Lord, I am your servant,
    and now I can die in peace,
because you have kept
    your promise to me.
[30]With my own eyes I have seen
what you have done
    to save your people,
[31]and foreign nations
    will also see this.
[32]Your mighty power is a light
    for all nations,
and it will bring honor
    to your people Israel."

[33]Jesus' parents were surprised at what Simeon had said. [34]Then he blessed them and told Mary, "This child of yours will cause many people in Israel to fall and others to stand. The child will be like a warning sign. Many people will reject him, [35]and you, Mary, will suffer as though you had been stabbed by a dagger. But all this will show what people are really thinking."

n2.22 after her baby is born: After a Jewish mother gave birth to a son, she was considered "unclean" and had to stay home until he was circumcised (see the note at 1.59). Then she had to stay home for another 33 days, before offering a sacrifice to the Lord.   o2.23 first-born: See the note at 2.7.

Anna Speaks About the Child Jesus

[36]The prophet Anna was also there in the temple. She was the daughter of
Phanuel from the tribe of Asher, and she was very old. In her youth she had
been married for seven years, but her husband died. [37]And now she was 84
years old.[p] Night and day she served God in the temple by praying and often
going without eating.[q]
[38]At this time Anna came in and praised God. She spoke about the child
Jesus to everyone who hoped for Jerusalem to be set free.

The Return to Nazareth

[39]After Joseph and Mary had done everything that the Law of the Lord commands, they returned home to Nazareth in Galilee. [40]The child Jesus grew.
He became strong and wise, and God blessed him.

The Boy Jesus in the Temple

[41]Every year Jesus' parents went to Jerusalem for Passover. [42]And when Jesus
was twelve years old, they all went there as usual for the celebration. [43]After
Passover his parents left, but they did not know that Jesus had stayed on in
the city. [44]They thought he was traveling with some other people, and they
went a whole day before they started looking for him. [45]When they could not
find him with their relatives and friends, they went back to Jerusalem and
started looking for him there.
[46]Three days later they found Jesus sitting in the temple, listening to the
teachers and asking them questions. [47]Everyone who heard him was surprised
at how much he knew and at the answers he gave.
[48]When his parents found him, they were amazed. His mother said, "Son,
why have you done this to us? Your father and I have been very worried, and
we have been searching for you!"
[49]Jesus answered, "Why did you have to look for me? Didn't you know
that I would be in my Father's house?"[r] [50]But they did not understand what
he meant.

p2.37 And now she was 84 years old: Or "And now she had been a widow for 84 years." q2.37 without eating: The Jewish people sometimes went without eating (also called "fasting") to show their love for God or to show sorrow for their sins. r2.49 in my Father's house: Or "doing my Father's work."

⁵¹Jesus went back to Nazareth with his parents and obeyed them. His mother kept on thinking about all that had happened.

⁵²Jesus became wise, and he grew strong. God was pleased with him and so were the people.

The Preaching of John the Baptist
(Matthew 3.1-12; Mark 1.1-8; John 1.19-28)

3 For 15 years' Emperor Tiberius had ruled that part of the world. Pontius Pilate was governor of Judea, and Herodᵗ was the ruler of Galilee. Herod's brother, Philip, was the ruler in the countries of Iturea and Trachonitis, and Lysanias was the ruler of Abilene. ²Annas and Caiaphas were the Jewish high priests.ᵘ

At that time God spoke to Zechariah's son John, who was living in the desert. ³So John went along the Jordan Valley, telling the people, "Turn back to God and be baptized! Then your sins will be forgiven." ⁴Isaiah the prophet wrote about John when he said,

"In the desert
   someone is shouting,
'Get the road ready
   for the Lord!
Make a straight path
   for him.
  ⁵Fill up every valley
and level every mountain
   and hill.
Straighten the crooked paths
and smooth out
   the rough roads.
   ⁶Then everyone will see
the saving power of God.'"

⁷Crowds of people came out to be baptized, but John said to them, "You bunch of snakes! Who warned you to run from the coming judgment? ⁸Do

s3.1 For 15 years: This was either A.D. 28 or 29, and Jesus was about 30 years old (see 3.23).   t3.1 Herod: Herod Antipas, the son of Herod the Great.   u3.2 Annas and Caiaphas . . . high priests: Annas was high priest from A.D. 6 until 15. His son-in-law Caiaphas was high priest from A.D. 18 until 37.

something to show that you really have given up your sins. Don't start saying you belong to Abraham's family. God can turn these stones into children for Abraham.[v] ⁹An ax is ready to cut the trees down at their roots. Any tree that doesn't produce good fruit will be cut down and thrown into a fire."

¹⁰The crowds asked John, "What should we do?"

¹¹John told them, "If you have two coats, give one to someone who doesn't have any. If you have food, share it with someone else."

¹²When tax collectors[w] came to be baptized, they asked John, "Teacher, what should we do?"

¹³John told them, "Don't make people pay more than they owe."

¹⁴Some soldiers asked him, "And what about us? What do we have to do?"

John told them, "Don't force people to pay money to make you leave them alone. Be satisfied with your pay."

¹⁵Everyone became excited and wondered, "Could John be the Messiah?"

¹⁶John said, "I am just baptizing with water. But someone more powerful is going to come, and I am not good enough even to untie his sandals.[x] He will baptize you with the Holy Spirit and with fire. ¹⁷His threshing fork[y] is in his hand, and he is ready to separate the wheat from the husks. He will store the wheat in his barn and burn the husks with a fire that never goes out."

¹⁸In many different ways John preached the good news to the people. ¹⁹But to Herod the ruler, he said, "It was wrong for you to take Herodias, your brother's wife." John also said Herod had done many other bad things. ²⁰Finally, Herod put John in jail, and this was the worst thing he had done.

The Baptism of Jesus
(Matthew 3.13-17; Mark 1.9-11)

²¹While everyone else was being baptized, Jesus himself was baptized. Then as he prayed, the sky opened up, ²²and the Holy Spirit came down upon him in the form of a dove. A voice from heaven said, "You are my own dear Son, and I am pleased with you."

v3.8 children for Abraham: The Jewish people thought they were God's chosen people because of God's promises to their ancestor Abraham.   w3.12 tax collectors: These were usually Jewish people who paid the Romans for the right to collect taxes. They were hated by other Jews who thought of them as traitors to their country and to their religion.   x3.16 untie his sandals: This was the duty of a slave.   y3.17 threshing fork: After Jewish farmers had trampled out the grain, they used a large fork to pitch the grain and the husks into the air. Wind would blow away the light husks, and the grain would fall back to the ground, where it could be gathered up.

The Ancestors of Jesus
(Matthew 1.1-17)

[23]When Jesus began to preach, he was about 30 years old. Everyone thought he was the son of Joseph. But his family went back through Heli, [24]Matthat, Levi, Melchi, Jannai, Joseph, [25]Mattathias, Amos, Nahum, Esli, Naggai, [26]Maath, Mattathias, Semein, Josech, Joda;

[27]Joanan, Rhesa, Zerubbabel, Shealtiel, Neri, [28]Melchi, Addi, Cosam, El-madam, Er, [29]Joshua, Eliezer, Jorim, Matthat, Levi;

[30]Simeon, Judah, Joseph, Jonam, Eliakim, [31]Melea, Menna, Mattatha, Nathan, David, [32]Jesse, Obed, Boaz, Salmon, Nahshon;

[33]Amminadab, Admin, Arni, Hezron, Perez, Judah, [34]Jacob, Isaac, Abra-ham, Terah, Nahor, [35]Serug, Reu, Peleg, Eber, Shelah;

[36]Cainan, Arphaxad, Shem, Noah, Lamech, [37]Methuselah, Enoch, Jared, Mahalaleel, Kenan, [38]Enosh, and Seth.

The family of Jesus went all the way back to Adam and then to God.

Jesus and the Devil
(Matthew 4.1-11; Mark 1.12,13)

4 When Jesus returned from the Jordan River, the power of the Holy Spirit was with him, and the Spirit led him into the desert. [2]For 40 days Jesus was tested by the devil, and during that time he went without eating.[z] When it was all over, he was hungry.

[3]The devil said to Jesus, "If you are God's Son, tell this stone to turn into bread."

[4]Jesus answered, "The Scriptures say, 'No one can live only on food.' "

[5]Then the devil led Jesus up to a high place and quickly showed him all the nations on earth. [6]The devil said, "I will give all this power and glory to you. It has been given to me, and I can give it to anyone I want to. [7]Just wor-ship me, and you can have it all."

[8]Jesus answered, "The Scriptures say:
'Worship the Lord your God
and serve only him!' "

[9]Finally, the devil took Jesus to Jerusalem and had him stand on top of

---

z4.2 went without eating: See the note at 2.37.

the temple. The devil said, "If you are God's Son, jump off. ¹⁰⁻¹¹The Scriptures say:

'God will tell his angels
   to take care of you.
They will catch you
   in their arms,
and you will not even hurt
   your feet on the stones.'"

¹²Jesus answered, "The Scriptures also say, 'Don't try to test the Lord your God!'"

¹³After the devil had finished testing Jesus in every way possible, he left him for a while.

Jesus Begins His Work
(Matthew 4.12-17; Mark 1.14,15)

¹⁴Jesus returned to Galilee with the power of the Spirit. News about him spread everywhere. ¹⁵He taught in the Jewish synagogues, and everyone praised him.

The People of Nazareth Turn Against Jesus
(Matthew 13.53-58; Mark 6.1-6)

¹⁶Jesus went back to Nazareth, where he had been brought up, and as usual he went to the synagogue on the Sabbath. When he stood up to read from the Scriptures, ¹⁷he was given the book of Isaiah the prophet. He opened it and read,

¹⁸"The Lord's Spirit
   has come to me,
because he has chosen me
to tell the good news
   to the poor.
The Lord has sent me
to announce freedom
   for prisoners,
to give sight to the blind,
to free everyone
   who suffers,

¹⁹and to say, 'This is the year
   the Lord has chosen.'"

²⁰Jesus closed the book, then handed it back to the man in charge and sat down. Everyone in the synagogue looked straight at Jesus. ²¹Then Jesus said to them, "What you have just heard me read has come true today."

²²All the people started talking about Jesus and were amazed at the wonderful things he said. They kept on asking, "Isn't he Joseph's son?"

²³Jesus answered:

You will certainly want to tell me this saying, "Doctor, first make yourself well." You will tell me to do the same things here in my own hometown that you heard I did in Capernaum. ²⁴But you can be sure that no prophets are liked by the people of their own hometown.

²⁵Once during the time of Elijah there was no rain for three and a half years, and people everywhere were starving. There were many widows in Israel, ²⁶but Elijah was sent only to a widow in the town of Zarephath near the city of Sidon. ²⁷During the time of the prophet Elisha, many men in Israel had leprosy.ᵃ But no one was healed, except Naaman who lived in Syria.

²⁸When the people in the synagogue heard Jesus say this, they became so angry ²⁹that they got up and threw him out of town. They dragged him to the edge of the cliff on which the town was built, because they wanted to throw him down from there. ³⁰But Jesus slipped through the crowd and got away.

A Man with an Evil Spirit
(Mark 1.21-28)

³¹Jesus went to the town of Capernaum in Galilee and taught the people on the Sabbath. ³²His teaching amazed them because he spoke with power. ³³There in the synagogue was a man with an evil spirit. He yelled out, ³⁴"Hey, Jesus of Nazareth, what do you want with us? Are you here to get rid of us? I know who you are! You are God's Holy One."

³⁵Jesus ordered the evil spirit to be quiet and come out. The demon threw the man to the ground in front of everyone and left without harming him.

---

a4.27 leprosy: In biblical times the word "leprosy" was used for many different kinds of skin diseases.

³⁶They all were amazed and kept saying to each other, "What kind of teaching is this? He has power to order evil spirits out of people!" ³⁷News about Jesus spread all over that part of the country.

Jesus Heals Many People
(Matthew 8.14-17; Mark 1.29-34)

³⁸Jesus left the synagogue and went to Simon's home. When Jesus got there, he was told that Simon's mother-in-law was sick with a high fever. ³⁹So Jesus went over to her and ordered the fever to go away. Right then she was able to get up and serve them a meal.

⁴⁰After the sun had set, people with all kinds of diseases were brought to Jesus. He put his hands on each one of them and healed them. ⁴¹Demons went out of many people and shouted, "You are the Son of God!" But Jesus ordered the demons not to speak because they knew he was the Messiah.

⁴²The next morning Jesus went out to a place where he could be alone, and crowds came looking for him. When they found him, they tried to stop him from leaving. ⁴³But Jesus said, "People in other towns must hear the good news about God's kingdom. This is why I was sent." ⁴⁴So he kept on preaching in the synagogues in Judea.[b]

Jesus Chooses His First Disciples
(Matthew 4.18-22; Mark 1.16-20)

5 Jesus was standing on the shore of Lake Gennesaret,[c] teaching the people as they crowded around him to hear God's message. ²Near the shore he saw two boats left there by some fishermen who had gone to wash their nets. ³Jesus got into the boat that belonged to Simon and asked him to row it out a little way from the shore. Then Jesus sat down[d] in the boat to teach the crowd.

⁴When Jesus had finished speaking, he told Simon, "Row the boat out into the deep water and let your nets down to catch some fish."

⁵"Master," Simon answered, "we have worked hard all night long and have not caught a thing. But if you tell me to, I will let the nets down." ⁶They

---

b4.44 Judea: Some manuscripts have "Galilee."   c5.1 Lake Gennesaret: Another name for Lake Galilee.   d5.3 sat down: Teachers in the ancient world, including Jewish teachers, usually sat down when they taught.

did this and caught so many fish that their nets began ripping apart. [7]Then they signaled for their partners in the other boat to come and help them. The men came, and together they filled the two boats so full that they both began to sink.

[8]When Simon Peter saw this happen, he knelt down in front of Jesus and said, "Lord, don't come near me! I am a sinner." [9]Peter and everyone with him were completely surprised at all the fish they had caught. [10]His partners James and John, the sons of Zebedee, were surprised too.

Jesus told Simon, "Don't be afraid! From now on you will bring in people instead of fish." [11]The men pulled their boats up on the shore. Then they left everything and went with Jesus.

Jesus Heals a Man
(Matthew 8.1-4; Mark 1.40-45)

[12]Jesus came to a town where there was a man who had leprosy.[e] When the man saw Jesus, he knelt down to the ground in front of Jesus and begged, "Lord, you have the power to make me well, if only you wanted to."

[13]Jesus put his hand on him and said, "I want to! Now you are well." At once the man's leprosy disappeared. [14]Jesus told him, "Don't tell anyone about this, but go and show yourself to the priest. Offer a gift to the priest, just as Moses commanded, and everyone will know that you have been healed."[f]

[15]News about Jesus kept spreading. Large crowds came to listen to him teach and to be healed of their diseases. [16]But Jesus would often go to some place where he could be alone and pray.

Jesus Heals a Man Who Could Not Walk
(Matthew 9.1-8; Mark 2.1-12)

[17]One day some Pharisees and experts in the Law of Moses sat listening to Jesus teach. They had come from every village in Galilee and Judea and from Jerusalem.

God had given Jesus the power to heal the sick, [18]and some people came carrying a man on a mat because he could not walk. They tried to take him

---

e5.12 leprosy: See the note at 4.27.	f5.14 everyone will know that you have been healed: People with leprosy had to be examined by a priest and told they were well (that is, "clean") before they could once again live a normal life in the Jewish community. The gift that Moses commanded was the sacrifice of some lambs together with flour mixed with olive oil.

inside the house and put him in front of Jesus. ¹⁹But because of the crowd, they could not get him to Jesus. So they went up on the roof,ᵍ where they removed some tiles and let the mat down in the middle of the room.

²⁰When Jesus saw how much faith they had, he said to the man, "My friend, your sins are forgiven."

²¹The Pharisees and the experts began arguing, "Jesus must think he is God! Only God can forgive sins."

²²Jesus knew what they were thinking, and he said, "Why are you thinking this? ²³Is it easier for me to tell this man that his sins are forgiven or to tell him to get up and walk? ²⁴But now you will see that the Son of Man has the right to forgive sins here on earth." Jesus then said to the man, "Get up! Pick up your mat and walk home."

²⁵At once the man stood up in front of everyone. He picked up his mat and went home, giving thanks to God. ²⁶Everyone was amazed and praised God. What they saw surprised them, and they said, "We have seen a great miracle today!"

Jesus Chooses Levi
(Matthew 9.9-13; Mark 2.13-17)

²⁷Later, Jesus went out and saw a tax collectorʰ named Levi sitting at the place for paying taxes. Jesus said to him, "Follow me." ²⁸Levi left everything and went with Jesus.

²⁹In his home Levi gave a big dinner for Jesus. Many tax collectors and other guests were also there.

³⁰The Pharisees and some of their teachers of the Law of Moses grumbled to Jesus' disciples, "Why do you eat and drink with these tax collectors and other sinners?"

³¹Jesus answered, "Healthy people don't need a doctor, but sick people do. ³²I didn't come to invite good people to turn to God. I came to invite sinners."

g5.19 *roof:* In Palestine the houses usually had a flat roof. Stairs on the outside led up to the roof, which was made of beams and boards covered with packed earth. Luke says that the roof was made of (clay) tiles, which were also used for making roofs in New Testament times. h5.27 *tax collector:* See the note at 3.12.

People Ask About Going Without Eating
(Matthew 9.14-17; Mark 2.18-22)

[33]Some people said to Jesus, "John's followers often pray and go without eating,[i] and so do the followers of the Pharisees. But your disciples never go without eating or drinking."

[34]Jesus told them, "The friends of a bridegroom don't go without eating while he is still with them. [35]But the time will come when he will be taken from them. Then they will go without eating."

[36]Jesus then told them these sayings:

No one uses a new piece of cloth to patch old clothes. The patch would shrink and make the hole even bigger.

[37]No one pours new wine into old wineskins. The new wine would swell and burst the old skins.[j] Then the wine would be lost, and the skins would be ruined. [38]New wine must be put only into new wineskins.

[39]No one wants new wine after drinking old wine. They say, "The old wine is better."

A Question About the Sabbath
(Matthew 12.1-8; Mark 2.23-28)

6 One Sabbath when Jesus and his disciples were walking through some wheat fields,[k] the disciples picked some wheat. They rubbed the husks off with their hands and started eating the grain.

[2]Some Pharisees said, "Why are you picking grain on the Sabbath? You're not supposed to do that!"

[3]Jesus answered, "You surely have read what David did when he and his followers were hungry. [4]He went into the house of God and took the sacred loaves of bread that only priests were supposed to eat. He not only ate some himself, but even gave some to his followers."

[5]Jesus finished by saying, "The Son of Man is Lord over the Sabbath."

---

i5.33 *without eating:* See the note at 2.37.   j5.37 *swell and burst the old skins:* While the juice from grapes was becoming wine, it would swell and stretch the skins in which it had been stored. If the skins were old and stiff, they would burst.   k6.1 *walking through some wheat fields:* It was the custom to let hungry travelers pick grains of wheat.

A Man with a Paralyzed Hand
(Matthew 12.9-14; Mark 3.1-6)

[6]On another Sabbath[l] Jesus was teaching in a synagogue, and a man with a paralyzed right hand was there. [7]Some Pharisees and teachers of the Law of Moses kept watching Jesus to see if he would heal the man. They did this because they wanted to accuse Jesus of doing something wrong.

[8]Jesus knew what they were thinking, so he told the man to stand up where everyone could see him. And the man stood up. [9]Then Jesus asked, "On the Sabbath should we do good deeds or evil deeds? Should we save someone's life or destroy it?"

[10]After he had looked around at everyone, he told the man, "Stretch out your hand." He did, and his bad hand became completely well.

[11]The teachers and the Pharisees were furious and started saying to one another, "What can we do about Jesus?"

Jesus Chooses His Twelve Apostles
(Matthew 10.1-4; Mark 3.13-19)

[12]About that time Jesus went off to a mountain to pray, and he spent the whole night there. [13]The next morning he called his disciples together and chose twelve of them to be his apostles. [14]One was Simon, and Jesus named him Peter. Another was Andrew, Peter's brother. There were also James, John, Philip, Bartholomew, [15]Matthew, Thomas, and James the son of Alphaeus. The rest of the apostles were Simon, known as the Eager One,[m] [16]Jude, who was the son of James, and Judas Iscariot,[n] who later betrayed Jesus.

Jesus Teaches, Preaches, and Heals
(Matthew 4.23-25)

[17]Jesus and his apostles went down from the mountain and came to some flat, level ground. Many other disciples were there to meet him. Large crowds of people from all over Judea, Jerusalem, and the coastal towns of Tyre and

---

l6.6 On another Sabbath: Some manuscripts have a reading which may mean "the Sabbath after the next." m6.15 known as the Eager One: The word "eager" translates the Greek word "zealot," which was a name later given to the members of a Jewish group that resisted and fought against the Romans. n6.16 Iscariot: This may mean "a man from Kerioth" (a place in Judea). But more probably it means "a man who was a liar" or "a man who was a betrayer."

Sidon were there too. [18]These people had come to listen to Jesus and to be healed of their diseases. All who were troubled by evil spirits were also healed. [19]Everyone was trying to touch Jesus, because power was going out from him and healing them all.

Blessings and Troubles
(Matthew 5.1-12)

[20]Jesus looked at his disciples and said:
    God will bless you people
who are poor.
    His kingdom belongs to you!
[21]God will bless
    you hungry people.
You will have plenty
    to eat!
God will bless you people
who are now crying.
    You will laugh!

[22]God will bless you when others hate you and won't have anything to do with you. God will bless you when people insult you and say cruel things about you, all because you are a follower of the Son of Man. [23]Long ago your own people did these same things to the prophets. So when this happens to you, be happy and jump for joy! You will have a great reward in heaven.
[24]But you rich people
    are in for trouble.
You have already had
    an easy life!
[25]You well-fed people
are in for trouble.
    You will go hungry!
You people
who are laughing now
    are in for trouble.
You are going to cry
    and weep!

[26]You are in for trouble when everyone says good things about you. That is what your own people said about those prophets who told lies.

Love for Enemies
(Matthew 5.38-48; 7.12a)

[27]This is what I say to all who will listen to me:

Love your enemies, and be good to everyone who hates you. [28]Ask God to bless anyone who curses you, and pray for everyone who is cruel to you. [29]If someone slaps you on one cheek, don't stop that person from slapping you on the other cheek. If someone wants to take your coat, don't try to keep back your shirt. [30]Give to everyone who asks and don't ask people to return what they have taken from you. [31]Treat others just as you want to be treated.

[32]If you love only someone who loves you, will God praise you for that? Even sinners love people who love them. [33]If you are kind only to someone who is kind to you, will God be pleased with you for that? Even sinners are kind to people who are kind to them. [34]If you lend money only to someone you think will pay you back, will God be pleased with you for that? Even sinners lend to sinners because they think they will get it all back.

[35]But love your enemies and be good to them. Lend without expecting to be paid back.[o] Then you will get a great reward, and you will be the true children of God in heaven. He is good even to people who are unthankful and cruel. [36]Have pity on others, just as your Father has pity on you.

Judging Others
(Matthew 7.1-5)

[37]Jesus said:

Don't judge others, and God won't judge you. Don't be hard on others, and God won't be hard on you. Forgive others, and God will forgive you. [38]If you give to others, you will be given a full amount in return. It will be packed down, shaken together, and spilling over into your lap. The way you treat others is the way you will be treated.

[39]Jesus also used some sayings as he spoke to the people. He said:

o6.35 *without expecting to be paid back:* Some manuscripts have "without giving up on anyone."

Can one blind person lead another blind person? Won't they both fall into a ditch? ⁴⁰Are students better than their teacher? But when they are fully trained, they will be like their teacher.

⁴¹You can see the speck in your friend's eye, but you don't notice the log in your own eye. ⁴²How can you say, "My friend, let me take the speck out of your eye," when you don't see the log in your own eye? You show-offs! First, get the log out of your own eye; then you can see how to take the speck out of your friend's eye.

A Tree and Its Fruit
(Matthew 7.17-20; 12.34b,35)

⁴³A good tree cannot produce bad fruit, and a bad tree cannot produce good fruit. ⁴⁴You can tell what a tree is like by the fruit it produces. You cannot pick figs or grapes from thornbushes. ⁴⁵Good people do good things because of the good in their hearts, but bad people do bad things because of the evil in their hearts. Your words show what is in your heart.

Two Builders
(Matthew 7.24-27)

⁴⁶Why do you keep on saying that I am your Lord, when you refuse to do what I say? ⁴⁷Anyone who comes and listens to me and obeys me ⁴⁸is like someone who dug down deep and built a house on solid rock. When a flood came and the river rushed against the house, it was built so well that it didn't even shake. ⁴⁹But anyone who hears what I say and doesn't obey me is like someone whose house wasn't built on solid rock. As soon as the river rushed against that house, it was smashed to pieces!

Jesus Heals an Army Officer's Servant
(Matthew 8.5-13; John 4.43-54)

7 After Jesus had finished teaching the people, he went to Capernaum. ²In this town an army officer's servant was sick and about to die. The officer liked his servant very much. ³And when he heard about Jesus, he sent some Jewish leaders to ask him to come and heal the servant.

⁴The leaders went to Jesus and begged him to do something. They said,

"This man deserves your help! ⁵He loves our nation and even built us a synagogue." ⁶So Jesus went with them.

When Jesus wasn't far from the house, the officer sent some friends to tell him, "Lord, don't go to any trouble for me! I am not good enough for you to come into my house. ⁷And I am certainly not worthy to come to you. Just say the word, and my servant will get well. ⁸I have officers who give orders to me, and I have soldiers who take orders from me. I can say to one of them, 'Go!' and he goes. I can say to another, 'Come!' and he comes. I can say to my servant, 'Do this!' and he will do it."

⁹When Jesus heard this, he was so surprised that he turned and said to the crowd following him, "In all of Israel I've never found anyone with this much faith!"

¹⁰The officer's friends returned and found the servant well.

A Widow's Son

¹¹Soon Jesus and his disciples were on their way to the town of Nain, and a big crowd was going along with them. ¹²As they came near the gate of the town, they saw people carrying out the body of a widow's only son. Many people from the town were walking along with her.

¹³When the Lord saw the woman, he felt sorry for her and said, "Don't cry!"

¹⁴Jesus went over and touched the stretcher on which the people were carrying the dead boy. They stopped, and Jesus said, "Young man, get up!" ¹⁵The boy sat up and began to speak. Jesus then gave him back to his mother.

¹⁶Everyone was frightened and praised God. They said, "A great prophet is here with us! God has come to his people."

¹⁷News about Jesus spread all over Judea and everywhere else in that part of the country.

John the Baptist
(Matthew 11.1-19)

¹⁸⁻¹⁹John's followers told John everything that was being said about Jesus. So he sent two of them to ask the Lord, "Are you the one we should be looking for? Or must we wait for someone else?"

²⁰When these messengers came to Jesus, they said, "John the Baptist sent us to ask, 'Are you the one we should be looking for? Or are we supposed to wait for someone else?'"

²¹At that time Jesus was healing many people who were sick or in pain or were troubled by evil spirits, and he was giving sight to a lot of blind people. ²²Jesus said to the messengers sent by John, "Go and tell John what you have seen and heard. Blind people are now able to see, and the lame can walk. People who have leprosy[p] are being healed, and the deaf can now hear. The dead are raised to life, and the poor are hearing the good news. ²³God will bless everyone who doesn't reject me because of what I do."

²⁴After John's messengers had gone, Jesus began speaking to the crowds about John:

What kind of person did you go out to the desert to see? Was he like tall grass blown about by the wind? ²⁵What kind of man did you really go out to see? Was he someone dressed in fine clothes? People who wear expensive clothes and live in luxury are in the king's palace. ²⁶What then did you go out to see? Was he a prophet? He certainly was! I tell you that he was more than a prophet. ²⁷In the Scriptures, God calls John his messenger and says, "I am sending my messenger ahead of you to get things ready for you." ²⁸No one ever born on this earth is greater than John. But whoever is least important in God's kingdom is greater than John.

²⁹Everyone had been listening to John. Even the tax collectors[q] had obeyed God and had done what was right by letting John baptize them. ³⁰But the Pharisees and the experts in the Law of Moses refused to obey God and be baptized by John.

³¹Jesus went on to say:

What are you people like? What kind of people are you? ³²You are like children sitting in the market and shouting to each other,

"We played the flute,
    but you would not dance!
We sang a funeral song,
    but you would not cry!"

³³John the Baptist did not go around eating and drinking, and you said, "John has a demon in him!" ³⁴But because the Son of Man goes around eating and drinking, you say, "Jesus eats and drinks too much! He is even a friend of tax collectors and sinners." ³⁵Yet Wisdom is shown to be right by what its followers do.

p7.22 leprosy: See the note at 4.27.   q7.29 tax collectors: See the note at 3.12.

Simon the Pharisee

[36]A Pharisee invited Jesus to have dinner with him. So Jesus went to the Pharisee's home and got ready to eat.[r]

[37]When a sinful woman in that town found out that Jesus was there, she bought an expensive bottle of perfume. [38]Then she came and stood behind Jesus. She cried and started washing his feet with her tears and drying them with her hair. The woman kissed his feet and poured the perfume on them.

[39]The Pharisee who had invited Jesus saw this and said to himself, "If this man really were a prophet, he would know what kind of woman is touching him! He would know that she is a sinner."

[40]Jesus said to the Pharisee, "Simon, I have something to say to you."

"Teacher, what is it?" Simon replied.

[41]Jesus told him, "Two people were in debt to a moneylender. One of them owed him 500 silver coins, and the other owed him 50. [42]Since neither of them could pay him back, the moneylender said that they didn't have to pay him anything. Which one of them will like him more?"

[43]Simon answered, "I suppose it would be the one who had owed more and didn't have to pay it back."

"You are right," Jesus said.

[44]He turned toward the woman and said to Simon, "Have you noticed this woman? When I came into your home, you didn't give me any water so I could wash my feet. But she has washed my feet with her tears and dried them with her hair. [45]You didn't greet me with a kiss, but from the time I came in, she has not stopped kissing my feet. [46]You didn't even pour olive oil on my head,[s] but she has poured expensive perfume on my feet. [47]So I tell you that all her sins are forgiven, and that is why she has shown great love. But anyone who has been forgiven for only a little will show only a little love."

[48]Then Jesus said to the woman, "Your sins are forgiven."

[49]Some other guests started saying to one another, "Who is this who dares to forgive sins?"

---

r7.36 got ready to eat: On special occasions the Jewish people often followed the Greek and Roman custom of lying down on their left side and leaning on their left elbow, while eating with their right hand. This is how the woman could come up behind Jesus and wash his feet (see verse 38). s7.44-46 washed my feet . . . greet me with a kiss . . . pour olive oil on my head: Guests in a home were usually offered water so they could wash their feet, because most people either went barefoot or wore sandals and would come in the house with very dusty feet. Guests were also greeted with a kiss on the cheek, and special ones often had sweet-smelling olive oil poured on their head.

⁵⁰But Jesus told the woman, "Because of your faith, you are now saved.ᵗ May God give you peace!"

Women Who Helped Jesus

8 Soon after this, Jesus was going through towns and villages, telling the good news about God's kingdom. His twelve apostles were with him, ²and so were some women who had been healed of evil spirits and all sorts of diseases. One of the women was Mary Magdalene,ᵘ who once had seven demons in her. ³Joanna, Susanna, and many others had also used what they ownedᵛ to help Jesus and his disciples. Joanna's husband Chuza was one of Herod's officials.ʷ

A Story About a Farmer
(Matthew 13.1-9; Mark 4.1-9)

⁴When a large crowd from several towns had gathered around Jesus, he told them this story:

⁵A farmer went out to scatter seed in a field. While the farmer was doing this, some of the seeds fell along the road and were stepped on or eaten by birds. ⁶Other seeds fell on rocky ground and started growing. But the plants did not have enough water and soon dried up. ⁷Some other seeds fell where thornbushes grew up and choked the plants. ⁸The rest of the seeds fell on good ground where they grew and produced a hundred times as many seeds.

When Jesus had finished speaking, he said, "If you have ears, pay attention!"

Why Jesus Used Stories
(Matthew 13.10-17; Mark 4.10-12)

⁹Jesus' disciples asked him what the story meant. ¹⁰So he answered:

I have explained the secrets about God's kingdom to you. But for others I use stories, so they will look, but not see, and they will hear, but not understand.

---

t7.50 *saved:* Or "healed." The Greek word may have either meaning.   u8.2 *Magdalene:* Meaning "from Magdala," a small town on the western shore of Lake Galilee. There is no hint that she is the sinful woman in 7.36-50.   v8.3 *used what they owned to help Jesus:* Women often helped Jewish teachers by giving them money.   w8.3 *Herod's officials:* Herod Antipas, the son of Herod the Great.

Jesus Explains the Story About a Farmer
(Matthew 13.18-23; Mark 4.13-20)

[11]This is what the story means: The seed is God's message, [12]and the seeds that fell along the road are the people who hear the message. But the devil comes and snatches the message out of their hearts, so they will not believe and be saved. [13]The seeds that fell on rocky ground are the people who gladly hear the message and accept it. But they don't have deep roots, and they believe only for a little while. As soon as life gets hard, they give up.

[14]The seeds that fell among the thornbushes are also people who hear the message. But they are so eager for riches and pleasures that they never produce anything. [15]Those seeds that fell on good ground are the people who listen to the message and keep it in good and honest hearts. They last and produce a harvest.

Light
(Mark 4.21-25)

[16]No one lights a lamp and puts it under a bowl or under a bed. A lamp is always put on a lampstand, so people who come into a house will see the light. [17]There is nothing hidden that will not be found. There is no secret that will not be well known. [18]Pay attention to how you listen! Everyone who has something will be given more, but people who have nothing will lose what little they think they have.

Jesus' Mother and Brothers
(Matthew 12.46-50; Mark 3.31-35)

[19]Jesus' mother and brothers went to see him, but because of the crowd they could not get near him. [20]Someone told Jesus, "Your mother and brothers are standing outside and want to see you."

[21]Jesus answered, "My mother and my brothers are those people who hear and obey God's message."

A Storm
(Matthew 8.23-27; Mark 4.35-41)

[22]One day, Jesus and his disciples got into a boat, and he said, "Let's cross the lake."[x] They started out, [23]and while they were sailing across, he went to sleep.

Suddenly a storm struck the lake, and the boat started sinking. They were in danger. [24]So they went to Jesus and woke him up, "Master, Master! We are about to drown!"

Jesus got up and ordered the wind and waves to stop. They obeyed, and everything was calm. [25]Then Jesus asked the disciples, "Don't you have any faith?"

But they were frightened and amazed. They said to each other, "Who is this? He can give orders to the wind and the waves, and they obey him!"

A Man with Demons in Him
(Matthew 8.28-34; Mark 5.1-20)

[26]Jesus and his disciples sailed across Lake Galilee and came to shore near the town of Gerasa.[y] [27]As Jesus was getting out of the boat, he was met by a man from this town. The man had demons in him. He had gone naked for a long time and no longer lived in a house, but in the graveyard.[z]

[28]The man saw Jesus and screamed. He knelt down in front of him and shouted, "Jesus, Son of God Most High, what do you want with me? I beg you not to torture me!" [29]He said this because Jesus had already told the evil spirit to go out of him.

The man had often been attacked by the demon. And even though he had been bound with chains and leg irons and kept under guard, he smashed whatever bound him. Then the demon would force him out into lonely places.

[30]Jesus asked the man, "What is your name?"

He answered, "My name is Lots." He said this because there were "lots" of demons in him. [31]They begged Jesus not to send them to the deep pit,[a] where they would be punished.

[32]A large herd of pigs was feeding there on the hillside. So the demons begged Jesus to let them go into the pigs, and Jesus let them go. [33]Then the

x8.22 cross the lake: To the eastern shore of Lake Galilee, where most of the people were not Jewish.   y8.26 Gerasa: Some manuscripts have "Gergesa."   z8.27 graveyard: It was thought that demons and evil spirits lived in graveyards.   a8.31 deep pit: The place where evil spirits are kept and punished.

demons left the man and went into the pigs. The whole herd rushed down the steep bank into the lake and drowned.

³⁴When the men taking care of the pigs saw this, they ran to spread the news in the town and on the farms. ³⁵The people went out to see what had happened, and when they came to Jesus, they also found the man. The demons had gone out of him, and he was sitting there at the feet of Jesus. He had clothes on and was in his right mind. But the people were terrified.

³⁶Then all who had seen the man healed told about it. ³⁷Everyone from around Gerasa[b] begged Jesus to leave, because they were so frightened.

When Jesus got into the boat to start back, ³⁸the man who had been healed begged to go with him. But Jesus sent him off and said, ³⁹"Go back home and tell everyone how much God has done for you." The man then went all over town, telling everything that Jesus had done for him.

A Dying Girl and a Sick Woman
(Matthew 9.18-26; Mark 5.21-43)

⁴⁰Everyone had been waiting for Jesus, and when he came back, a crowd was there to welcome him. ⁴¹Just then the man in charge of the synagogue came and knelt down in front of Jesus. His name was Jairus, and he begged Jesus to come to his home ⁴²because his twelve-year-old child was dying. She was his only daughter.

While Jesus was on his way, people were crowding all around him. ⁴³In the crowd was a woman who had been bleeding for twelve years. She had spent everything she had on doctors,[c] but none of them could make her well.

⁴⁴As soon as she came up behind Jesus and barely touched his clothes, her bleeding stopped.

⁴⁵"Who touched me?" Jesus asked.

While everyone was denying it, Peter said, "Master, people are crowding all around and pushing you from every side."[d]

⁴⁶But Jesus answered, "Someone touched me, because I felt power going out from me." ⁴⁷The woman knew that she could not hide, so she came trembling and knelt down in front of Jesus. She told everyone why she had touched him and that she had been healed at once.

b8.37 Gerasa: See the note at 8.26. c8.43 She had spent everything she had on doctors: Some manuscripts do not have these words. d8.45 from every side: Some manuscripts add "and you ask, 'Who touched me?'"

⁴⁸Jesus said to the woman, "You are now well because of your faith. May God give you peace!"

⁴⁹While Jesus was speaking, someone came from Jairus' home and said, "Your daughter has died! Why bother the teacher anymore?"

⁵⁰When Jesus heard this, he told Jairus, "Don't worry! Have faith, and your daughter will get well."

⁵¹Jesus went into the house, but he did not let anyone else go with him, except Peter, John, James, and the girl's father and mother. ⁵²Everyone was crying and weeping for the girl. But Jesus said, "The child isn't dead. She is just asleep." ⁵³The people laughed at him because they knew she was dead.

⁵⁴Jesus took hold of the girl's hand and said, "Child, get up!" ⁵⁵She came back to life and got right up. Jesus told them to give her something to eat. ⁵⁶Her parents were surprised, but Jesus ordered them not to tell anyone what had happened.

Instructions for the Twelve Apostles
(Matthew 10.5-15; Mark 6.7-13)

9 Jesus called together his twelve apostles and gave them complete power over all demons and diseases. ²Then he sent them to tell about God's kingdom and to heal the sick. ³He told them, "Don't take anything with you! Don't take a walking stick or a traveling bag or food or money or even a change of clothes. ⁴When you are welcomed into a home, stay there until you leave that town. ⁵If people won't welcome you, leave the town and shake the dust from your feet^e as a warning to them."

⁶The apostles left and went from village to village, telling the good news and healing people everywhere.

Herod Is Worried
(Matthew 14.1-12; Mark 6.14-29)

⁷Herod^f the ruler heard about all that was happening, and he was worried. Some people were saying John the Baptist had come back to life. ⁸Others were saying Elijah had come^g or one of the prophets from long ago had come back

---

e9.5 shake the dust from your feet: This was a way of showing rejection.   f9.7 Herod: Herod Antipas, the son of Herod the Great.   g9.8 Elijah had come: Many of the Jewish people expected the prophet Elijah to come and prepare the way for the Messiah.

to life. ⁹But Herod said, "I had John's head cut off! Who is this I hear so much about?" Herod was eager to meet Jesus.

Jesus Feeds Five Thousand
(Matthew 14.13-21; Mark 6.30-44; John 6.1-14)

¹⁰The apostles came back and told Jesus everything they had done. He then took them with him to the village of Bethsaida, where they could be alone. ¹¹But a lot of people found out about this and followed him. Jesus welcomed them. He spoke about God's kingdom and healed everyone who was sick.

¹²Late in the afternoon the twelve apostles came to Jesus and said, "Send the crowd to the villages and farms around here. They need to find a place to stay and something to eat. There is nothing in this place. It's like a desert!"

¹³Jesus answered, "You give them something to eat."

But they replied, "We have only five small loaves of bread*ʰ* and two fish. If we are going to feed all these people, we will have to go and buy food." ¹⁴There were about 5,000 men in the crowd.

Jesus said to his disciples, "Tell the people to sit in groups of 50." ¹⁵They did this, and all the people sat down. ¹⁶Jesus took the five loaves and the two fish. He looked up toward heaven and blessed the food. Then he broke the bread and fish and handed them to his disciples to give to the people.

¹⁷Everyone ate all they wanted. What was left over filled twelve baskets.

Who Is Jesus?
(Matthew 16.13-19; Mark 8.27-29)

¹⁸When Jesus was alone praying, his disciples came to him, and he asked them, "What do people say about me?"

¹⁹They answered, "Some say you are John the Baptist or Elijah*ⁱ* or a prophet from long ago who has come back to life."

²⁰Jesus then asked, "But who do you say I am?"

Peter answered, "You are the Messiah sent from God."

²¹Jesus strictly warned his disciples not to tell anyone about this.

h9.13 *small loaves of bread:* These would have been flat and round or in the shape of a bun.
i9.19 *Elijah:* See the note at 9.8.

Jesus Speaks About His Suffering and Death
(Matthew 16.20-28; Mark 8.30—9.1)

[22]Jesus told his disciples, "The nation's leaders, the chief priests, and the teachers of the Law of Moses will make the Son of Man suffer terribly. They will reject him and kill him, but three days later he will rise to life."

[23]Then Jesus said to all the people:

If any of you want to be my followers, you must forget about yourself. You must take up your cross every day and follow me. [24]If you want to save your life,[j] you will destroy it. But if you give up your life for me, you will save it. [25]What will you gain, if you own the whole world but destroy yourself or waste your life? [26]If you are ashamed of me and my message, the Son of Man will be ashamed of you when he comes in his glory and in the glory of his Father and the holy angels. [27]You can be sure some of the people standing here will not die before they see God's kingdom.

The True Glory of Jesus
(Matthew 17.1-8; Mark 9.2-8)

[28]About eight days later Jesus took Peter, John, and James with him and went up on a mountain to pray. [29]While he was praying, his face changed, and his clothes became shining white. [30]Suddenly Moses and Elijah were there speaking with him. [31]They appeared in heavenly glory and talked about all that Jesus' death[k] in Jerusalem would mean.

[32]Peter and the other two disciples had been sound asleep. All at once they woke up and saw how glorious Jesus was. They also saw the two men who were with him.

[33]Moses and Elijah were about to leave, when Peter said to Jesus, "Master, it is good for us to be here! Let us make three shelters, one for you, one for Moses, and one for Elijah." But Peter did not know what he was talking about.

[34]While Peter was still speaking, a shadow from a cloud passed over, and they were frightened as the cloud covered them. [35]From the cloud a voice spoke, "This is my chosen Son. Listen to what he says!"

j9.24 life: In verses 24,25 a Greek word which often means "soul" is translated "life" and "yourself."
k9.31 Jesus' death: In Greek this is "his departure," which probably includes his rising to life and his return to heaven.

³⁶After the voice had spoken, Peter, John, and James saw only Jesus. For some time they kept quiet and did not say anything about what they had seen.

Jesus Heals a Boy
(Matthew 17.14-18; Mark 9.14-27)

³⁷The next day Jesus and his three disciples came down from the mountain and were met by a large crowd. ³⁸Just then someone in the crowd shouted, "Teacher, please do something for my son! He is my only child! ³⁹A demon often attacks him and makes him scream. It shakes him until he foams at the mouth, and it won't leave him until it has completely worn the boy out. ⁴⁰I begged your disciples to force out the demon, but they couldn't do it."

⁴¹Jesus said to them, "You people are stubborn and don't have any faith! How much longer must I be with you? Why do I have to put up with you?"

Then Jesus said to the man, "Bring your son to me." ⁴²While the boy was being brought, the demon attacked him and made him shake all over. Jesus ordered the demon to stop. Then he healed the boy and gave him back to his father. ⁴³Everyone was amazed at God's great power.

Jesus Again Speaks About His Death
(Matthew 17.22,23; Mark 9.30-32)

While everyone was still amazed at what Jesus was doing, he said to his disciples, ⁴⁴"Pay close attention to what I am telling you! The Son of Man will be handed over to his enemies." ⁴⁵But the disciples did not know what he meant. The meaning was hidden from them. They could not understand it, and they were afraid to ask.

Who Is the Greatest?
(Matthew 18.1-5; Mark 9.33-37)

⁴⁶Jesus' disciples were arguing about which one of them was the greatest. ⁴⁷Jesus knew what they were thinking, and he had a child stand there beside him. ⁴⁸Then he said to his disciples, "When you welcome even a child because of me, you welcome me. And when you welcome me, you welcome the one who sent me. Whichever one of you is the most humble is the greatest."

For or Against Jesus
(Mark 9.38-40)

⁴⁹John said, "Master, we saw a man using your name to force demons out of people. But we told him to stop, because he isn't one of us."

⁵⁰"Don't stop him!" Jesus said. "Anyone who isn't against you is for you."

A Samaritan Village Refuses to Receive Jesus

⁵¹Not long before it was time for Jesus to be taken up to heaven, he made up his mind to go to Jerusalem. ⁵²He sent some messengers on ahead to a Samaritan village to get things ready for him. ⁵³But he was on his way to Jerusalem, so the people there refused to welcome him. ⁵⁴When the disciples James and John saw what was happening, they asked, "Lord, do you want us to call down fire from heaven to destroy these people?"[l]

⁵⁵But Jesus turned and corrected them for what they had said.[m] ⁵⁶Then they all went on to another village.

Three People Who Wanted to Be Followers
(Matthew 8.19-22)

⁵⁷Along the way someone said to Jesus, "I'll follow you anywhere!"

⁵⁸Jesus said, "Foxes have dens, and birds have nests, but the Son of Man doesn't have a place to call his own."

⁵⁹Jesus told someone else to come with him. But the man said, "Lord, let me wait until I bury my father."[n]

⁶⁰Jesus answered, "Let the dead take care of the dead, while you go and tell about God's kingdom."

⁶¹Then someone said to Jesus, "I want to follow you, Lord, but first let me go back and take care of things at home."

⁶²Jesus answered, "Anyone who starts plowing and keeps looking back isn't worth a thing to God's kingdom!"

l9.54 to destroy these people: Some manuscripts add "as Elijah did." m9.55 what they had said: Some manuscripts add, "and said, 'Don't you know what spirit you belong to? The Son of Man did not come to destroy people's lives, but to save them.' " n9.59 bury my father: The Jewish people taught that giving someone a proper burial was even more important than helping the poor.

The Work of the Seventy-two Followers

10 Later the Lord chose 72[o] other followers and sent them out two by two to every town and village where he was about to go. [2]He said to them:

A large crop is in the fields, but there are only a few workers. Ask the Lord in charge of the harvest to send out workers to bring it in. [3]Now go, but remember, I am sending you like lambs into a pack of wolves. [4]Don't take along a moneybag or a traveling bag or sandals. And don't waste time greeting people on the road.[p] [5]As soon as you enter a home, say, "God bless this home with peace." [6]If the people living there are peace-loving, your prayer for peace will bless them. But if they are not peace-loving, your prayer will return to you. [7]Stay with the same family, eating and drinking whatever they give you, because workers are worth what they earn. Don't move around from house to house.

[8]If the people of a town welcome you, eat whatever they offer. [9]Heal their sick and say, "God's kingdom will soon be here!"[q]

[10]But if the people of a town refuse to welcome you, go out into the street and say, [11]"We are shaking the dust from our feet[r] as a warning to you. And you can be sure that God's kingdom will soon be here!"[s] [12]I tell you that on the day of judgment the people of Sodom will get off easier than the people of that town!

The Unbelieving Towns
(Matthew 11.20-24)

[13]You people of Chorazin are in for trouble! You people of Bethsaida are also in for trouble! If the miracles that took place in your towns had happened in Tyre and Sidon, the people there would have turned to God long ago. They would have dressed in sackcloth and put ashes

---

o10.1 72: Some manuscripts have "70." According to Jewish tradition, there were 70 nations on earth. But the ancient Greek translation of the Old Testament has "72" in place of "70." Jesus probably chose this number of followers to show that his message was for everyone in the world.   p10.4 waste time greeting people on the road: In those days a polite greeting could take a long time.   q10.9 will soon be here: Or "is already here."   r10.11 shaking the dust from our feet: This was a way of showing rejection.   s10.11 will soon be here: Or "is already here."

on their heads.[t] [14]On the day of judgment the people of Tyre and Sidon will get off easier than you will. [15]People of Capernaum, do you think you will be honored in heaven? Well, you will go down to hell!

[16]My followers, whoever listens to you is listening to me. Anyone who says "No" to you is saying "No" to me. And anyone who says "No" to me is really saying "No" to the one who sent me.

The Return of the Seventy-two

[17]When the 72[u] followers returned, they were excited and said, "Lord, even the demons obeyed when we spoke in your name!"

[18]Jesus told them:

I saw Satan fall from heaven like a flash of lightning. [19]I have given you the power to trample on snakes and scorpions and to defeat the power of your enemy Satan. Nothing can harm you. [20]But don't be happy because evil spirits obey you. Be happy that your names are written in heaven!

Jesus Thanks His Father
(Matthew 11.25-27; 13.16,17)

[21]At that same time, Jesus felt the joy that comes from the Holy Spirit,[v] and he said:

My Father, Lord of heaven and earth, I am grateful that you hid all this from wise and educated people and showed it to ordinary people. Yes, Father, this is what pleased you.

[22]My Father has given me everything, and he is the only one who knows the Son. The only one who really knows the Father is the Son. But the Son wants to tell others about the Father, so they can know him too.

[23]Jesus then turned to his disciples and said to them in private, "You are really blessed to see what you see! [24]Many prophets and kings were eager to see what you see and to hear what you hear. But I tell you they did not see or hear."

---

t10.13 dressed in sackcloth . . . ashes on their heads: This was one way that people showed how sorry they were for their sins.   u10.17 72: See the note at 10.1.   v10.21 the Holy Spirit: Some manuscripts have "his spirit."

The Good Samaritan

²⁵An expert in the Law of Moses stood up and asked Jesus a question to see what he would say. "Teacher," he asked, "what must I do to have eternal life?"

²⁶Jesus answered, "What is written in the Scriptures? How do you understand them?"

²⁷The man replied, "The Scriptures say, 'Love the Lord your God with all your heart, soul, strength, and mind.' They also say, 'Love your neighbors as much as you love yourself.' "

²⁸Jesus said, "You have given the right answer. If you do this, you will have eternal life."

²⁹But the man wanted to show that he knew what he was talking about. So he asked Jesus, "Who are my neighbors?"

³⁰Jesus replied:

As a man was going down from Jerusalem to Jericho, robbers attacked him and grabbed everything he had. They beat him up and ran off, leaving him half dead.

³¹A priest happened to be going down the same road. But when he saw the man, he walked by on the other side. ³²Later a temple helper[w] came to the same place. But when he saw the man who had been beaten up, he also went by on the other side.

³³A man from Samaria then came traveling along that road. When he saw the man, he felt sorry for him ³⁴and went over to him. He treated his wounds with olive oil and wine[x] and bandaged them. Then he put him on his own donkey and took him to an inn, where he took care of him. ³⁵The next morning he gave the innkeeper two silver coins and said, "Please take care of the man. If you spend more than this on him, I will pay you when I return."

³⁶Then Jesus asked, "Which one of these three people was a real neighbor to the man who was beaten up by robbers?"

³⁷The expert in the Law of Moses answered, "The one who showed pity." Jesus said, "Go and do the same!"

---

w10.32 temple helper: A man from the tribe of Levi, whose job it was to work around the temple. x10.34 olive oil and wine: In New Testament times these were used as medicine. Sometimes olive oil is a symbol for healing by means of a miracle (see James 5.14).

Martha and Mary

³⁸The Lord and his disciples were traveling along and came to a village. When they got there, a woman named Martha welcomed him into her home. ³⁹She had a sister named Mary, who sat down in front of the Lord and was listening to what he said. ⁴⁰Martha was worried about all that had to be done. Finally, she went to Jesus and said, "Lord, doesn't it bother you that my sister has left me to do all the work by myself? Tell her to come and help me!"

⁴¹The Lord answered, "Martha, Martha! You are worried and upset about so many things, ⁴²but only one thing is necessary. Mary has chosen what is best, and it will not be taken away from her."

Prayer
(Matthew 6.9-13; 7.7-11)

11 When Jesus had finished praying, one of his disciples said to him, "Lord, teach us to pray, just as John taught his followers to pray."

²So Jesus told them, "Pray in this way:
'Father, help us
   to honor your name.
Come and set up
   your kingdom.
³Give us each day
   the food we need.ʸ
⁴Forgive our sins,
as we forgive everyone
   who has done wrong to us.
And keep us
   from being tempted.'"

⁵Then Jesus went on to say:

   Suppose one of you goes to a friend in the middle of the night and says, "Let me borrow three loaves of bread. ⁶A friend of mine has dropped in, and I don't have a thing for him to eat." ⁷And suppose your friend answers, "Don't bother me! The door is bolted, and my children and I are in bed. I cannot get up to give you something."

ʸ11.3 the food we need: Or "food for today" or "food for the coming day."

⁸He may not get up and give you the bread, just because you are his friend. But he will get up and give you as much as you need, simply because you are not ashamed to keep on asking.

⁹So I tell you to ask and you will receive, search and you will find, knock and the door will be opened for you. ¹⁰Everyone who asks will receive, everyone who searches will find, and the door will be opened for everyone who knocks. ¹¹Which one of you fathers would give your hungry child a snake if the child asked for a fish? ¹²Which one of you would give your child a scorpion if the child asked for an egg? ¹³As bad as you are, you still know how to give good gifts to your children. But your heavenly Father is even more ready to give the Holy Spirit to anyone who asks.

Jesus and the Ruler of Demons
(Matthew 12.22-30; Mark 3.20-27)

¹⁴Jesus forced a demon out of a man who could not talk. And after the demon had gone out, the man started speaking, and the crowds were amazed. ¹⁵But some people said, "He forces out demons by the power of Beelzebul, the ruler of the demons!"

¹⁶Others wanted to put Jesus to the test. So they asked him to show them a sign from God. ¹⁷Jesus knew what they were thinking, and he said:

A kingdom where people fight each other will end up in ruin. And a family that fights will break up. ¹⁸If Satan fights against himself, how can his kingdom last? Yet you say that I force out demons by the power of Beelzebul. ¹⁹If I use his power to force out demons, whose power do your own followers use to force them out? They are the ones who will judge you. ²⁰But if I use God's power to force out demons, it proves that God's kingdom has already come to you.

²¹When a strong man arms himself and guards his home, everything he owns is safe. ²²But if a stronger man comes and defeats him, he will carry off the weapons in which the strong man trusted. Then he will divide with others what he has taken. ²³If you are not on my side, you are against me. If you don't gather in the crop with me, you scatter it.

Return of an Evil Spirit
(Matthew 12.43-45)

[24]When an evil spirit leaves a person, it travels through the desert, looking for a place to rest. But when it doesn't find a place, it says, "I will go back to the home I left." [25]When it gets there and finds the place clean and fixed up, [26]it goes off and finds seven other evil spirits even worse than itself. They all come and make their home there, and that person ends up in worse shape than before.

Being Really Blessed

[27]While Jesus was still talking, a woman in the crowd spoke up, "The woman who gave birth to you and nursed you is blessed!"

[28]Jesus replied, "That's true, but the people who are really blessed are the ones who hear and obey God's message!"[z]

A Sign from God
(Matthew 12.38-42; Mark 8.12)

[29]As crowds were gathering around Jesus, he said:

You people of today are evil! You keep looking for a sign from God. But what happened to Jonah[a] is the only sign you will be given. [30]Just as Jonah was a sign to the people of Nineveh, the Son of Man will be a sign to the people of today. [31]When the judgment comes, the Queen of the South[b] will stand there with you and condemn you. She traveled a long way to hear Solomon's wisdom, and yet here is something far greater than Solomon. [32]The people of Nineveh will also stand there with you and condemn you. They turned to God when Jonah preached, and yet here is something far greater than Jonah.

---

z11.28 That's true, but the people who are really blessed . . . message: Or "That's not true, the people who are blessed . . . message." a11.29 what happened to Jonah: Jonah was in the stomach of a big fish for three days and nights (see Matthew 12.40). b11.31 South: Sheba, probably a country in southern Arabia.

Light
(Matthew 5.15; 6.22,23)

³³No one lights a lamp and then hides it or puts it under a clay pot.
A lamp is put on a lampstand, so everyone who comes into the house
can see the light. ³⁴Your eyes are the lamp for your body. When your
eyes are good, you have all the light you need. But when your eyes
are bad, everything is dark. ³⁵So be sure your light isn't darkness. ³⁶If
you have light, and nothing is dark, then light will be everywhere, as
when a lamp shines brightly on you.

Jesus Condemns the Pharisees and
Teachers of the Law of Moses
(Matthew 23.1-36; Mark 12.38-40; Luke 20.45-47)

³⁷When Jesus finished speaking, a Pharisee invited him home for a meal. Jesus
went and sat down to eat.ᶜ ³⁸The Pharisee was surprised that he did not wash
his handsᵈ before eating. ³⁹So the Lord said to him:

You Pharisees clean the outside of cups and dishes, but on the inside you are greedy and evil. ⁴⁰You fools! Didn't God make both the
outside and the inside?ᵉ ⁴¹If you would only give what you have to the
poor, everything you do would please God.

⁴²You Pharisees are in for trouble! You give God a tenth of the
spices from your gardens, such as mint and rue. But you cheat people, and you don't love God. You should be fair and kind to others
and still give a tenth to God.

⁴³You Pharisees are in for trouble! You love the front seats in the
synagogues, and you like to be greeted with honor in the market.
⁴⁴But you are in for trouble! You are like unmarked gravesᶠ that people walk on without even knowing it.

⁴⁵A teacher of the Law of Moses spoke up, "Teacher, you said cruel things
about us."

c11.37 sat down to eat: See the note at 7.36.   d11.38 did not wash his hands: The Jewish people
had strict laws about washing their hands before eating, especially if they had been out in public.
e11.40 Didn't God make both the outside and the inside: Or "Doesn't the person who washes the
outside always wash the inside too?"   f11.44 unmarked graves: Tombs were whitewashed to keep
anyone from accidentally touching them. A person who touched a dead body or a tomb was considered unclean and could not worship with other Jewish people.

⁴⁶Jesus replied:

You teachers are also in for trouble! You load people down with heavy burdens, but you won't lift a finger to help them carry the loads. ⁴⁷Yes, you are really in for trouble. You build monuments to honor the prophets your own people murdered long ago. ⁴⁸You must think that was the right thing for your people to do, or else you would not have built monuments for the prophets they murdered.

⁴⁹Because of your evil deeds, the Wisdom of God said, "I will send prophets and apostles to you. But you will murder some and mistreat others." ⁵⁰You people living today will be punished for all the prophets who have been murdered since the beginning of the world. ⁵¹This includes every prophet from the time of Abel to the time of Zechariah,ᵍ who was murdered between the altar and the temple. You people will certainly be punished for all of this.

⁵²You teachers of the Law of Moses are really in for trouble! You carry the keys to the door of knowledge about God. But you never go in, and you keep others from going in.

⁵³Jesus was about to leave, but the teachers and the Pharisees wanted to get even with him. They tried to make him say what he thought about other things, ⁵⁴so they could catch him saying something wrong.

Warnings

12 As thousands of people crowded around Jesus and were stepping on each other, he told his disciples:

Be sure to guard against the dishonest teachingʰ of the Pharisees! It is their way of fooling people. ²Everything that is hidden will be found out, and every secret will be known. ³Whatever you say in the dark will be heard when it is day. Whatever you whisper in a closed room will be shouted from the housetops.

g11.51 *from the time of Abel . . . Zechariah:* Genesis is the first book in the Jewish Scriptures, and it tells that Abel was the first person to be murdered. Second Chronicles is the last book in the Jewish Scriptures, and the last murder that it tells about is that of Zechariah. h12.1 *dishonest teaching:* The Greek text has "yeast," which is used here of a teaching that is not true (see Matthew 16.6,12).

The One to Fear
(Matthew 10.28-31)

[4]My friends, don't be afraid of people. They can kill you, but after that, there is nothing else they can do. [5]God is the one you must fear. Not only can he take your life, but he can throw you into hell. God is certainly the one you should fear!

[6]Five sparrows are sold for only a few cents, but God doesn't forget a single one of them. [7]Even the hairs on your head are counted. So don't be afraid! You are worth much more than many sparrows.

Telling Others About Christ
(Matthew 10.32,33; 12.32; 10.19,20)

[8]If you tell others that you belong to me, the Son of Man will tell God's angels that you are my followers. [9]But if you reject me, you will be rejected in front of them. [10]If you speak against the Son of Man, you can be forgiven, but if you speak against the Holy Spirit, you cannot be forgiven.

[11]When you are brought to trial in the synagogues or before rulers or officials, don't worry about how you will defend yourselves or what you will say. [12]At that time the Holy Spirit will tell you what to say.

A Rich Fool

[13]A man in a crowd said to Jesus, "Teacher, tell my brother to give me my share of what our father left us when he died."

[14]Jesus answered, "Who gave me the right to settle arguments between you and your brother?"

[15]Then he said to the crowd, "Don't be greedy! Owning a lot of things won't make your life safe."

[16]So Jesus told them this story:

A rich man's farm produced a big crop, [17]and he said to himself, "What can I do? I don't have a place large enough to store everything."

[18]Later, he said, "Now I know what I'll do. I'll tear down my barns and build bigger ones, where I can store all my grain and other goods. [19]Then I'll say to myself, 'You have stored up enough good things to last for years to come. Live it up! Eat, drink, and enjoy yourself.'"

²⁰But God said to him, "You fool! Tonight you will die. Then who will get what you have stored up?"

²¹"This is what happens to people who store up everything for themselves, but are poor in the sight of God."

Worry
(Matthew 6.25-34)

²²Jesus said to his disciples:

I tell you not to worry about your life! Don't worry about having something to eat or wear. ²³Life is more than food or clothing. ²⁴Look at the crows! They don't plant or harvest, and they don't have storehouses or barns. But God takes care of them. You are much more important than any birds. ²⁵Can worry make you live longer?[i] ²⁶If you don't have power over small things, why worry about everything else?

²⁷Look how the wild flowers grow! They don't work hard to make their clothes. But I tell you Solomon with all his wealth[j] wasn't as well clothed as one of these flowers. ²⁸God gives such beauty to everything that grows in the fields, even though it is here today and thrown into a fire tomorrow. Won't he do even more for you? You have such little faith!

²⁹Don't keep worrying about having something to eat or drink. ³⁰Only people who don't know God are always worrying about such things. Your Father knows what you need. ³¹But put God's work first, and these things will be yours as well.

Treasures in Heaven
(Matthew 6.19-21)

³²My little group of disciples, don't be afraid! Your Father wants to give you the kingdom. ³³Sell what you have and give the money to the poor. Make yourselves moneybags that never wear out. Make sure your treasure is safe in heaven, where thieves cannot steal it and moths cannot destroy it. ³⁴Your heart will always be where your treasure is.

---

i12.25 live longer: Or "grow taller."   j12.27 Solomon with all his wealth: The Jewish people thought that Solomon was the richest person who had ever lived.

Faithful and Unfaithful Servants
(Matthew 24.45-51)

35Be ready and keep your lamps burning 36just like those servants who wait up for their master to return from a wedding feast. As soon as he comes and knocks, they open the door for him. 37Servants are fortunate if their master finds them awake and ready when he comes! I promise you he will get ready and let his servants sit down so he can serve them. 38Those servants are really fortunate if their master finds them ready, even though he comes late at night or early in the morning. 39You would surely not let a thief break into your home, if you knew when the thief was coming. 40So always be ready! You don't know when the Son of Man will come.

41Peter asked Jesus, "Did you say this just for us or for everyone?" 42The Lord answered:

Who are faithful and wise servants? Who are the ones the master will put in charge of giving the other servants their food supplies at the proper time? 43Servants are fortunate if their master comes and finds them doing their job. 44A servant who is always faithful will surely be put in charge of everything the master owns.

45But suppose one of the servants thinks that the master won't return until late. Suppose that servant starts beating all the other servants and eats and drinks and gets drunk. 46If that happens, the master will come on a day and at a time when the servant least expects him. That servant will then be punished and thrown out with the servants who cannot be trusted.

47If servants are not ready or willing to do what their master wants them to do, they will be beaten hard. 48But servants who don't know what their master wants them to do will not be beaten so hard for doing wrong. If God has been generous with you, he will expect you to serve him well. But if he has been more than generous, he will expect you to serve him even better.

Not Peace, but Trouble
(Matthew 10.34-36)

49I came to set fire to the earth, and I wish it were already on fire! 50I am going to be put to a hard test. And I will have to suffer a lot of pain until it is over. ⁵¹Do you think that I came to bring peace to earth? No indeed! I came to make people choose sides. ⁵²A family of five will be divided, with two of them against the other three. ⁵³Fathers and sons will turn against one another, and mothers and daughters will do the same. Mothers-in-law and daughters-in-law will also turn against each other.

Knowing What to Do
(Matthew 16.2, 3; 5.25, 26)

⁵⁴Jesus said to all the people:

As soon as you see a cloud coming up in the west, you say, "It's going to rain," and it does. ⁵⁵When the south wind blows, you say, "It's going to get hot," and it does. ⁵⁶Are you trying to fool someone? You can predict the weather by looking at the earth and sky, but you don't really know what's going on right now. ⁵⁷Why don't you understand the right thing to do? ⁵⁸When someone accuses you of something, try to settle things before you are taken to court. If you don't, you will be dragged before the judge. Then the judge will hand you over to the jailer, and you will be locked up. ⁵⁹You won't get out until you have paid the last cent you owe.

Turn Back to God

13 About this same time Jesus was told that Pilate had given orders for some people from Galilee to be killed while they were offering sacrifices. ²Jesus replied:

Do you think that these people were worse sinners than everyone else in Galilee just because of what happened to them? ³Not at all! But you can be sure that if you don't turn back to God, every one of you will also be killed. ⁴What about those 18 people who died when the tower in Siloam fell on them? Do you think they were worse than everyone else in Jerusalem? ⁵Not at all! But you can be sure that if you don't turn back to God, every one of you will also die.

A Story About a Fig Tree

⁶Jesus then told them this story:

A man had a fig tree growing in his vineyard. One day he went out to pick some figs, but he didn't find any. ⁷So he said to the gardener, "For three years I have come looking for figs on this tree, and I haven't found any yet. Chop it down! Why should it take up space?"

⁸The gardener answered, "Master, leave it for another year. I'll dig around it and put some manure on it to make it grow. ⁹Maybe it will have figs on it next year. If it doesn't, you can have it cut down."

Healing a Woman on the Sabbath

¹⁰One Sabbath, Jesus was teaching in a synagogue, ¹¹and a woman was there who had been crippled by an evil spirit for 18 years. She was completely bent over and could not straighten up. ¹²When Jesus saw the woman, he called her over and said, "You are now well." ¹³He placed his hands on her, and at once she stood up straight and praised God.

¹⁴The man in charge of the synagogue was angry because Jesus had healed someone on the Sabbath. So he said to the people, "Each week has six days when we can work. Come and be healed on one of those days, but not on the Sabbath."

¹⁵The Lord replied, "Are you trying to fool someone? Won't any one of you untie your ox or donkey and lead it out to drink on a Sabbath? ¹⁶This woman belongs to the family of Abraham, but Satan has kept her bound for 18 years. Isn't it right to set her free on the Sabbath?" ¹⁷Jesus' words made his enemies ashamed. But everyone else in the crowd was happy about the wonderful things he was doing.

A Mustard Seed and Yeast
(Matthew 13.31-33; Mark 4.30-32)

¹⁸Jesus said, "What is God's kingdom like? What can I compare it with? ¹⁹It is like what happens when someone plants a mustard seed in a garden. The seed grows as big as a tree, and birds nest in its branches."

²⁰Then Jesus said, "What can I compare God's kingdom with? ²¹It is like

what happens when a woman mixes yeast into three batches of flour. Finally, all the dough rises."

The Narrow Door
(Matthew 7.13,14,21-23)

[22]As Jesus was on his way to Jerusalem, he taught the people in the towns and villages. [23]Someone asked him, "Lord, are only a few people going to be saved?"

Jesus answered:

[24]Do all you can to go in by the narrow door! A lot of people will try to get in, but will not be able to. [25]Once the owner of the house gets up and locks the door, you will be left standing outside. You will knock on the door and say, "Sir, open the door for us!"

But the owner will answer, "I don't know a thing about you!"

[26]Then you will start saying, "We dined with you, and you taught in our streets."

[27]But he will say, "I really don't know who you are! Get away from me, you evil people!"

[28]Then when you have been thrown outside, you will weep and grit your teeth because you will see Abraham, Isaac, Jacob, and all the prophets in God's kingdom. [29]People will come from all directions and sit down to feast in God's kingdom. [30]There the ones who are now least important will be the most important, and those who are now most important will be least important.

Jesus and Herod

[31]At that time some Pharisees came to Jesus and said, "You had better get away from here, because Herod[k] wants to kill you!"

[32]Jesus said to them:

Go tell that fox, "I am going to force out demons and heal people today and tomorrow, and three days later I'll be through." [33]But I am going on my way today and tomorrow and the next day. After all, Jerusalem is the place where prophets are killed.

k13.31 Herod: Herod Antipas, the son of Herod the Great.

Jesus Loves Jerusalem
(Matthew 23.37-39)

34Jerusalem, Jerusalem! Your people have killed the prophets and have stoned the messengers who were sent to you. I have often wanted to gather your people, as a hen gathers her chicks under her wings. But you wouldn't let me. 35Now your temple will be deserted. You won't see me again until the time when you say,

"Blessed is the one who comes
   in the name of the Lord."

Jesus Heals a Sick Man

14 One Sabbath, Jesus was having dinner in the home of an important Pharisee, and everyone was carefully watching Jesus. 2All of a sudden a man with swollen legs stood up in front of him. 3Jesus turned and asked the Pharisees and the teachers of the Law of Moses, "Is it right to heal on the Sabbath?" 4But they did not say a word.

Jesus took hold of the man. Then he healed him and sent him away. 5Afterwards, Jesus asked the people, "If your son or ox falls into a well, wouldn't you pull him out at once, even on the Sabbath?" 6There was nothing they could say.

How to Be a Guest

7Jesus saw how the guests had tried to take the best seats. So he told them:

8When you are invited to a wedding feast, don't sit in the best place. Someone more important may have been invited. 9Then the one who invited you will come and say, "Give your place to this other guest!" You will be embarrassed and will have to sit in the worst place.

10When you are invited to be a guest, go and sit in the worst place. Then the one who invited you may come and say, "My friend, take a better seat!" You will then be honored in front of all the other guests. 11If you put yourself above others, you will be put down. But if you humble yourself, you will be honored.

12Then Jesus said to the man who had invited him:

When you give a dinner or a banquet, don't invite your friends and family and relatives and rich neighbors. If you do, they will invite you in return, and you will be paid back. 13When you give a feast, invite the poor, the paralyzed, the lame, and the blind. [14]They cannot pay you back. But God will bless you and reward you when his people rise from death.

The Great Banquet
(Matthew 22.1-10)

[15]After Jesus had finished speaking, one of the guests said, "The greatest blessing of all is to be at the banquet in God's kingdom!"

[16]Jesus told him:

A man once gave a great banquet and invited a lot of guests. [17]When the banquet was ready, he sent a servant to tell the guests, "Everything is ready! Please come."

[18]One guest after another started making excuses. The first one said, "I bought some land, and I've got to look it over. Please excuse me."

[19]Another guest said, "I bought five teams of oxen, and I need to try them out. Please excuse me."

[20]Still another guest said, "I've just now married, and I can't be there."

[21]The servant told his master what happened, and the master became so angry he said, "Go as fast as you can to every street and alley in town! Bring in everyone who is poor or paralyzed or blind or lame."

[22]When the servant returned, he said, "Master, I've done what you told me, and there is still plenty of room for more people."

[23]His master then told him, "Go out along the back roads and make people come in, so my house will be full. [24]Not one of the guests I first invited will get even a bite of my food!"

Being a Disciple
(Matthew 10.37, 38)

[25]Large crowds were walking along with Jesus, when he turned and said:

[26]You cannot be my disciple, unless you love me more than you love your father and mother, your wife and children, and your brothers and sisters. You cannot follow me unless you love me more than you love your own life.

[27]You cannot be my disciple unless you carry your own cross and follow me.

²⁸Suppose one of you wants to build a tower. What is the first thing you will do? Won't you sit down and figure out how much it will cost and if you have enough money to pay for it? ²⁹Otherwise, you will start building the tower, but not be able to finish. Then everyone who sees what is happening will laugh at you. ³⁰They will say, "You started building, but could not finish the job."

³¹What will a king do if he has only 10,000 soldiers to defend himself against a king who is about to attack him with 20,000 soldiers? Before he goes out to battle, won't he first sit down and decide if he can win? ³²If he thinks he won't be able to defend himself, he will send messengers and ask for peace while the other king is still a long way off. ³³So then, you cannot be my disciple unless you give away everything you own.

Salt and Light
(Matthew 5.13; Mark 9.50)

³⁴Salt is good, but if it no longer tastes like salt, how can it be made to taste salty again? ³⁵It is no longer good for the soil or even for the manure pile. People simply throw it out. If you have ears, pay attention!

One Sheep
(Matthew 18.12-14)

15 Tax collectors¹ and sinners were all crowding around to listen to Jesus. ²So the Pharisees and the teachers of the Law of Moses started grumbling, "This man is friendly with sinners. He even eats with them."

³Then Jesus told them this story:

⁴If any of you has 100 sheep, and one of them gets lost, what will you do? Won't you leave the 99 in the field and go look for the lost sheep until you find it? ⁵And when you find it, you will be so glad that you will put it on your shoulder ⁶and carry it home. Then you will call in your friends and neighbors and say, "Let's celebrate! I've found my lost sheep."

⁷Jesus said, "In the same way there is more happiness in heaven because of one sinner who turns to God than over 99 good people who don't need to."

115.1 Tax collectors: See the note at 3.12.

One Coin

⁸Jesus told the people another story:

What will a woman do if she has ten silver coins and loses one of them? Won't she light a lamp, sweep the floor, and look carefully until she finds it? ⁹Then she will call in her friends and neighbors and say, "Let's celebrate! I've found the coin I lost."

¹⁰Jesus said, "In the same way God's angels are happy when even one person turns to him."

Two Sons

¹¹Jesus told them yet another story:

Once a man had two sons. ¹²The younger son said to his father, "Give me my share of the property." So the father divided his property between his two sons.

¹³Not long after that, the younger son packed up everything he owned and left for a foreign country, where he wasted all his money in wild living. ¹⁴He had spent everything, when a bad famine spread through that whole land. Soon he had nothing to eat.

¹⁵He went to work for a man in that country, and the man sent him out to take care of his pigs.ᵐ ¹⁶He would have been glad to eat what the pigs were eating,ⁿ but no one gave him a thing.

¹⁷Finally, he came to his senses and said, "My father's workers have plenty to eat, and here I am, starving to death! ¹⁸I will go to my father and say to him, 'Father, I have sinned against God in heaven and against you. ¹⁹I am no longer good enough to be called your son. Treat me like one of your workers.'"

²⁰The younger son got up and started back to his father. But when he was still a long way off, his father saw him and felt sorry for him. He ran to his son and hugged and kissed him.

²¹The son said, "Father, I have sinned against God in heaven and against you. I am no longer good enough to be called your son."

²²But his father said to the servants, "Hurry and bring the best

---

m15.15 pigs: The Jewish religion taught that pigs were not fit to eat or even to touch. A Jewish man would have felt terribly insulted if he had to feed pigs, much less eat with them. n15.16 what the pigs were eating: The Greek text has "(bean) pods," which came from a tree in Palestine. These were used to feed animals. Poor people sometimes ate them too.

clothes and put them on him. Give him a ring for his finger and sandals[o] for his feet. ²³Get the best calf and prepare it, so we can eat and celebrate. ²⁴This son of mine was dead, but has now come back to life. He was lost and has now been found." And they began to celebrate.

²⁵The older son had been out in the field. But when he came near the house, he heard the music and dancing. ²⁶So he called one of the servants over and asked, "What's going on here?"

²⁷The servant answered, "Your brother has come home safe and sound, and your father ordered us to kill the best calf." ²⁸The older brother got so angry that he would not even go into the house.

His father came out and begged him to go in. ²⁹But he said to his father, "For years I have worked for you like a slave and have always obeyed you. But you have never even given me a little goat, so that I could give a dinner for my friends. ³⁰This other son of yours wasted your money on prostitutes. And now that he has come home, you ordered the best calf to be killed for a feast."

³¹His father replied, "My son, you are always with me, and everything I have is yours. ³²But we should be glad and celebrate! Your brother was dead, but he is now alive. He was lost and has now been found."

A Dishonest Manager

16 Jesus said to his disciples:

A rich man once had a manager to take care of his business. But he was told that his manager was wasting money. ²So the rich man called him in and said, "What is this I hear about you? Tell me what you have done! You are no longer going to work for me."

³The manager said to himself, "What shall I do now that my master is going to fire me? I can't dig ditches, and I'm ashamed to beg. ⁴I know what I'll do, so that people will welcome me into their homes after I've lost my job."

⁵Then one by one he called in the people who were in debt to his master. He asked the first one, "How much do you owe my master?"

⁶"A hundred barrels of olive oil," the man answered.

o15.22 ring . . . sandals: These show that the young man's father fully accepted him as his son. A ring was a sign of high position in the family. Sandals showed that he was a son instead of a slave, since slaves did not usually wear sandals.

So the manager said, "Take your bill and sit down and quickly write '50.' "

[7]The manager asked someone else who was in debt to his master, "How much do you owe?"

"A thousand sacks[p] of wheat," the man replied.

The manager said, "Take your bill and write '800.' "

[8]The master praised his dishonest manager for looking out for himself so well. That's how it is! The people of this world look out for themselves better than the people who belong to the light.

[9]My disciples, I tell you to use wicked wealth to make friends for yourselves. Then when it is gone, you will be welcomed into an eternal home. [10]Anyone who can be trusted in little matters can also be trusted in important matters. But anyone who is dishonest in little matters will be dishonest in important matters. [11]If you cannot be trusted with this wicked wealth, who will trust you with true wealth? [12]And if you cannot be trusted with what belongs to someone else, who will give you something that will be your own? [13]You cannot be the slave of two masters. You will like one more than the other or be more loyal to one than to the other. You cannot serve God and money.

Some Sayings of Jesus
(Matthew 11.12, 13; 5.31, 32; Mark 10.11, 12)

[14]The Pharisees really loved money. So when they heard what Jesus said, they made fun of him. [15]But Jesus told them:

You are always making yourselves look good, but God sees what is in your heart. The things that most people think are important are worthless as far as God is concerned.

[16]Until the time of John the Baptist, people had to obey the Law of Moses and the Books of the Prophets.[q] But since God's kingdom has been preached, everyone is trying hard to get in. [17]Heaven and earth will disappear before the smallest letter of the Law does.

[18]It is a terrible sin[r] for a man to divorce his wife and marry an-

p16.7 A thousand sacks: The Greek text has "100 measures," and each measure is about 10 or 12 sacks.   q16.16 the Law of Moses and the Books of the Prophets: The Jewish Scriptures, that is, the Old Testament.   r16.18 a terrible sin: The Greek text uses a word that means the sin of being unfaithful in marriage.

other woman. It is also a terrible sin for a man to marry a divorced woman.

Lazarus and the Rich Man

[19]There was once a rich man who wore expensive clothes and every day ate the best food. [20]But a poor beggar named Lazarus was brought to the gate of the rich man's house. [21]He was happy just to eat the scraps that fell from the rich man's table. His body was covered with sores, and dogs kept coming up to lick them. [22]The poor man died, and angels took him to the place of honor next to Abraham.[s]

The rich man also died and was buried. [23]He went to hell[t] and was suffering terribly. When he looked up and saw Abraham far off and Lazarus at his side, [24]he said to Abraham, "Have pity on me! Send Lazarus to dip his finger in water and touch my tongue. I'm suffering terribly in this fire."

[25]Abraham answered, "My friend, remember that while you lived, you had everything good, and Lazarus had everything bad. Now he is happy, and you are in pain. [26]And besides, there is a deep ditch between us, and no one from either side can cross over."

[27]But the rich man said, "Abraham, then please send Lazarus to my father's home. [28]Let him warn my five brothers, so they won't come to this horrible place."

[29]Abraham answered, "Your brothers can read what Moses and the prophets[u] wrote. They should pay attention to that."

[30]Then the rich man said, "No, that's not enough! If only someone from the dead would go to them, they would listen and turn to God."

[31]So Abraham said, "If they won't pay attention to Moses and the prophets, they won't listen even to someone who comes back from the dead."

s16.22 the place of honor next to Abraham: The Jewish people thought that heaven would be a banquet that God would give for them. Abraham would be the most important person there, and the guest of honor would sit next to him.   t16.23 hell: The Greek text has "hades," which the Jewish people often thought of as the place where the dead wait for the final judgment.   u16.29 Moses and the prophets: The Jewish Scriptures, that is, the Old Testament.

Faith and Service

(Matthew 18.6, 7, 21, 22; Mark 9.42)

17 Jesus said to his disciples:

There will always be something that causes people to sin. But anyone who causes them to sin is in for trouble. A person who causes even one of my little followers to sin ²would be better off thrown into the ocean with a heavy stone tied around their neck. ³So be careful what you do.

Correct any followers[v] of mine who sin, and forgive the ones who say they are sorry. ⁴Even if one of them mistreats you seven times in one day and says, "I am sorry," you should still forgive that person. ⁵The apostles said to the Lord, "Make our faith stronger!"

⁶Jesus replied:

If you had faith no bigger than a tiny mustard seed, you could tell this mulberry tree to pull itself up, roots and all, and to plant itself in the ocean. And it would!

⁷If your servant comes in from plowing or from taking care of the sheep, would you say, "Welcome! Come on in and have something to eat"? ⁸No, you wouldn't say that. You would say, "Prepare me something to eat. Get ready to serve me, so I can have my meal. Then later on you can eat and drink." ⁹Servants don't deserve special thanks for doing what they are supposed to do. ¹⁰And that's how it should be with you. When you've done all you should, then say, "We are merely servants, and we have simply done our duty."

Ten Men with Leprosy

¹¹On his way to Jerusalem, Jesus went along the border between Samaria and Galilee. ¹²As he was going into a village, ten men with leprosy[w] came toward him. They stood at a distance ¹³and shouted, "Jesus, Master, have pity on us!"

¹⁴Jesus looked at them and said, "Go show yourselves to the priests."[x]

On their way they were healed. ¹⁵When one of them discovered that he

v17.3 *followers:* The Greek text has "brothers," which is often used in the New Testament for followers of Jesus. w17.12 *leprosy:* See the note at 4.27. x17.14 *show yourselves to the priests:* See the note at 5.14.

was healed, he came back, shouting praises to God. [16]He bowed down at the feet of Jesus and thanked him. The man was from the country of Samaria.

[17]Jesus asked, "Weren't ten men healed? Where are the other nine? [18]Why was this foreigner the only one who came back to thank God?" [19]Then Jesus told the man, "You may get up and go. Your faith has made you well."

God's Kingdom
(Matthew 24.23-28, 37-41)

[20]Some Pharisees asked Jesus when God's kingdom would come. He answered, "God's kingdom isn't something you can see. [21]There is no use saying, 'Look! Here it is' or 'Look! There it is.' God's kingdom is here with you."[y]

[22]Jesus said to his disciples:

The time will come when you will long to see one of the days of the Son of Man, but you will not. [23]When people say to you, "Look there," or "Look here," don't go looking for him. [24]The day of the Son of Man will be like lightning flashing across the sky. [25]But first he must suffer terribly and be rejected by the people of today. [26]When the Son of Man comes, things will be just as they were when Noah lived. [27]People were eating, drinking, and getting married right up to the day when Noah went into the big boat. Then the flood came and drowned everyone on earth.

[28]When Lot[z] lived, people were also eating and drinking. They were buying, selling, planting, and building. [29]But on the very day Lot left Sodom, fiery flames poured down from the sky and killed everyone. [30]The same will happen on the day when the Son of Man appears.

[31]At that time no one on a rooftop[a] should go down into the house to get anything. No one in a field should go back to the house for anything. [32]Remember what happened to Lot's wife.[b]

[33]People who try to save their lives will lose them, and those who lose their lives will save them. [34]On that night two people will be sleeping in the same bed, but only one will be taken. The other will

y17.21 *here with you:* Or "in your hearts." z17.27,28 *Noah . . . Lot:* When God destroyed the earth by a flood, he saved Noah and his family. And when God destroyed the cities of Sodom and Gomorrah and the evil people who lived there, he rescued Lot and his family (see Genesis 19.1-29). a17.31 *rooftop:* See the note at 5.19. b17.32 *what happened to Lot's wife:* She turned into a block of salt when she disobeyed God (see Genesis 19.26).

be left. [35-36]Two women will be together grinding wheat, but only one will be taken. The other will be left.[c]

[37]Then Jesus' disciples spoke up, "But where will this happen, Lord?" Jesus said, "Where there is a corpse, there will always be vultures."[d]

A Widow and a Judge

18 Jesus told his disciples a story about how they should keep on praying and never give up:

[2]In a town there was once a judge who didn't fear God or care about people. [3]In that same town there was a widow who kept going to the judge and saying, "Make sure that I get fair treatment in court."

[4]For a while the judge refused to do anything. Finally, he said to himself, "Even though I don't fear God or care about people, [5]I will help this widow because she keeps on bothering me. If I don't help her, she will wear me out."

[6]The Lord said:

Think about what that crooked judge said. [7]Won't God protect his chosen ones who pray to him day and night? Won't he be concerned for them? [8]He will surely hurry and help them. But when the Son of Man comes, will he find on this earth anyone with faith?

A Pharisee and a Tax Collector

[9]Jesus told a story to some people who thought they were better than others and who looked down on everyone else:

[10]Two men went into the temple to pray.[e] One was a Pharisee and the other a tax collector.[f] [11]The Pharisee stood over by himself and prayed,[g] "God, I thank you that I am not greedy, dishonest, and unfaithful in marriage like other people. And I am really glad that I am

---

c17.35,36 will be left: Some manuscripts add, "Two men will be in the same field, but only one will be taken. The other will be left." d17.37 Where there is a corpse, there will always be vultures: This saying may mean that when anything important happens, people soon know about it. Or the saying may mean that whenever something bad happens, curious people gather around and stare. But the word translated "vulture" also means "eagle" and may refer to the Roman army, which had an eagle as its symbol. e18.10 into the temple to pray: Jewish people usually prayed there early in the morning and late in the afternoon. f18.10 tax collector: See the note at 3.12. g18.11 stood over by himself and prayed: Some manuscripts have "stood up and prayed to himself."

not like that tax collector over there. [12]I go without eating[h] for two days a week, and I give you one tenth of all I earn."

[13]The tax collector stood off at a distance and did not think he was good enough even to look up toward heaven. He was so sorry for what he had done that he pounded his chest and prayed, "God, have pity on me! I am such a sinner."

[14]Then Jesus said, "When the two men went home, it was the tax collector and not the Pharisee who was pleasing to God. If you put yourself above others, you will be put down. But if you humble yourself, you will be honored."

Jesus Blesses Little Children
(Matthew 19.13-15; Mark 10.13-16)

[15]Some people brought their little children for Jesus to bless. But when his disciples saw them doing this, they told the people to stop bothering him. [16]So Jesus called the children over to him and said, "Let the children come to me! Don't try to stop them. People who are like these children belong to God's kingdom.[i] [17]You will never get into God's kingdom unless you enter it like a child!"

A Rich and Important Man
(Matthew 19.16-30; Mark 10.17-31)

[18]An important man asked Jesus, "Good Teacher, what must I do to have eternal life?"

[19]Jesus said, "Why do you call me good? Only God is good. [20]You know the commandments: 'Be faithful in marriage. Do not murder. Do not steal. Do not tell lies about others. Respect your father and mother.'"

[21]He told Jesus, "I have obeyed all these commandments since I was a young man."

[22]When Jesus heard this, he said, "There is one thing you still need to do. Go and sell everything you own! Give the money to the poor, and you will have riches in heaven. Then come and be my follower." [23]When the man heard this, he was sad, because he was very rich.

h18.12 *without eating:* See the note at 2.37.   i18.16 *People who are like these children belong to God's kingdom:* Or "God's kingdom belongs to people who are like these children."

²⁴Jesus saw how sad the man was. So he said, "It's terribly hard for rich people to get into God's kingdom! ²⁵In fact, it's easier for a camel to go through the eye of a needle than for a rich person to get into God's kingdom."

²⁶When the crowd heard this, they asked, "How can anyone ever be saved?"

²⁷Jesus replied, "There are some things that people cannot do, but God can do anything."

²⁸Peter said, "Remember, we left everything to be your followers!"

²⁹Jesus answered, "You can be sure that anyone who gives up home or wife or brothers or family or children because of God's kingdom ³⁰will be given much more in this life. And in the future world they will have eternal life."

Jesus Again Tells About His Death
(Matthew 20.17-19; Mark 10.32-34)

³¹Jesus took the twelve apostles aside and said:

We are now on our way to Jerusalem. Everything that the prophets wrote about the Son of Man will happen there. ³²He will be handed over to foreigners,ʲ who will make fun of him, mistreat him, and spit on him. ³³They will beat him and kill him, but three days later he will rise to life.

³⁴The apostles did not understand what Jesus was talking about. They could not understand, because the meaning of what he said was hidden from them.

Jesus Heals a Blind Beggar
(Matthew 20.29-34; Mark 10.46-52)

³⁵When Jesus was coming close to Jericho, a blind man sat begging beside the road. ³⁶The man heard the crowd walking by and asked what was happening. ³⁷Some people told him that Jesus from Nazareth was passing by. ³⁸So the blind man shouted, "Jesus, Son of David,ᵏ have pity on me!" ³⁹The people who were going along with Jesus told the man to be quiet. But he shouted even louder, "Son of David, have pity on me!"

⁴⁰Jesus stopped and told some people to bring the blind man over to him.

j18.32 foreigners: The Romans, who ruled Judea at this time.   k18.38 Son of David: The Jewish people expected the Messiah to be from the family of King David, and for this reason the Messiah was often called the "Son of David."

When the blind man was getting near, Jesus asked, [41]"What do you want me to do for you?"

"Lord, I want to see!" he answered.

[42]Jesus replied, "Look and you will see! Your eyes are healed because of your faith." [43]At once the man could see, and he went with Jesus and started thanking God. When the crowds saw what happened, they praised God.

Zacchaeus

19 Jesus was going through Jericho, [2]where a man named Zacchaeus lived. He was in charge of collecting taxes[l] and was very rich. [3-4]Jesus was heading his way, and Zacchaeus wanted to see what he was like. But Zacchaeus was a short man and could not see over the crowd. So he ran ahead and climbed up into a sycamore tree.

[5]When Jesus got there, he looked up and said, "Zacchaeus, hurry down! I want to stay with you today." [6]Zacchaeus hurried down and gladly welcomed Jesus.

[7]Everyone who saw this started grumbling, "This man Zacchaeus is a sinner! And Jesus is going home to eat with him."

[8]Later that day Zacchaeus stood up and said to the Lord, "I will give half of my property to the poor. And I will now pay back four times as much[m] to everyone I have ever cheated."

[9]Jesus said to Zacchaeus, "Today you and your family have been saved,[n] because you are a true son of Abraham.[o] [10]The Son of Man came to look for and to save people who are lost."

A Story About Ten Servants
(Matthew 25.14-30)

[11]The crowd was still listening to Jesus as he was getting close to Jerusalem. Many of them thought that God's kingdom would soon appear, [12]and Jesus told them this story:

l19.2 in charge of collecting taxes: See the note at 3.12.   m19.8 pay back four times as much: Both Jewish and Roman law said that a person must pay back four times the amount that was taken. n19.9 saved: Zacchaeus was Jewish, but it is only now that he is rescued from sin and placed under God's care.   o19.9 son of Abraham: As used in this verse, the words mean that Zacchaeus is truly one of God's special people.

A prince once went to a foreign country to be crowned king and then to return. ¹³But before leaving, he called in ten servants and gave each of them some money. He told them, "Use this to earn more money until I get back."

¹⁴But the people of his country hated him, and they sent messengers to the foreign country to say, "We don't want this man to be our king."

¹⁵After the prince had been made king, he returned and called in his servants. He asked them how much they had earned with the money they had been given.

¹⁶The first servant came and said, "Sir, with the money you gave me I have earned ten times as much."

¹⁷"That's fine, my good servant!" the king said. "Since you have shown that you can be trusted with a small amount, you will be given ten cities to rule."

¹⁸The second one came and said, "Sir, with the money you gave me, I have earned five times as much."

¹⁹The king said, "You will be given five cities."

²⁰Another servant came and said, "Sir, here is your money. I kept it safe in a handkerchief. ²¹You are a hard man, and I was afraid of you. You take what isn't yours, and you harvest crops you didn't plant."

²²"You worthless servant!" the king told him. "You have condemned yourself by what you have just said. You knew I am a hard man, taking what isn't mine and harvesting what I've not planted. ²³Why didn't you put my money in the bank? On my return, I could have had the money together with interest."

²⁴Then he said to some other servants standing there, "Take the money away from him and give it to the servant who earned ten times as much."

²⁵But they said, "Sir, he already has ten times as much!"

²⁶The king replied, "Those who have something will be given more. But everything will be taken away from those who don't have anything. ²⁷Now bring me the enemies who didn't want me to be their king. Kill them while I watch!"

Jesus Enters Jerusalem
(Matthew 21.1-11; Mark 11.1-11; John 12.12-19)

[28]When Jesus had finished saying all this, he went on toward Jerusalem. [29]As he was getting near Bethphage and Bethany on the Mount of Olives, he sent two of his disciples on ahead. [30]He told them, "Go into the next village, where you will find a young donkey that has never been ridden. Untie the donkey and bring it here. [31]If anyone asks why you are doing this, just say, 'The Lord[p] needs it.'"

[32]They went off and found everything just as Jesus had said. [33]While they were untying the donkey, its owners asked, "Why are you doing that?"

[34]They answered, "The Lord[p] needs it."

[35]Then they led the donkey to Jesus. They put some of their clothes on its back and helped Jesus get on. [36]And as he rode along, the people spread clothes on the road[q] in front of him. [37]When Jesus started down the Mount of Olives, his large crowd of disciples were happy and praised God because of all the miracles they had seen. [38]They shouted,

"Blessed is the king who comes
    in the name of the Lord!
Peace in heaven
    and glory to God."

[39]Some Pharisees in the crowd said to Jesus, "Teacher, make your disciples stop shouting!"

[40]But Jesus answered, "If they keep quiet, these stones will start shouting."

[41]When Jesus came closer and could see Jerusalem, he cried [42]and said:

It is too bad that today your people don't know what will bring them peace! Now it is hidden from them. [43]Jerusalem, the time will come when your enemies will build walls around you to attack you. Armies will surround you and close in on you from every side. [44]They will level you to the ground and kill your people. Not one stone in your buildings will be left on top of another. This will happen because you did not see that God had come to save you.[r]

p19.31,34 *The Lord:* Or "The master of the donkey." q19.36 *spread clothes on the road:* This was one way that the Jewish people welcomed a famous person. r19.44 *that God had come to save you:* The Jewish people looked for the time when God would come and rescue them from their enemies. But when Jesus came, many of them refused to obey him.

Jesus in the Temple
(Matthew 21.12-17; Mark 11.15-19; John 2.13-22)

⁴⁵When Jesus entered the temple, he started chasing out the people who were selling things. ⁴⁶He told them, "The Scriptures say, 'My house should be a place of worship.' But you have made it a place where robbers hide!"

⁴⁷Each day, Jesus kept on teaching in the temple. So the chief priests, the teachers of the Law of Moses, and some other important people tried to have him killed. ⁴⁸But they could not find a way to do it, because everyone else was eager to listen to him.

A Question About Jesus' Authority
(Matthew 21.23-27; Mark 11.27-33)

20 One day, Jesus was teaching in the temple and telling the good news. So the chief priests, the teachers, and the nation's leaders ²asked him, "What right do you have to do these things? Who gave you this authority?"

³Jesus replied, "I want to ask you a question. ⁴Who gave John the right to baptize? Was it God in heaven or merely some human being?"

⁵They talked this over and said to each other, "We can't say God gave John this right. Jesus will ask us why we didn't believe John. ⁶And we can't say it was merely some human who gave John the right to baptize. The crowd will stone us to death, because they think John was a prophet."

⁷So they told Jesus, "We don't know who gave John the right to baptize."

⁸Jesus replied, "Then I won't tell you who gave me the right to do what I do."

Renters of a Vineyard
(Matthew 21.33-46; Mark 12.1-12)

⁹Jesus told the people this story:

A man once planted a vineyard and rented it out. Then he left the country for a long time. ¹⁰When it was time to harvest the crop, he sent a servant to ask the renters for his share of the grapes. But they beat up the servant and sent him away without anything. ¹¹So the owner sent another servant. The renters also beat him up. They insulted him terribly and sent him away without a thing. ¹²The owner sent a third servant. He was also beaten terribly and thrown out of the vineyard.

¹³The owner then said to himself, "What am I going to do? I know what. I'll send my son, the one I love so much. They will surely respect him!"

¹⁴When the renters saw the owner's son, they said to one another, "Someday he will own the vineyard. Let's kill him! Then we can have it all for ourselves." ¹⁵So they threw him out of the vineyard and killed him.

Jesus asked, "What do you think the owner of the vineyard will do? ¹⁶I'll tell you what. He will come and kill those renters and let someone else have his vineyard."

When the people heard this, they said, "This must never happen!"

¹⁷But Jesus looked straight at them and said, "Then what do the Scriptures mean when they say, 'The stone the builders tossed aside is now the most important stone of all'? ¹⁸Anyone who stumbles over this stone will get hurt, and anyone it falls on will be smashed to pieces."

¹⁹The chief priests and the teachers of the Law of Moses knew that Jesus was talking about them when he was telling this story. They wanted to arrest him right then, but they were afraid of the people.

Paying Taxes
(Matthew 22.15-22; Mark 12.13-17)

²⁰Jesus' enemies kept watching him closely, because they wanted to hand him over to the Roman governor. So they sent some men who pretended to be good. But they were really spies trying to catch Jesus saying something wrong. ²¹The spies said to him, "Teacher, we know you teach the truth about what God wants people to do. And you treat everyone with the same respect, no matter who they are. ²²Tell us, should we pay taxes to the Emperor or not?"

²³Jesus knew they were trying to trick him. So he told them, ²⁴"Show me a coin." Then he asked, "Whose picture and name are on it?"

"The Emperor's," they answered.

²⁵Then he told them, "Give the Emperor what belongs to him and give God what belongs to God." ²⁶Jesus' enemies could not catch him saying anything wrong there in front of the people. They were amazed at his answer and kept quiet.

Life in the Future World
(Matthew 22.23-33; Mark 12.18-27)

[27]The Sadducees did not believe that people would rise to life after death. So some of them came to Jesus [28]and said:

Teacher, Moses wrote that if a married man dies and has no children, his brother should marry the widow. Their first son would then be thought of as the son of the dead brother.

[29]There were once seven brothers. The first one married, but died without having any children. [30]The second one married his brother's widow, and he also died without having any children. [31]The same thing happened to the third one. Finally, all seven brothers married this woman and died without having any children. [32]At last the woman died. [33]When God raises people from death, whose wife will this woman be? All seven brothers had married her.

[34]Jesus answered:

The people in this world get married. [35]But in the future world no one who is worthy to rise from death will either marry [36]or die. They will be like the angels and will be God's children, because they have been raised to life.

[37]In the story about the burning bush, Moses clearly shows that people will live again. He said, "The Lord is the God worshiped by Abraham, Isaac, and Jacob."[s] [38]So the Lord isn't the God of the dead, but of the living. This means that everyone is alive as far as God is concerned.

[39]Some of the teachers of the Law of Moses said, "Teacher, you have given a good answer!" [40]From then on, no one dared to ask Jesus any questions.

About David's Son
(Matthew 22.41-46; Mark 12.35-37)

[41]Jesus asked, "Why do people say that the Messiah will be the son of King David?[t] [42]In the book of Psalms, David himself says,

'The Lord said to my Lord,
Sit at my right side[u]

---

s20.37 *The Lord is the God worshiped by Abraham, Isaac, and Jacob:* Jesus argues that if God is worshiped by these three, they must be alive, because he is the God of the living.   t20.41 *the son of King David:* See the note at 18.38.   u20.42 *right side:* The place of power and honor.

⁴³until I make your enemies
   into a footstool for you.'
⁴⁴David spoke of the Messiah as his Lord, so how can the Messiah be his son?"

Jesus and the Teachers of the Law of Moses
(Matthew 23.1-36; Mark 12.38-40; Luke 11.37-54)

⁴⁵While everyone was listening to Jesus, he said to his disciples:
   ⁴⁶Guard against the teachers of the Law of Moses! They love to walk around in long robes, and they like to be greeted in the market. They want the front seats in the synagogues and the best seats at banquets. ⁴⁷But they cheat widows out of their homes and then pray long prayers just to show off. These teachers will be punished most of all.

A Widow's Offering
(Mark 12.41-44)

21 Jesus looked up and saw some rich people tossing their gifts into the offering box. ²He also saw a poor widow putting in a few cents. ³And he said, "I tell you that this poor woman has put in more than all the others. ⁴Everyone else gave what they didn't need. But she is very poor and gave everything she had."

The Temple Will Be Destroyed
(Matthew 24.1,2; Mark 13.1,2)

⁵Some people were talking about the beautiful stones used to build the temple and about the gifts that had been placed in it. Jesus said, ⁶"Do you see these stones? The time is coming when not one of them will be left in place. They will all be knocked down."

Warning About Trouble
(Matthew 24.3-14; Mark 13.3-13)

⁷Some people asked, "Teacher, when will all this happen? How can we know when these things are about to take place?"
   ⁸Jesus replied:
      Don't be fooled by those who will come and claim to be me. They will say, "I am Christ!" and "Now is the time!" But don't fol-

low them. ⁹When you hear about wars and riots, don't be afraid. These things will have to happen first, but this isn't the end.

¹⁰Nations will go to war against one another, and kingdoms will attack each other. ¹¹There will be great earthquakes, and in many places people will starve to death and suffer terrible diseases. All sorts of frightening things will be seen in the sky.

¹²Before all this happens, you will be arrested and punished. You will be tried in your synagogues and put in jail. Because of me you will be placed on trial before kings and governors. ¹³But this will be your chance to tell about your faith.

¹⁴Don't worry about what you will say to defend yourselves. ¹⁵I will give you the wisdom to know what to say. None of your enemies will be able to oppose you or to say that you are wrong. ¹⁶You will be betrayed by your own parents, brothers, family, and friends. Some of you will even be killed. ¹⁷Because of me, you will be hated by everyone. ¹⁸But don't worry!ᵛ ¹⁹You will be saved by being faithful to me.

Jerusalem Will Be Destroyed
(Matthew 24.15-21; Mark 13.14-19)

²⁰When you see Jerusalem surrounded by soldiers, you will know that it will soon be destroyed. ²¹If you are living in Judea at this time, run to the mountains. If you are in the city, leave it. And if you are out in the country, don't go back into the city. ²²This time of punishment is what is written about in the Scriptures. ²³It will be an awful time for women who are expecting babies or nursing young children! Everywhere in the land people will suffer horribly and be punished. ²⁴Some of them will be killed by swords. Others will be carried off to foreign countries. Jerusalem will be overrun by foreign nations until their time comes to an end.

When the Son of Man Appears
(Matthew 24.29-31; Mark 13.24-27)

²⁵Strange things will happen to the sun, moon, and stars. The nations on earth will be afraid of the roaring sea and tides, and they won't

---

v21.18 But don't worry: The Greek text has "Not a hair of your head will be lost," which means, "There's no need to worry."

know what to do. [26]People will be so frightened that they will faint because of what is happening to the world. Every power in the sky will be shaken.[w] [27]Then the Son of Man will be seen, coming in a cloud with power and great glory. [28]When all of this starts happening, stand up straight and be brave. You will soon be set free.

A Lesson from a Fig Tree
(Matthew 24.32-35; Mark 13.28-31)

[29]Then Jesus told them a story:

When you see a fig tree or any other tree [30]putting out leaves, you know that summer will soon come. [31]So, when you see these things happening, you know that God's kingdom will soon be here. [32]You can be sure that some of the people of this generation will still be alive when all of this takes place. [33]The sky and the earth won't last forever, but my words will.

A Warning

[34]Don't spend all of your time thinking about eating or drinking or worrying about life. If you do, the final day will suddenly catch you [35]like a trap. This day will surprise everyone on earth. [36]Watch out and keep praying that you can escape all that is going to happen and that the Son of Man will be pleased with you.

[37]Jesus taught in the temple each day, and he spent each night on the Mount of Olives. [38]Everyone got up early and came to the temple to hear him teach.

A Plot to Kill Jesus
(Matthew 26.1-5,14,16; Mark 14.1,2,10,11; John 11.45-53)

22 The Festival of Thin Bread, also called Passover, was near. [2]The chief priests and the teachers of the Law of Moses were looking for a way to get rid of Jesus, because they were afraid of what the people might do. [3]Then Satan entered the heart of Judas Iscariot,[x] who was one of the twelve apostles.

w21.26 Every power in the sky will be shaken: In ancient times people thought that the stars were spiritual powers.   x22.3 Iscariot: See the note at 6.16.

4Judas went to talk with the chief priests and the officers of the temple police about how he could help them arrest Jesus. 5They were very pleased and offered to pay Judas some money. 6He agreed and started looking for a good chance to betray Jesus when the crowds were not around.

Jesus Eats with His Disciples
(Matthew 26.17-25; Mark 14.12-21; John 13.21-30)

7The day had come for the Festival of Thin Bread, and it was time to kill the Passover lambs. 8So Jesus said to Peter and John, "Go and prepare the Passover meal for us to eat."

9But they asked, "Where do you want us to prepare it?"

10Jesus told them, "As you go into the city, you will meet a man carrying a jar of water.y Follow him into the house 11and say to the owner, 'Our teacher wants to know where he can eat the Passover meal with his disciples.' 12The owner will take you upstairs and show you a large room ready for you to use. Prepare the meal there."

13Peter and John left. They found everything just as Jesus had told them, and they prepared the Passover meal.

The Lord's Supper
(Matthew 26.26-30; Mark 14.22-26; 1 Corinthians 11.23-25)

14When the time came for Jesus and the apostles to eat, 15he said to them, "I have very much wanted to eat this Passover meal with you before I suffer. 16I tell you I will not eat another Passover meal until it is finally eaten in God's kingdom."

17Jesus took a cup of wine in his hands and gave thanks to God. Then he told the apostles, "Take this wine and share it with each other. 18I tell you that I will not drink any more wine until God's kingdom comes."

19Jesus took some bread in his hands and gave thanks for it. He broke the bread and handed it to his apostles. Then he said, "This is my body, which is given for you. Eat this as a way of remembering me!"

20After the meal he took another cup of wine in his hands. Then he said, "This is my blood. It is poured out for you, and with it God makes his new

y22.10 a man carrying a jar of water: A male slave carrying water would probably mean that the family was rich.

agreement. [21]The one who will betray me is here at the table with me! [22]The Son of Man will die in the way that has been decided for him, but it will be terrible for the one who betrays him!"

[23]Then the apostles started arguing about who would ever do such a thing.

An Argument About Greatness

[24]The apostles got into an argument about which one of them was the greatest. [25]So Jesus told them:

Foreign kings order their people around, and powerful rulers call themselves everyone's friends.[z] [26]But don't be like them. The most important one of you should be like the least important, and your leader should be like a servant. [27]Who do people think is the greatest, a person who is served or one who serves? Isn't it the one who is served? But I have been with you as a servant.

[28]You have stayed with me in all my troubles. [29]So I will give you the right to rule as kings, just as my Father has given me the right to rule as a king. [30]You will eat and drink with me in my kingdom, and you will each sit on a throne to judge the twelve tribes of Israel.

Jesus' Disciples Will Be Tested
(Matthew 26.31-35; Mark 14.27-31; John 13.36-38)

[31]Jesus said, "Simon, listen to me! Satan has demanded the right to test each one of you, as a farmer does when he separates wheat from the husks.[a] [32]But Simon, I have prayed that your faith will be strong. And when you have come back to me, help the others."

[33]Peter said, "Lord, I am ready to go with you to jail and even to die with you."

[34]Jesus replied, "Peter, I tell you that before a rooster crows tomorrow morning, you will say three times that you don't know me."

Moneybags, Traveling Bags, and Swords

[35]Jesus asked his disciples, "When I sent you out without a moneybag or a traveling bag or sandals, did you need anything?"

z22.25 everyone's friends: This translates a Greek word that rulers sometimes used as a title for themselves or for special friends. a22.31 separates wheat from the husks: See the note at 3.17.

"No!" they answered.

³⁶Jesus told them, "But now, if you have a moneybag, take it with you. Also take a traveling bag, and if you don't have a sword,[b] sell some of your clothes and buy one. ³⁷Do this because the Scriptures say, 'He was considered a criminal.' This was written about me, and it will soon come true."

³⁸The disciples said, "Lord, here are two swords!"

"Enough of that!" Jesus replied.

Jesus Prays
(Matthew 26.36-46; Mark 14.32-42)

³⁹Jesus went out to the Mount of Olives, as he often did, and his disciples went with him. ⁴⁰When they got there, he told them, "Pray that you won't be tested."

⁴¹Jesus walked on a little way before he knelt down and prayed, ⁴²"Father, if you will, please don't make me suffer by drinking from this cup.[c] But do what you want, and not what I want."

⁴³Then an angel from heaven came to help him. ⁴⁴Jesus was in great pain and prayed so sincerely that his sweat fell to the ground like drops of blood.[d]

⁴⁵Jesus got up from praying and went over to his disciples. They were asleep and worn out from being so sad. ⁴⁶He said to them, "Why are you asleep? Wake up and pray that you won't be tested."

Jesus Is Arrested
(Matthew 26.47-56; Mark 14.43-50; John 18.3-11)

⁴⁷While Jesus was still speaking, a crowd came up. It was led by Judas, one of the twelve apostles. He went over to Jesus and greeted him with a kiss.[e]

⁴⁸Jesus asked Judas, "Are you betraying the Son of Man with a kiss?"

⁴⁹When Jesus' disciples saw what was about to happen, they asked, "Lord, should we attack them with a sword?" ⁵⁰One of the disciples even struck at the high priest's servant with his sword and cut off the servant's right ear.

---

b22.36 moneybag . . . traveling bag . . . sword: These were things that someone would take on a dangerous journey. Jesus was telling his disciples to be ready for anything that might happen. They seem to have understood what he meant (see 22.49-51).   c22.42 drinking from this cup: In the Scriptures "to drink from a cup" sometimes means to suffer.   d22.43,44 Then an angel . . . like drops of blood: Verses 43,44 are not in some manuscripts.   e22.47 greeted him with a kiss: It was the custom for people to greet each other with a kiss on the cheek.

[51]"Enough of that!" Jesus said. Then he touched the servant's ear and healed it.

[52]Jesus spoke to the chief priests, the temple police, and the leaders who had come to arrest him. He said, "Why do you come out with swords and clubs and treat me like a criminal? [53]I was with you every day in the temple, and you didn't arrest me. But this is your time, and darkness[f] is in control."

Peter Says He Doesn't Know Jesus
(Matthew 26.57, 58, 67-75; Mark 14.53, 54, 66-72; John 18.12-18, 25-27)

[54]Jesus was arrested and led away to the house of the high priest, while Peter followed at a distance. [55]Some people built a fire in the middle of the courtyard and were sitting around it. Peter sat there with them, [56]and a servant girl saw him. Then after she had looked at him carefully, she said, "This man was with Jesus!"

[57]Peter said, "Woman, I don't even know that man!"

[58]A little later someone else saw Peter and said, "You are one of them!"

"No, I'm not!" Peter replied.

[59]About an hour later another man insisted, "This man must have been with Jesus. They both come from Galilee."

[60]Peter replied, "I don't know what you are talking about!" Right then, while Peter was still speaking, a rooster crowed.

[61]The Lord turned and looked at Peter. And Peter remembered that the Lord had said, "Before a rooster crows tomorrow morning, you will say three times that you don't know me." [62]Then Peter went out and cried bitterly.

[63]The men who were guarding Jesus made fun of him and beat him. [64]They put a blindfold on him and said, "Tell us who struck you!" [65]They kept on insulting Jesus in many other ways.

Jesus Is Questioned by the Council
(Matthew 26.59-66; Mark 14.55-64; John 18.19-24)

[66]At daybreak the nation's leaders, the chief priests, and the teachers of the Law of Moses got together and brought Jesus before their council. [67]They said, "Tell us! Are you the Messiah?"

Jesus replied, "If I said so, you wouldn't believe me. [68]And if I asked you

---

f22.53 darkness: Darkness stands for the power of the devil.

a question, you wouldn't answer. ⁶⁹But from now on, the Son of Man will be seated at the right side of God All-Powerful."

⁷⁰Then they asked, "Are you the Son of God?"ᵍ

Jesus answered, "You say I am!"ʰ

⁷¹They replied, "Why do we need more witnesses? He said it himself!"

Pilate Questions Jesus
(Matthew 27.1, 2, 11-14; Mark 15.1-5; John 18.28-38)

23 Everyone in the council got up and led Jesus off to Pilate. ²They started accusing him and said, "We caught this man trying to get our people to riot and to stop paying taxes to the Emperor. He also claims that he is the Messiah, our king."

³Pilate asked Jesus, "Are you the king of the Jews?"

"Those are your words," Jesus answered.

⁴Pilate told the chief priests and the crowd, "I don't find him guilty of anything."

⁵But they all kept on saying, "He has been teaching and causing trouble all over Judea. He started in Galilee and has now come all the way here."

Jesus Is Brought Before Herod

⁶When Pilate heard this, he asked, "Is this man from Galilee?" ⁷After Pilate learned that Jesus came from the region ruled by Herod,ⁱ he sent him to Herod, who was in Jerusalem at that time.

⁸For a long time Herod had wanted to see Jesus and was very happy because he finally had this chance. He had heard many things about Jesus and hoped to see him work a miracle.

⁹Herod asked him a lot of questions, but Jesus did not answer. ¹⁰Then the chief priests and the teachers of the Law of Moses stood up and accused him of all kinds of bad things.

¹¹Herod and his soldiers made fun of Jesus and insulted him. They put a fine robe on him and sent him back to Pilate. ¹²That same day Herod and Pilate became friends, even though they had been enemies before this.

g22.70 *Son of God:* This was one of the titles used for the kings of Israel.   h22.70 *You say I am:* Or "That's what you say."   i23.7 *Herod:* Herod Antipas, the son of Herod the Great.

The Death Sentence
(Matthew 27.15-26; Mark 15.6-15; John 18.39—19.16)

[13]Pilate called together the chief priests, the leaders, and the people. [14]He told them, "You brought Jesus to me and said he was a troublemaker. But I have questioned him here in front of you, and I have not found him guilty of anything that you say he has done. [15]Herod didn't find him guilty either and sent him back. This man doesn't deserve to be put to death! [16-17]I will just have him beaten with a whip and set free."[j]

[18]But the whole crowd shouted, "Kill Jesus! Give us Barabbas!" [19]Now Barabbas was in jail because he had started a riot in the city and had murdered someone.

[20]Pilate wanted to set Jesus free, so he spoke again to the crowds. [21]But they kept shouting, "Nail him to a cross! Nail him to a cross!"

[22]Pilate spoke to them a third time, "But what crime has he done? I have not found him guilty of anything for which he should be put to death. I will have him beaten with a whip and set free."

[23]The people kept on shouting as loud as they could for Jesus to be put to death. [24]Finally, Pilate gave in. [25]He freed the man who was in jail for rioting and murder, because he was the one the crowd wanted to be set free. Then Pilate handed Jesus over for them to do what they wanted with him.

Jesus Is Nailed to a Cross
(Matthew 27.31-44; Mark 15.21-32; John 19.17-27)

[26]As Jesus was being led away, some soldiers grabbed hold of a man named Simon who was from Cyrene. He was coming in from the fields, but they put the cross on him and made him carry it behind Jesus.

[27]A large crowd was following Jesus, and in the crowd a lot of women were crying and weeping for him. [28]Jesus turned to the women and said:

Women of Jerusalem, don't cry for me! Cry for yourselves and for your children. [29]Someday people will say, "Women who never had children are really fortunate!" [30]At that time everyone will say to the mountains, "Fall on us!" They will say to the hills, "Hide us!" [31]If this

---

j23.16,17 *set free:* Some manuscripts add, "Pilate said this, because at every Passover he was supposed to set one prisoner free for the Jewish people."

can happen when the wood is green, what do you think will happen when it is dry?[k]

[32]Two criminals were led out to be put to death with Jesus. [33]When the soldiers came to the place called "The Skull,"[l] they nailed Jesus to a cross. They also nailed the two criminals to crosses, one on each side of Jesus.

[34-35]Jesus said, "Father, forgive these people! They don't know what they're doing."[m]

While the crowd stood there watching Jesus, the soldiers gambled for his clothes. The leaders insulted him by saying, "He saved others. Now he should save himself, if he really is God's chosen Messiah!"

[36]The soldiers made fun of Jesus and brought him some wine. [37]They said, "If you are the king of the Jews, save yourself!"

[38]Above him was a sign that said, "This is the King of the Jews."

[39]One of the criminals hanging there also insulted Jesus by saying, "Aren't you the Messiah? Save yourself and save us!"

[40]But the other criminal told the first one off, "Don't you fear God? Aren't you getting the same punishment as this man? [41]We got what was coming to us, but he didn't do anything wrong." [42]Then he said to Jesus, "Remember me when you come into power!"

[43]Jesus replied, "I promise that today you will be with me in paradise."[n]

The Death of Jesus
(Matthew 27.45-56; Mark 15.33-41; John 19.28-30)

[44]Around noon the sky turned dark and stayed that way until the middle of the afternoon. [45]The sun stopped shining, and the curtain in the temple[o] split down the middle. [46]Jesus shouted, "Father, I put myself in your hands!" Then he died.

k23.31 If this can happen when the wood is green, what do you think will happen when it is dry: This saying probably means, "If this can happen to an innocent person, what do you think will happen to one who is guilty?"   l23.33 "The Skull": The place was probably given this name because it was near a large rock in the shape of a human skull.   m23.34,35 Jesus said, "Father, forgive these people! They don't know what they're doing": These words are not in some manuscripts. n23.43 paradise: In the Greek translation of the Old Testament, this word is used for the Garden of Eden. In New Testament times it was sometimes used for the place where God's people are happy and at rest, as they wait for the final judgment.   o23.45 curtain in the temple: There were two curtains in the temple. One was at the entrance, and the other separated the holy place from the most holy place that the Jewish people thought of as God's home on earth. The second curtain is probably the one which is meant.

47When the Roman officer saw what had happened, he praised God and
said, "Jesus must really have been a good man!"
48A crowd had gathered to see the terrible sight. Then after they had seen
it, they felt brokenhearted and went home. 49All of Jesus' close friends and the
women who had come with him from Galilee stood at a distance and watched.

Jesus Is Buried

(Matthew 27.57-61; Mark 15.42-47; John 19.38-42)

50-51There was a man named Joseph, who was from Arimathea in Judea. Joseph
was a good and honest man, and he was eager for God's kingdom to come.
He was also a member of the council, but he did not agree with what they
had decided.
52Joseph went to Pilate and asked for Jesus' body. 53He took the body
down from the cross and wrapped it in fine cloth. Then he put it in a tomb
that had been cut out of solid rock and had never been used. 54It was Friday,
and the Sabbath was about to begin.[p]
55The women who had come with Jesus from Galilee followed Joseph and
watched how Jesus' body was placed in the tomb. 56Then they went to prepare some sweet-smelling spices for his burial. But on the Sabbath they rested,
as the Law of Moses commands.

Jesus Is Alive

(Matthew 28.1-10; Mark 16.1-8; John 20.1-10)

24 Very early on Sunday morning the women went to the tomb, carrying the spices they had prepared. 2When they found the stone rolled
away from the entrance, 3they went in. But they did not find the body of the
Lord[q] Jesus, 4and they did not know what to think.
Suddenly two men in shining white clothes stood beside them. 5The
women were afraid and bowed to the ground. But the men said, "Why are
you looking in the place of the dead for someone who is alive? 6Jesus isn't here!
He has been raised from death. Remember that while he was still in Galilee,
he told you, 7'The Son of Man will be handed over to sinners who will nail
him to a cross. But three days later he will rise to life.' " 8Then they remembered what Jesus had said.

p23.54 the Sabbath was about to begin: The Sabbath begins at sunset on Friday. q24.3 the Lord: These words are not in some manuscripts.

⁹⁻¹⁰Mary Magdalene, Joanna, Mary the mother of James, and some other women were the ones who had gone to the tomb. When they returned, they told the eleven apostles and the others what had happened. ¹¹The apostles thought it was all nonsense, and they would not believe.

¹²But Peter ran to the tomb. And when he stooped down and looked in, he saw only the burial clothes. Then he returned, wondering what had happened.ʳ

Jesus Appears to Two Disciples
(Mark 16.12,13)

¹³That same day two of Jesus' disciples were going to the village of Emmaus, which was about seven miles from Jerusalem. ¹⁴As they were talking and thinking about what had happened, ¹⁵Jesus came near and started walking along beside them. ¹⁶But they did not know who he was.

¹⁷Jesus asked them, "What were you talking about as you walked along?"

The two of them stood there looking sad and gloomy. ¹⁸Then the one named Cleopas asked Jesus, "Are you the only person from Jerusalem who didn't know what was happening there these last few days?"

¹⁹"What do you mean?" Jesus asked.

They answered:

Those things that happened to Jesus from Nazareth. By what he did and said he showed that he was a powerful prophet, who pleased God and all the people. ²⁰Then the chief priests and our leaders had him arrested and sentenced to die on a cross. ²¹We had hoped that he would be the one to set Israel free! But it has already been three days since all this happened.

²²Some women in our group surprised us. They had gone to the tomb early in the morning, ²³but did not find the body of Jesus. They came back, saying they had seen a vision of angels who told them that he is alive. ²⁴Some men from our group went to the tomb and found it just as the women had said. But they didn't see Jesus either.

²⁵Then Jesus asked the two disciples, "Why can't you understand? How can you be so slow to believe all that the prophets said? ²⁶Didn't you know that the Messiah would have to suffer before he was given his glory?" ²⁷Jesus

---

r24.12 what had happened: Verse 12 is not in some manuscripts.

then explained everything written about himself in the Scriptures, beginning with the Law of Moses and the Books of the Prophets.[s]

²⁸When the two of them came near the village where they were going, Jesus seemed to be going farther. ²⁹They begged him, "Stay with us! It's already late, and the sun is going down." So Jesus went into the house to stay with them.

³⁰After Jesus sat down to eat, he took some bread. He blessed it and broke it. Then he gave it to them. ³¹At once they knew who he was, but he disappeared. ³²They said to each other, "When he talked with us along the road and explained the Scriptures to us, didn't it warm our hearts?" ³³So they got up and returned to Jerusalem.

The two disciples found the eleven apostles and the others gathered together. ³⁴And they learned from the group that the Lord was really alive and had appeared to Peter. ³⁵Then the disciples from Emmaus told what happened on the road and how they knew he was the Lord when he broke the bread.

What Jesus' Followers Must Do
(Matthew 28.16-20; Mark 16.14-18; John 20.19-23; Acts 1.6-8)

³⁶While Jesus' disciples were talking about what had happened, Jesus appeared and greeted them. ³⁷They were frightened and terrified because they thought they were seeing a ghost.

³⁸But Jesus said, "Why are you so frightened? Why do you doubt? ³⁹Look at my hands and my feet and see who I am! Touch me and find out for yourselves. Ghosts don't have flesh and bones as you see I have."

⁴⁰After Jesus said this, he showed them his hands and his feet. ⁴¹The disciples were so glad and amazed that they could not believe it. Jesus then asked them, "Do you have something to eat?" ⁴²They gave him a piece of broiled fish. ⁴³He took it and ate it as they watched.

⁴⁴Jesus said to them, "While I was still with you, I told you that everything written about me in the Law of Moses, the Books of the Prophets, and in the Psalms[t] had to happen."

⁴⁵Then he helped them understand the Scriptures. ⁴⁶He told them:

The Scriptures say that the Messiah must suffer, then three days

---

s24.27 the Law of Moses and the Books of the Prophets: See the note at 16.16.   t24.44 Psalms: The Jewish Scriptures were made up of three parts: (1) the Law of Moses, (2) the Books of the Prophets, (3) and the Writings, which included the Psalms. Sometimes the Scriptures were just called the Law or the Law (of Moses) and the Books of the Prophets.

later he will rise from death. ⁴⁷They also say that all people of every nation must be told in my name to turn to God, in order to be forgiven. So beginning in Jerusalem, ⁴⁸you must tell everything that has happened. ⁴⁹I will send you the one my Father has promised,^u but you must stay in the city until you are given power from heaven.

Jesus Returns to Heaven
(Mark 16.19, 20; Acts 1.9-11)

⁵⁰Jesus led his disciples out to Bethany, where he raised his hands and blessed them. ⁵¹As he was doing this, he left and was taken up to heaven.^v ⁵²After his disciples had worshiped him,^w they returned to Jerusalem and were very happy. ⁵³They spent their time in the temple, praising God.

u24.49 the one my Father has promised: Jesus means the Holy Spirit.   v24.51 and was taken up to heaven: These words are not in some manuscripts.   w24.52 After his disciples had worshiped him: These words are not in some manuscripts.

IV.

John

John, the fourth Gospel, focuses on Jesus' role as the Messiah and as the eternal Word of God who was present with God at the beginning of creation. This makes John quite different from the previous three Gospels—Matthew, Mark, and Luke—which focus on providing historical accounts to show that Jesus was the fulfillment of God's promise to Israel. For this reason, many scholars believe John was written to answer those who doubted Jesus was the Messiah. John describes seven miracles ("signs") of Jesus and uses these miracles to show the profound teachings of Jesus and to point to him as the Son of God. By using metaphors to describe Jesus—such as water, light, a gate, and bread—John tries to lead readers into the kingdom of God that Jesus has prepared for them.

Outline

The Word of Life

1 In the beginning was the one
who is called the Word.
The Word was with God
and was truly God.
[2]From the very beginning
the Word was with God.

[3]And with this Word,
God created all things.
Nothing was made
without the Word.
Everything that was created
[4]received its life from him,
and his life gave light
to everyone.
[5]The light keeps shining
in the dark,
and darkness has never
put it out.[a]
[6]God sent a man named John,

---

a1.5 put it out: Or "understood it."

[7]who came to tell
   about the light
and to lead all people
   to have faith.
[8]John wasn't this light.
He came only to tell
   about the light.

[9]The true light that shines
on everyone
   was coming into the world.
[10]The Word was in the world,
   but no one knew him,
though God had made the world
   with his Word.
[11]He came into his own world,
but his own nation
   did not welcome him.
[12]Yet some people accepted him
   and put their faith in him.
So he gave them the right
   to be the children of God.
[13]They were not God's children
   by nature or because
of any human desires.
God himself was the one
   who made them his children.

[14]The Word became
a human being
   and lived here with us.
We saw his true glory,
the glory of the only Son
   of the Father.
From him the complete gifts
of undeserved grace and truth
   have come down to us.

¹⁵John spoke about him and shouted, "This is the one I told you would come! He is greater than I am, because he was alive before I was born."

¹⁶Because of all that the Son is, we have been given one blessing after another.ᵇ ¹⁷The Law was given by Moses, but Jesus Christ brought us undeserved kindness and truth. ¹⁸No one has ever seen God. The only Son, who is truly God and is closest to the Father, has shown us what God is like.

John the Baptist Tells About Jesus
(Matthew 3.1-12; Mark 1.1-8; Luke 3.15-17)

¹⁹⁻²⁰The religious authorities in Jerusalem sent priests and temple helpers to ask John who he was. He told them plainly, "I am not the Messiah." ²¹Then when they asked him if he were Elijah, he said, "No, I am not!" And when they asked if he were the Prophet,ᶜ he also said "No!"

²²Finally, they said, "Who are you then? We have to give an answer to the ones who sent us. Tell us who you are!"

²³John answered in the words of the prophet Isaiah, "I am only someone shouting in the desert, 'Get the road ready for the Lord!'"

²⁴Some Pharisees had also been sent to John. ²⁵They asked him, "Why are you baptizing people, if you are not the Messiah or Elijah or the Prophet?"

²⁶John told them, "I use water to baptize people. But here with you is someone you don't know. ²⁷Even though I came first, I am not good enough to untie his sandals." ²⁸John said this as he was baptizing east of the Jordan River in Bethany.ᵈ

The Lamb of God

²⁹The next day, John saw Jesus coming toward him and said:

Here is the Lamb of God who takes away the sin of the world! ³⁰He is the one I told you about when I said, "Someone else will come, who is greater than I am, because he was alive before I was born." ³¹I didn't know who he was. But I came to baptize you with water, so that everyone in Israel would see him.

³²I was there and saw the Spirit come down on him like a dove

---

b1.16 one blessing after another: Or "one blessing in place of another." c1.21 the Prophet: Many of the Jewish people expected God to send them a prophet who would be like Moses, but with even greater power (see Deuteronomy 18.15,18). d1.28 Bethany: An unknown village east of the Jordan with the same name as the village near Jerusalem.

from heaven. And the Spirit stayed on him. [33]Before this I didn't know who he was. But the one who sent me to baptize with water had told me, "You will see the Spirit come down and stay on someone. Then you will know that he is the one who will baptize with the Holy Spirit." [34]I saw this happen, and I tell you that he is the Son of God.

The First Disciples of Jesus

[35]The next day, John was there again, and two of his followers were with him. [36]When he saw Jesus walking by, he said, "Here is the Lamb of God!" [37]John's two followers heard him, and they went with Jesus.

[38]When Jesus turned and saw them, he asked, "What do you want?"

They answered, "Rabbi, where do you live?" The Hebrew word "Rabbi" means "Teacher."

[39]Jesus replied, "Come and see!" It was already about four o'clock in the afternoon when they went with him and saw where he lived. So they stayed on for the rest of the day.

[40]One of the two men who had heard John and had gone with Jesus was Andrew, the brother of Simon Peter. [41]The first thing Andrew did was to find his brother and tell him, "We have found the Messiah!" The Hebrew word "Messiah" means the same as the Greek word "Christ."

[42]Andrew brought his brother to Jesus. And when Jesus saw him, he said, "Simon son of John, you will be called Cephas." This name can be translated as "Peter."[e]

Jesus Chooses Philip and Nathanael

[43-44]The next day Jesus decided to go to Galilee. There he met Philip, who was from Bethsaida, the hometown of Andrew and Peter. Jesus said to Philip, "Follow me."

[45]Philip then found Nathanael and said, "We have found the one that Moses and the Prophets[f] wrote about. He is Jesus, the son of Joseph from Nazareth."

[46]Nathanael asked, "Can anything good come from Nazareth?"

e1.42 Peter: The Aramaic name "Cephas" and the Greek name "Peter" each mean "rock."   f1.45 Moses and the Prophets: The Jewish Scriptures, that is, the Old Testament.

Philip answered, "Come and see."

⁴⁷When Jesus saw Nathanael coming toward him, he said, "Here is a true descendant of our ancestor Israel. And he isn't deceitful."ᵍ

⁴⁸"How do you know me?" Nathanael asked.

Jesus answered, "Before Philip called you, I saw you under the fig tree."

⁴⁹Nathanael said, "Rabbi, you are the Son of God and the King of Israel!"

⁵⁰Jesus answered, "Did you believe me just because I said that I saw you under the fig tree? You will see something even greater. ⁵¹I tell you for certain you will see heaven open and God's angels going up and coming down on the Son of Man."ʰ

Jesus at a Wedding in Cana

2 Three days later Mary, the mother of Jesus, was at a wedding feast in the village of Cana in Galilee. ²Jesus and his disciples had also been invited and were there.

³When the wine was all gone, Mary said to Jesus, "They don't have any more wine."

⁴Jesus replied, "Mother, my time hasn't yet come!ⁱ You must not tell me what to do."

⁵Mary then said to the servants, "Do whatever Jesus tells you to do."

⁶At the feast there were six stone water jars that were used by the people for washing themselves in the way that their religion said they must. Each jar held about 20 or 30 gallons. ⁷Jesus told the servants to fill them to the top with water. Then after the jars had been filled, ⁸he said, "Now take some water and give it to the man in charge of the feast."

The servants did as Jesus told them, ⁹and the man in charge drank some of the water that had now turned into wine. He did not know where the wine had come from, but the servants did. He called the bridegroom over ¹⁰and said, "The best wine is always served first. Then after the guests have had plenty, the other wine is served. But you have kept the best until last!"

---

g1.47 Israel . . . isn't deceitful: Israel (meaning "a man who wrestled with God" or "a prince of God") was the name that the Lord gave to Jacob (meaning "cheater" or "deceiver"), the famous ancestor of the Jewish people.   h1.51 going up and coming down on the Son of Man: When Jacob (see the note at verse 47) was running from his brother Esau, he had a dream in which he saw angels going up and down on a ladder from earth to heaven (see Genesis 28.10-22).   i2.4 my time hasn't yet come: The time when the true glory of Jesus would be seen, and he would be recognized as God's Son (see 12.23).

[11]This was Jesus' first miracle,[j] and he did it in the village of Cana in Galilee. There Jesus showed his glory, and his disciples put their faith in him. [12]After this, he went with his mother, his brothers, and his disciples to the town of Capernaum, where they stayed for a few days.

Jesus in the Temple
(Matthew 21.12,13; Mark 11.15-17; Luke 19.45,46)

[13]Not long before the Jewish festival of Passover, Jesus went to Jerusalem. [14]There he found people selling cattle, sheep, and doves in the temple. He also saw moneychangers sitting at their tables. [15]So he took some rope and made a whip. Then he chased everyone out of the temple, together with their sheep and cattle. He turned over the tables of the moneychangers and scattered their coins.

[16]Jesus said to the people who had been selling doves, "Get those doves out of here! Don't make my Father's house a marketplace."

[17]The disciples then remembered that the Scriptures say, "My love for your house burns in me like a fire."

[18]The Jewish leaders asked Jesus, "What miracle[j] will you work to show us why you have done this?"

[19] "Destroy this temple," Jesus answered, "and in three days I will build it again!"

[20]The leaders replied, "It took 46 years to build this temple. What makes you think you can rebuild it in three days?"

[21]But Jesus was talking about his body as a temple. [22]And when he was raised from death, his disciples remembered what he had told them. Then they believed the Scriptures and the words of Jesus.

Jesus Knows What People Are Like

[23]In Jerusalem during Passover many people put their faith in Jesus, because they saw him work miracles.[j] [24]But Jesus knew what was in their hearts, and he would not let them have power over him. [25]No one had to tell him what people were like. He already knew.

---

j2.11,18,23 miracle: The Greek text has "sign." In the Gospel of John the word "sign" is used for the miracle itself and as a way of pointing to Jesus as the Son of God.

Jesus and Nicodemus

3 There was a man named Nicodemus who was a Pharisee and a Jewish leader. [2]One night he went to Jesus and said, "Rabbi, we know that God has sent you to teach us. You could not work these miracles, unless God were with you."

[3]Jesus replied, "I tell you for certain that you must be born from above[k] before you can see God's kingdom!"

[4]Nicodemus asked, "How can a grown man ever be born a second time?" [5]Jesus answered:

I tell you for certain that before you can get into God's kingdom, you must be born not only by water, but by the Spirit. [6]Humans give life to their children. Yet only God's Spirit can change you into a child of God. [7]Don't be surprised when I say that you must be born from above. [8]Only God's Spirit gives new life. The Spirit is like the wind that blows wherever it wants to. You can hear the wind, but you don't know where it comes from or where it is going.

[9]"How can this be?" Nicodemus asked.

[10]Jesus replied:

How can you be a teacher of Israel and not know these things? [11]I tell you for certain we know what we are talking about because we have seen it ourselves. But none of you will accept what we say. [12]If you don't believe when I talk to you about things on earth, how can you possibly believe if I talk to you about things in heaven?

[13] No one has gone up to heaven except the Son of Man, who came down from there. [14]And the Son of Man must be lifted up, just as the metal snake was lifted up by Moses in the desert.[l] [15]Then everyone who has faith in the Son of Man will have eternal life.

[16]God loved the people of this world so much that he gave his only Son, so that everyone who has faith in him will have eternal life and never really die. [17]God did not send his Son into the world to condemn its people. He sent him to save them! [18]No one who has faith in God's Son will be condemned. But everyone who doesn't have

---

k3.3 *from above:* Or "in a new way." The same Greek word is used in verses 7, 31. l3.14 *just as the metal snake was lifted up by Moses in the desert:* When the Lord punished the people of Israel by sending snakes to bite them, he told Moses to hold a metal snake up on a pole. Everyone who looked at the snake was cured of the snake bites (see Numbers 21.4-9).

faith in him has already been condemned for not having faith in God's only Son.

[19]The light has come into the world, and people who do evil things are judged guilty because they love the dark more than the light. [20]People who do evil hate the light and won't come to the light, because it clearly shows what they have done. [21]But everyone who lives by the truth will come to the light, because they want others to know that God is really the one doing what they do.

Jesus and John the Baptist

[22]Later, Jesus and his disciples went to Judea, where he stayed with them for a while and was baptizing people.

[23-24]John had not yet been put in jail. He was at Aenon near Salim, where there was a lot of water, and people were coming there for John to baptize them.

[25]John's followers got into an argument with a Jewish man[m] about a ceremony of washing.[n] [26]They went to John and said, "Rabbi, you spoke about a man when you were with him east of the Jordan. He is now baptizing people, and everyone is going to him."

[27]John replied:

No one can do anything unless God in heaven allows it. [28]You surely remember how I told you that I am not the Messiah. I am only the one sent ahead of him.

[29]At a wedding the groom is the one who gets married. The best man is glad just to be there and to hear the groom's voice. That's why I am so glad. [30]Jesus must become more important, while I become less important.

The One Who Comes from Heaven

[31]God's Son comes from heaven and is above all others. Everyone who comes from the earth belongs to the earth and speaks about earthly things. The one who comes from heaven is above all others.

---

m3.25 a Jewish man: Some manuscripts have "some Jewish men." n3.25 about a ceremony of washing: The Jewish people had many rules about washing themselves and their dishes, in order to make themselves fit to worship God.

³²He speaks about what he has seen and heard, and yet no one believes him. ³³But everyone who does believe him has shown that God is truthful. ³⁴The Son was sent to speak God's message, and he has been given the full power of God's Spirit.

³⁵The Father loves the Son and has given him everything. ³⁶Everyone who has faith in the Son has eternal life. But no one who rejects him will ever share in that life, and God will be angry with them forever.

4 Jesus knew that the Pharisees had heard that he was winning and baptizing more followers than John was. ²But Jesus' disciples were really the ones doing the baptizing, and not Jesus himself.

Jesus and the Samaritan Woman

³Jesus left Judea and started for Galilee again. ⁴This time he had to go through Samaria, ⁵and on his way he came to the town of Sychar. It was near the field that Jacob had long ago given to his son Joseph. ⁶⁻⁸The well that Jacob had dug was still there, and Jesus sat down beside it because he was tired from traveling. It was noon, and after Jesus' disciples had gone into town to buy some food, a Samaritan woman came to draw water from the well.

Jesus asked her, "Would you please give me a drink of water?"

⁹"You are a Jew," she replied, "and I am a Samaritan woman. How can you ask me for a drink of water when Jews and Samaritans won't have anything to do with each other?"°

¹⁰Jesus answered, "You don't know what God wants to give you, and you don't know who is asking you for a drink. If you did, you would ask me for the water that gives life."

¹¹"Sir," the woman said, "you don't even have a bucket, and the well is deep. Where are you going to get this life-giving water? ¹²Our ancestor Jacob dug this well for us, and his family and animals got water from it. Are you greater than Jacob?"

¹³Jesus answered, "Everyone who drinks this water will get thirsty again. ¹⁴But no one who drinks the water I give will ever be thirsty again. The water I give will become in that person a flowing fountain that gives eternal life."

---

o4.9 won't have anything to do with each other: Or "won't use the same cups." The Samaritans lived in the land between Judea and Galilee. They worshiped God differently from the Jews and did not get along with them.

[15]The woman replied, "Sir, please give me a drink of that water! Then I won't get thirsty and have to come to this well again."

[16]Jesus told her, "Go and bring your husband."

[17-18]The woman answered, "I don't have a husband."

"That's right," Jesus replied, "you're telling the truth. You don't have a husband. You have already been married five times, and the man you are now living with isn't your husband."

[19]The woman said, "Sir, I can see that you are a prophet. [20]My ancestors worshiped on this mountain,[p] but you Jews say Jerusalem is the only place to worship."

[21]Jesus said to her:

Believe me, the time is coming when you won't worship the Father either on this mountain or in Jerusalem. [22]You Samaritans don't really know the one you worship. But we Jews do know the God we worship, and by using us, God will save the world. [23]But a time is coming, and it is already here! Even now the true worshipers are being led by the Spirit to worship the Father according to the truth. These are the ones the Father is seeking to worship him. [24]God is Spirit, and those who worship God must be led by the Spirit to worship him according to the truth.

[25]The woman said, "I know that the Messiah will come. He is the one we call Christ. When he comes, he will explain everything to us."

[26]"I am that one," Jesus told her, "and I am speaking to you now."

[27]The disciples returned about this time and were surprised to find Jesus talking with a woman. But none of them asked him what he wanted or why he was talking with her.

[28]The woman left her water jar and ran back into town, where she said to the people, [29]"Come and see a man who told me everything I have ever done! Could he be the Messiah?" [30]Everyone in town went out to see Jesus.

[31]While this was happening, Jesus' disciples were saying to him, "Teacher, please eat something."

[32]But Jesus told them, "I have food you don't know anything about."

[33]His disciples started asking each other, "Has someone brought him something to eat?"

[34]Jesus said:

p4.20 this mountain: Mount Gerizim, near the city of Shechem.

My food is to do what God wants! He is the one who sent me, and I must finish the work that he gave me to do. ³⁵You may say there are still four months until harvest time. But I tell you to look, and you will see that the fields are ripe and ready to harvest.

³⁶Even now the harvest workers are receiving their reward by gathering a harvest that brings eternal life. Then everyone who planted the seed and everyone who harvests the crop will celebrate together. ³⁷So the saying proves true, "Some plant the seed, and others harvest the crop." ³⁸I am sending you to harvest crops in fields where others have done all the hard work.

³⁹A lot of Samaritans in that town put their faith in Jesus because the woman had said, "This man told me everything I have ever done." ⁴⁰They came and asked him to stay in their town, and he stayed on for two days.

⁴¹Many more Samaritans put their faith in Jesus because of what they heard him say. ⁴²They told the woman, "We no longer have faith in Jesus just because of what you told us. We have heard him ourselves, and we are certain that he is the Savior of the world!"

Jesus Heals an Official's Son
(Matthew 8.5-13; Luke 7.1-10)

⁴³⁻⁴⁴Jesus had said, "Prophets are honored everywhere, except in their own country." Then two days later he left ⁴⁵and went to Galilee. The people there welcomed him, because they had gone to the festival in Jerusalem and had seen everything he had done.

⁴⁶While Jesus was in Galilee, he returned to the village of Cana, where he had turned the water into wine. There was an official in Capernaum whose son was sick. ⁴⁷And when the man heard that Jesus had come from Judea, he went and begged him to keep his son from dying.

⁴⁸Jesus told the official, "You won't have faith unless you see miracles and wonders!"

⁴⁹The man replied, "Lord, please come before my son dies!"

⁵⁰Jesus then said, "Your son will live. Go on home to him." The man believed Jesus and started back home.

⁵¹Some of the official's servants met him along the road and told him, "Your son is better!" ⁵²He asked them when the boy got better, and they answered, "The fever left him yesterday at one o'clock."

⁵³The boy's father realized that at one o'clock the day before, Jesus had told him, "Your son will live!" So the man and everyone in his family put their faith in Jesus.

⁵⁴This was the second miracle⁹ that Jesus worked after he left Judea and went to Galilee.

Jesus Heals a Sick Man

5 Later, Jesus went to Jerusalem for another Jewish festival.ʳ ²In the city near the sheep gate was a pool with five porches, and its name in Hebrew was Bethzatha.ˢ

³⁻⁴Many sick, blind, lame, and paralyzed people were lying close to the pool.ᵗ

⁵Beside the pool was a man who had been sick for 38 years. ⁶When Jesus saw the man and realized that he had been crippled for a long time, he asked him, "Do you want to be healed?"

⁷The man answered, "Sir, I don't have anyone to put me in the pool when the water is stirred up. I try to get in, but someone else always gets there first."

⁸Jesus told him, "Pick up your mat and walk!" ⁹Right then the man was healed. He picked up his mat and started walking around. The day on which this happened was a Sabbath.

¹⁰When the Jewish leaders saw the man carrying his mat, they said to him, "This is the Sabbath! No one is allowed to carry a mat on the Sabbath."

¹¹But he replied, "The man who healed me told me to pick up my mat and walk."

¹²They asked him, "Who is this man that told you to pick up your mat and walk?" ¹³But he did not know who Jesus was, and Jesus had left because of the crowd.

¹⁴Later, Jesus met the man in the temple and told him, "You are now well. But don't sin anymore or something worse might happen to you." ¹⁵The man left and told the leaders that Jesus was the one who had healed him. ¹⁶They started making a lot of trouble for Jesus because he did things like this on the Sabbath.

q4.54 miracle: See the note at 2.11.   r5.1 another Jewish festival: Either the Festival of Shelters or Passover.   s5.2 Bethzatha: Some manuscripts have "Bethesda" and others have "Bethsaida."   t5.3,4 pool: Some manuscripts add, "They were waiting for the water to be stirred, because an angel from the Lord would sometimes come down and stir it. The first person to get into the pool after that would be healed."

¹⁷But Jesus said, "My Father has never stopped working, and this is why I keep on working." ¹⁸Now the leaders wanted to kill Jesus for two reasons. First, he had broken the law of the Sabbath. But even worse, he had said God was his Father, which made him equal with God.

The Son's Authority

¹⁹Jesus told the people:

I tell you for certain the Son cannot do anything on his own. He can do only what he sees the Father doing, and he does exactly what he sees the Father do. ²⁰The Father loves the Son and has shown him everything he does. The Father will show him even greater things, and you will be amazed. ²¹Just as the Father raises the dead and gives life, so the Son gives life to anyone he wants to.

²²The Father doesn't judge anyone, but he has made his Son the judge of everyone. ²³The Father wants all people to honor the Son as much as they honor him. When anyone refuses to honor the Son, this is the same as refusing to honor the Father who sent him. ²⁴I tell you for certain that everyone who hears my message and has faith in the one who sent me has eternal life and will never be condemned. They have already gone from death to life.

²⁵I tell you for certain the time will come, and it is already here, when all of the dead will hear the voice of the Son of God. And those who listen to it will live! ²⁶The Father has the power to give life, and he has given that same power to the Son. ²⁷And he has given his Son the right to judge everyone, because he is the Son of Man.

²⁸Don't be surprised! The time will come when all of the dead will hear the voice of the Son of Man, ²⁹and they will come out of their graves. Everyone who has done good things will rise to life, but everyone who has done evil things will rise and be condemned.

³⁰I cannot do anything on my own. The Father sent me, and he is the one who told me how to judge. I judge with fairness, because I obey him, and I don't just try to please myself.

Witnesses to Jesus

³¹If I speak for myself, there is no way to prove I am telling the truth. ³²But there is someone else who speaks for me, and I know what he

says is true. [33]You sent messengers to John, and he told them the truth. [34]I don't depend on what people say about me, but I tell you these things so that you may be saved. [35]John was a lamp that gave a lot of light, and you were glad to enjoy his light for a while.

[36]But something more important than John speaks for me. I mean the things that the Father has given me to do! All of these speak for me and prove that the Father sent me.

[37]The Father who sent me also speaks for me, but you have never heard his voice or seen him face to face. [38]You have not believed his message, because you refused to have faith in the one he sent.

[39]You search the Scriptures, because you think you will find eternal life in them. The Scriptures tell about me, [40]but you refuse to come to me for eternal life.

[41]I don't care about human praise, [42]but I do know that none of you love God. [43]I have come with my Father's authority, and you have not welcomed me. But you will welcome people who come on their own. [44]How could you possibly believe? You like to have your friends praise you, and you don't care about praise that the only God can give!

[45]Don't think that I will be the one to accuse you to the Father. You have put your hope in Moses, yet he is the very one who will accuse you. [46]Moses wrote about me, and if you had believed Moses, you would have believed me. [47]But if you don't believe what Moses wrote, how can you believe what I say?

Feeding Five Thousand
(Matthew 14.13-21; Mark 6.30-44; Luke 9.10-17)

6 Jesus crossed Lake Galilee, which was also known as Lake Tiberias. [2]A large crowd had seen him work miracles to heal the sick, and those people went with him. [3-4]It was almost time for the Jewish festival of Passover, and Jesus went up on a mountain with his disciples and sat down.[u]

[5]When Jesus saw the large crowd coming toward him, he asked Philip, "Where will we get enough food to feed all these people?" [6]He said this to test Philip, since he already knew what he was going to do.

u6.3,4 sat down: Possibly to teach. Teachers in the ancient world, including Jewish teachers, usually sat down to teach.

⁷Philip answered, "Don't you know that it would take almost a year's wagesᵛ just to buy only a little bread for each of these people?"

⁸Andrew, the brother of Simon Peter, was one of the disciples. He spoke up and said, ⁹"There is a boy here who has five small loavesʷ of barley bread and two fish. But what good is that with all these people?"

¹⁰The ground was covered with grass, and Jesus told his disciples to tell everyone to sit down. About 5,000 men were in the crowd. ¹¹Jesus took the bread in his hands and gave thanks to God. Then he passed the bread to the people, and he did the same with the fish, until everyone had plenty to eat.

¹²The people ate all they wanted, and Jesus told his disciples to gather up the leftovers, so that nothing would be wasted. ¹³The disciples gathered them up and filled twelve large baskets with what was left over from the five barley loaves.

¹⁴After the people had seen Jesus work this miracle,ˣ they began saying, "This must be the Prophetʸ who is to come into the world!" ¹⁵Jesus realized that they would try to force him to be their king. So he went up on a mountain, where he could be alone.

Jesus Walks on the Water
(Matthew 14.22-27; Mark 6.45-52)

¹⁶That evening, Jesus' disciples went down to the lake. ¹⁷They got into a boat and started across for Capernaum. Later that evening Jesus had still not come to them, ¹⁸and a strong wind was making the water rough.

¹⁹When the disciples had rowed for three or four miles, they saw Jesus walking on the water. He kept coming closer to the boat, and they were terrified. ²⁰But he said, "I am Jesus!ᶻ Don't be afraid!" ²¹The disciples wanted to take him into the boat, but suddenly the boat reached the shore where they were headed.

The Bread that Gives Life

²²The people who had stayed on the east side of the lake knew that only one boat had been there. They also knew that Jesus had not left in it with his dis-

v6.7 almost a year's wages: The Greek text has "200 silver coins." Each coin was worth the average day's wages for a worker.   w6.9 small loaves: These would have been flat and round or in the shape of a bun.   x6.14 miracle: See the note at 2.11.   y6.14 the Prophet: See the note at 1.21.   z6.20 I am Jesus: The Greek text has "I am" (see the note at 8.24).

ciples. But the next day [23]some boats from Tiberias sailed near the place where the crowd had eaten the bread for which the Lord had given thanks. [24]They saw that Jesus and his disciples had left. Then they got into the boats and went to Capernaum to look for Jesus. [25]They found him on the west side of the lake and asked, "Rabbi, when did you get here?"

[26]Jesus answered, "I tell you for certain that you are not looking for me because you saw the miracles,[a] but because you ate all the food you wanted. [27]Don't work for food that spoils. Work for food that gives eternal life. The Son of Man will give you this food, because God the Father has given him the right to do so."

[28]"What exactly does God want us to do?" the people asked.

[29]Jesus answered, "God wants you to have faith in the one he sent."

[30]They replied, "What miracle will you work, so that we can have faith in you? What will you do? [31]For example, when our ancestors were in the desert, they were given manna[b] to eat. It happened just as the Scriptures say, 'God gave them bread from heaven to eat.' "

[32]Jesus then told them, "I tell you for certain that Moses wasn't the one who gave you bread from heaven. My Father is the one who gives you the true bread from heaven. [33]And the bread that God gives is the one who came down from heaven to give life to the world."

[34]The people said, "Sir, give us this bread and don't ever stop!"

[35]Jesus replied:

I am the bread that gives life! No one who comes to me will ever be hungry. No one who has faith in me will ever be thirsty. [36]I have told you already that you have seen me and still do not have faith in me. [37]Everything and everyone that the Father has given me will come to me, and I won't turn any of them away.

[38]I didn't come from heaven to do what I want! I came to do what the Father wants me to do. He sent me, [39]and he wants to make certain that none of the ones he has given me will be lost. Instead, he wants me to raise them to life on the last day.[c] [40]My Father wants everyone who sees the Son to have faith in him and to have eternal life. Then I will raise them to life on the last day.

a6.26 miracles: The Greek text has "signs" here and "sign" in verse 30 (see the note at 2.11).
b6.31 manna: When the people of Israel were wandering through the desert, the Lord gave them a special kind of food to eat. It tasted like a wafer and was called "manna," which in Hebrew means, "What is this?"   c6.39 the last day: When God will judge all people.

⁴¹The people started grumbling because Jesus had said he was the bread that had come down from heaven. ⁴²They were asking each other, "Isn't he Jesus, the son of Joseph? Don't we know his father and mother? How can he say that he has come down from heaven?"

⁴³Jesus told them:

Stop grumbling! ⁴⁴No one can come to me, unless the Father who sent me makes them want to come. But if they do come, I will raise them to life on the last day. ⁴⁵One of the prophets wrote, "God will teach all of them." And so everyone who listens to the Father and learns from him will come to me.

⁴⁶The only one who has seen the Father is the one who has come from him. No one else has ever seen the Father. ⁴⁷I tell you for certain that everyone who has faith in me has eternal life.

⁴⁸I am the bread that gives life! ⁴⁹Your ancestors ate manna[d] in the desert, and later they died. ⁵⁰But the bread from heaven has come down, so that no one who eats it will ever die. ⁵¹I am that bread from heaven! Everyone who eats it will live forever. My flesh is the life-giving bread I give to the people of this world.

⁵²They started arguing with each other and asked, "How can he give us his flesh to eat?"

⁵³Jesus answered:

I tell you for certain that you won't live unless you eat the flesh and drink the blood of the Son of Man. ⁵⁴But if you do eat my flesh and drink my blood, you will have eternal life, and I will raise you to life on the last day. ⁵⁵My flesh is the true food, and my blood is the true drink. ⁵⁶If you eat my flesh and drink my blood, you are one with me, and I am one with you.

⁵⁷The living Father sent me, and I have life because of him. Now everyone who eats my flesh will live because of me. ⁵⁸The bread that comes down from heaven isn't like what your ancestors ate. They died, but whoever eats this bread will live forever.

⁵⁹Jesus was teaching in a synagogue in Capernaum when he said these things.

d6.49 manna: See the note at 6.31.

The Words of Eternal Life

⁶⁰Many of Jesus' disciples heard him and said, "This is too hard for anyone to understand."

⁶¹Jesus knew that his disciples were grumbling. So he asked, "Does this bother you? ⁶²What if you should see the Son of Man go up to heaven where he came from? ⁶³The Spirit is the one who gives life! Human strength can do nothing. The words that I have spoken to you are from that life-giving Spirit. ⁶⁴But some of you refuse to have faith in me." Jesus said this, because from the beginning he knew who would have faith in him. He also knew which one would betray him.

⁶⁵Then Jesus said, "You cannot come to me, unless the Father makes you want to come. That is why I have told these things to all of you."

⁶⁶Because of what Jesus said, many of his disciples turned their backs on him and stopped following him. ⁶⁷Jesus then asked his twelve disciples if they also were going to leave him. ⁶⁸Simon Peter answered, "Lord, there is no one else that we can go to! Your words give eternal life. ⁶⁹We have faith in you, and we are sure that you are God's Holy One."

⁷⁰Jesus told his disciples, "I chose all twelve of you, but one of you is a demon!" ⁷¹Jesus was talking about Judas, the son of Simon Iscariot.ᵉ He would later betray Jesus, even though he was one of the twelve disciples.

Jesus' Brothers Don't Have Faith in Him

7 Jesus decided to leave Judea and to start going through Galilee because the leaders of the people wanted to kill him. ² It was almost time for the Festival of Shelters, ³and Jesus' brothers said to him, "Why don't you go to Judea? Then your disciples can see what you are doing. ⁴No one does anything in secret, if they want others to know about them. So let the world know what you are doing!" ⁵Even Jesus' own brothers had not yet become his followers.

⁶Jesus answered, "My time hasn't yet come,ᶠ but your time is always here. ⁷The people of this world cannot hate you. They hate me, because I tell them that they do evil things. ⁸Go on to the festival. My time hasn't yet come, and I am not going." ⁹Jesus said this and stayed on in Galilee.

e6.71 Iscariot: This may mean "a man from Kerioth" (a place in Judea). But more probably it means "a man who was a liar" or "a man who was a betrayer."   f7.6 My time hasn't yet come: See the note at 2.4.

Jesus at the Festival of Shelters

[10]After Jesus' brothers had gone to the festival, he went secretly, without telling anyone.

[11]During the festival the leaders of the people looked for Jesus and asked, "Where is he?" [12]The crowds even got into an argument about him. Some were saying, "Jesus is a good man," while others were saying, "He is lying to everyone." [13]But the people were afraid of their leaders, and none of them talked in public about him.

[14]When the festival was about half over, Jesus went into the temple and started teaching. [15]The leaders were surprised and said, "How does this man know so much? He has never been taught!"

[16]Jesus replied:

I am not teaching something I thought up. What I teach comes from the one who sent me. [17]If you really want to obey God, you will know if what I teach comes from God or from me. [18]If I wanted to bring honor to myself, I would speak for myself. But I want to honor the one who sent me. This is why I tell the truth and not a lie. [19]Didn't Moses give you the Law? Yet none of you obey it! So why do you want to kill me?

[20]The crowd replied, "You're crazy! What makes you think someone wants to kill you?"

[21]Jesus answered:

I worked one miracle,[g] and it amazed you. [22]Moses commanded you to circumcise your sons. But it wasn't really Moses who gave you this command. It was your ancestors, and even on the Sabbath you circumcise your sons [23]in order to obey the Law of Moses. Why are you angry with me for making someone completely well on the Sabbath? [24]Don't judge by appearances. Judge by what is right.

[25]Some of the people from Jerusalem were saying, "Isn't this the man they want to kill? [26]Yet here he is, speaking for everyone to hear. And no one is arguing with him. Do you suppose the authorities know he is the Messiah? [27]But how could that be? No one knows where the Messiah will come from, but we know where this man comes from."

[28]As Jesus was teaching in the temple, he shouted, "Do you really think you know me and where I came from? I didn't come on my own! The one

g7.21 *one miracle:* The healing of the sick man (5.1-18; see also the note at 2.11).

who sent me is truthful, and you don't know him. [29]But I know the one who sent me, because I came from him."

[30]Some of the people wanted to arrest Jesus right then. But no one even laid a hand on him, because his time had not yet come.[h] [31]A lot of people in the crowd put their faith in him and said, "When the Messiah comes, he surely won't perform more miracles[i] than this man has done!"

Officers Sent to Arrest Jesus

[32]When the Pharisees heard the crowd arguing about Jesus, they got together with the chief priests and sent some temple police to arrest him. [33]But Jesus told them, "I will be with you a little while longer, and then I will return to the one who sent me. [34]You will look for me, but you won't find me. You cannot go where I am going."

[35]The people asked each other, "Where can he go to keep us from finding him? Is he going to some foreign country where our people live? Is he going there to teach the Greeks?[j] [36]What did he mean by saying that we will look for him, but won't find him? Why can't we go where he is going?"

Streams of Life-Giving Water

[37]On the last and most important day of the festival, Jesus stood up and shouted, "If you are thirsty, come to me and drink! [38]Have faith in me, and you will have life-giving water flowing from deep inside you, just as the Scriptures say." [39]Jesus was talking about the Holy Spirit, who would be given to everyone that had faith in him. The Spirit had not yet been given to anyone, since Jesus had not yet been given his full glory.[k]

The People Take Sides

[40]When the crowd heard Jesus say this, some of them said, "He must be the Prophet!"[l] [41]Others said, "He is the Messiah!" Others even said, "Can the Messiah come from Galilee? [42]The Scriptures say that the Messiah will come

h7.30 his time had not yet come: See the note at 2.4.   i7.31 miracles: See the note at 2.11.   j7.35 Greeks: Perhaps Gentiles or Jews who followed Greek customs.   k7.39 had not yet been given his full glory: In the Gospel of John, Jesus is given his full glory both when he is nailed to the cross and when he is raised from death to sit beside his Father in heaven.   l7.40 the Prophet: See the note at 1.21.

from the family of King David. Doesn't this mean that he will be born in David's hometown of Bethlehem?" [43]The people started taking sides against each other because of Jesus. [44]Some of them wanted to arrest him, but no one laid a hand on him.

The Leaders Refuse to Have Faith in Jesus

[45]When the temple police returned to the chief priests and Pharisees, they were asked, "Why didn't you bring Jesus here?"

[46]They answered, "No one has ever spoken like this man!"

[47]The Pharisees said to them, "Have you also been fooled? [48]Not one of the chief priests or the Pharisees has faith in him. [49]And these people who don't know the Law are under God's curse anyway."

[50]Nicodemus was there at the time. He was a member of the council, and was the same one who had earlier come to see Jesus.[m] He said, [51]"Our Law doesn't let us condemn people before we hear what they have to say. We cannot judge them before we know what they have done."

[52]Then they said, "Nicodemus, you must be from Galilee! Read the Scriptures, and you will find that no prophet is to come from Galilee."

A Woman Caught in Sin

8 [53]Everyone else went home, [1]but Jesus walked out to the Mount of Olives. [2]Then early the next morning he went to the temple. The people came to him, and he sat down[n] and started teaching them.

[3]The Pharisees and the teachers of the Law of Moses brought in a woman who had been caught in bed with a man who wasn't her husband. They made her stand in the middle of the crowd. [4]Then they said, "Teacher, this woman was caught sleeping with a man who isn't her husband. [5]The Law of Moses teaches that a woman like this should be stoned to death! What do you say?"

[6]They asked Jesus this question, because they wanted to test him and bring some charge against him. But Jesus simply bent over and started writing on the ground with his finger.

[7]They kept on asking Jesus about the woman. Finally, he stood up and said, "If any of you have never sinned, then go ahead and throw the first stone at her!" [8]Once again he bent over and began writing on the ground. [9]The peo-

m7.50 who had earlier come to see Jesus: See 3.1-21.   n8.2 sat down: See the note at 6.3,4.

ple left one by one, beginning with the oldest. Finally, Jesus and the woman were there alone.

[10]Jesus stood up and asked her, "Where is everyone? Isn't there anyone left to accuse you?"

[11]"No sir," the woman answered.

Then Jesus told her, "I am not going to accuse you either. You may go now, but don't sin anymore."[o]

Jesus Is the Light for the World

[12]Once again Jesus spoke to the people. This time he said, "I am the light for the world! Follow me, and you won't be walking in the dark. You will have the light that gives life."

[13]The Pharisees objected, "You are the only one speaking for yourself, and what you say isn't true!"

[14]Jesus replied:

Even if I do speak for myself, what I say is true! I know where I came from and where I am going. But you don't know where I am from or where I am going. [15]You judge in the same way that everyone else does, but I don't judge anyone. [16]If I did judge, I would judge fairly, because I would not be doing it alone. The Father who sent me is here with me. [17]Your Law requires two witnesses to prove that something is true. [18]I am one of my witnesses, and the Father who sent me is the other one.

[19]"Where is your Father?" they asked.

"You don't know me or my Father!" Jesus answered. "If you knew me, you would know my Father."

[20]Jesus said this while he was still teaching in the place where the temple treasures were stored. But no one arrested him, because his time had not yet come.[p]

You Cannot Go Where I Am Going

[21]Jesus also told them, "I am going away, and you will look for me. But you cannot go where I am going, and you will die with your sins unforgiven."

---

o8.11 don't sin anymore: Verses 1-11 are not in some manuscripts. In other manuscripts these verses are placed after 7.36 or after 21.25 or after Luke 21.38, with some differences in the text.   p8.20 his time had not yet come: See the note at 2.4.

²²The people asked, "Does he intend to kill himself? Is that what he means by saying we cannot go where he is going?"

²³Jesus answered, "You are from below, but I am from above. You belong to this world, but I don't. ²⁴This is why I said you will die with your sins unforgiven. If you don't have faith in me for who I am,^q you will die, and your sins will not be forgiven."

²⁵"Who are you?" they asked Jesus.

Jesus answered, "I am exactly who I told you at the beginning. ²⁶There is a lot more I could say to condemn you. But the one who sent me is truthful, and I tell the people of this world only what I have heard from him."

²⁷No one understood that Jesus was talking to them about the Father.

²⁸Jesus went on to say, "When you have lifted up the Son of Man,^r you will know who I am. You will also know that I don't do anything on my own. I say only what my Father taught me. ²⁹The one who sent me is with me. I always do what pleases him, and he will never leave me."

³⁰After Jesus said this, many of the people put their faith in him.

The Truth Will Set You Free

³¹Jesus told the people who had faith in him, "If you keep on obeying what I have said, you truly are my disciples. ³²You will know the truth, and the truth will set you free."

³³They answered, "We are Abraham's children! We have never been anyone's slaves. How can you say we will be set free?"

³⁴Jesus replied:

I tell you for certain that anyone who sins is a slave of sin! ³⁵And slaves don't stay in the family forever, though the Son will always remain in the family. ³⁶If the Son gives you freedom, you are free! ³⁷I know that you are from Abraham's family. Yet you want to kill me, because my message isn't really in your hearts. ³⁸I am telling you what my Father has shown me, just as you are doing what your father has taught you.

q8.24 I am: For the Jewish people the most holy name of God is "Yahweh," which may be translated "I am." In the Gospel of John "I am" is sometimes used by Jesus to show that he is that one.
r8.28 lifted up the Son of Man: See the note at 7.39.

Your Father Is the Devil

[39]The people said to Jesus, "Abraham is our father!"

Jesus replied, "If you were Abraham's children, you would do what Abraham did. [40]Instead, you want to kill me for telling you the truth that God gave me. Abraham never did anything like that. [41]But you are doing exactly what your father does."

"Don't accuse us of having someone else as our father!" they said. "We just have one father, and he is God."

[42]Jesus answered:

If God were your Father, you would love me, because I came from God and now I am here. He sent me. I did not come on my own. [43]Why can't you understand what I am talking about? Can't you stand to hear what I am saying? [44]Your father is the devil, and you do exactly what he wants. He has always been a murderer and a liar. There is nothing truthful about him. He speaks on his own, and everything he says is a lie. Not only is he a liar himself, but he is also the father of all lies.

[45]Everything I have told you is true, and you still refuse to have faith in me. [46]Can any of you accuse me of sin? If you cannot, why won't you have faith in me? After all, I am telling you the truth. [47]Anyone who belongs to God will listen to his message. But you refuse to listen, because you don't belong to God.

Jesus and Abraham

[48]The people told Jesus, "We were right to say that you are a Samaritan[s] and that you have a demon in you!"

[49]Jesus answered, "I don't have a demon in me. I honor my Father, and you refuse to honor me. [50]I don't want honor for myself. But there is one who wants me to be honored, and he is also the one who judges. [51]I tell you for certain that if you obey my words, you will never die."

[52]Then the people said, "Now we are sure that you have a demon. Abraham is dead, and so are the prophets. How can you say that no one who obeys your words will ever die? [53]Are you greater than our father Abraham? He died, and so did the prophets. Who do you think you are?"

s8.48 Samaritan: See 4.9 and the note there.

[54]Jesus replied, "If I honored myself, it would mean nothing. My Father is the one who honors me. You claim that he is your God, [55]even though you don't really know him. If I said I didn't know him, I would be a liar, just like all of you. But I know him, and I do what he says. [56]Your father Abraham was really glad to see me."

[57]"You are not even 50 years old!" they said. "How could you have seen Abraham?"

[58]Jesus answered, "I tell you for certain that even before Abraham was, I was, and I am."[t] [59]The people picked up stones to kill Jesus, but he hid and left the temple.

Jesus Heals a Man Born Blind

9 As Jesus walked along, he saw a man who had been blind since birth. [2]Jesus' disciples asked, "Teacher, why was this man born blind? Was it because he or his parents sinned?"

[3]"No, it wasn't!" Jesus answered. "But because of his blindness, you will see God work a miracle for him. [4]As long as it is day, we must do what the one who sent me wants me to do. When night comes, no one can work. [5]While I am in the world, I am the light for the world."

[6]After Jesus said this, he spit on the ground. He made some mud and smeared it on the man's eyes. [7]Then he said, "Go wash off the mud in Siloam Pool." The man went and washed in Siloam, which means "One Who Is Sent." When he had washed off the mud, he could see.

[8]The man's neighbors and the people who had seen him begging wondered if he really could be the same man. [9]Some of them said he was the same beggar, while others said he only looked like him. But he told them, "I am that man."

[10]"Then how can you see?" they asked.

[11]He answered, "Someone named Jesus made some mud and smeared it on my eyes. He told me to go and wash it off in Siloam Pool. When I did, I could see."

[12]"Where is he now?" they asked.

"I don't know," he answered.

---

t8.58 I am: See the note at 8.24.

The Pharisees Try to Find Out What Happened

[13-14]The day when Jesus made the mud and healed the man was a Sabbath. So the people took the man to the Pharisees. [15]They asked him how he was able to see, and he answered, "Jesus made some mud and smeared it on my eyes. Then after I washed it off, I could see."

[16]Some of the Pharisees said, "This man Jesus doesn't come from God. If he did, he would not break the law of the Sabbath."

Others asked, "How could someone who is a sinner work such a miracle?"[u]

Since the Pharisees could not agree among themselves, [17]they asked the man, "What do you say about this one who healed your eyes?"

"He is a prophet!" the man told them.

[18]But the Jewish leaders would not believe that the man had once been blind. They sent for his parents [19]and asked them, "Is this the son that you said was born blind? How can he now see?"

[20]The man's parents answered, "We are certain that he is our son, and we know that he was born blind. [21]But we don't know how he got his sight or who gave it to him. Ask him! He is old enough to speak for himself."

[22-23]The man's parents said this because they were afraid of their leaders. The leaders had already agreed that no one was to have anything to do with anyone who said Jesus was the Messiah.

[24]The leaders called the man back and said, "Swear by God to tell the truth! We know that Jesus is a sinner."

[25]The man replied, "I don't know if he is a sinner or not. All I know is that I used to be blind, but now I can see!"

[26]"What did he do to you?" they asked. "How did he heal your eyes?"

[27]The man answered, "I have already told you once, and you refused to listen. Why do you want me to tell you again? Do you also want to become his disciples?"

[28]The leaders insulted the man and said, "You are his follower! We are followers of Moses. [29]We are sure God spoke to Moses, but we don't even know where Jesus comes from."

[30]"How strange!" the man replied. "He healed my eyes, and yet you don't know where he comes from. [31]We know that God listens only to people who love and obey him. God doesn't listen to sinners. [32]And this is the first time

u9.16 miracle: See the note at 2.11.

in history anyone has ever given sight to someone born blind. [33]Jesus could not do anything unless he came from God."

[34]The leaders told the man, "You have been a sinner since the day you were born! Do you think you can teach us anything?" Then they said, "You can never come back into any of our synagogues!"

[35]When Jesus heard what had happened, he went and found the man. Then Jesus asked, "Do you have faith in the Son of Man?"

[36]He replied, "Sir, if you will tell me who he is, I will put my faith in him."

[37]"You have already seen him," Jesus answered, "and right now he is talking with you."

[38]The man said, "Lord, I put my faith in you!" Then he worshiped Jesus.

[39]Jesus told him, "I came to judge the people of this world. I am here to give sight to the blind and to make blind everyone who can see."

[40]When the Pharisees heard Jesus say this, they asked, "Are we blind?"

[41]Jesus answered, "If you were blind, you would not be guilty. But now that you claim to see, you will keep on being guilty."

A Story About Sheep

10 Jesus said:

I tell you for certain only thieves and robbers climb over the fence instead of going in through the gate to the sheep pen. [2-3]But the gatekeeper opens the gate for the shepherd, and he goes in through it. The sheep know their shepherd's voice. He calls each of them by name and leads them out.

[4]When he has led out all of his sheep, he walks in front of them, and they follow, because they know his voice. [5]The sheep will not follow strangers. They don't recognize a stranger's voice, and they run away.

[6]Jesus told the people this story. But they did not understand what he was talking about.

Jesus Is the Good Shepherd

[7]Jesus said:

I tell you for certain that I am the gate for the sheep. [8]Everyone who came before me was a thief or a robber, and the sheep did not listen to any of them. [9]I am the gate. All who come in through me will be saved. Through me they will come and go and find pasture.

¹⁰A thief comes only to rob, kill, and destroy. I came so everyone would have life, and have it fully. ¹¹I am the good shepherd, and the good shepherd gives up his life for his sheep. ¹²Hired workers are not like the shepherd. They don't own the sheep, and when they see a wolf coming, they run off and leave the sheep. Then the wolf attacks and scatters the flock. ¹³Hired workers run away because they don't care about the sheep.

¹⁴I am the good shepherd. I know my sheep, and they know me. ¹⁵Just as the Father knows me, I know the Father, and I give up my life for my sheep. ¹⁶I have other sheep that are not in this sheep pen. I must also bring them together, when they hear my voice. Then there will be one flock of sheep and one shepherd.

¹⁷The Father loves me, because I give up my life, so I may receive it back again. ¹⁸No one takes my life from me. I give it up willingly! I have the power to give it up and the power to receive it back again, just as my Father commanded me to do.

¹⁹The people took sides because of what Jesus had told them. ²⁰Many of them said, "He has a demon in him! He is crazy! Why listen to him?"

²¹But others said, "How could anyone with a demon in him say these things? No one like this could give sight to a blind person!"

Jesus Is Rejected

²²That winter, Jesus was in Jerusalem for the Temple Festival. ²³One day he was walking in the part of the temple known as Solomon's Porch,ᵛ ²⁴and the people gathered all around him. They said, "How long are you going to keep us guessing? If you are the Messiah, tell us plainly!"

²⁵Jesus answered:

I have told you, and you refused to believe me. The things I do by my Father's authority show who I am. ²⁶But since you are not my sheep, you don't believe me. ²⁷My sheep know my voice, and I know them. They follow me, ²⁸and I give them eternal life, so that they will never be lost. No one can snatch them out of my hand. ²⁹My Father gave them to me, and he is greater than all others.ʷ No one can snatch them from his hands, ³⁰and I am one with the Father.

---

v10.23 Solomon's Porch: A public place with tall columns along the east side of the temple.
w10.29 he is greater than all others: Some manuscripts have "they are greater than all others."

[31]Once again the people picked up stones in order to kill Jesus. [32]But he said, "I have shown you many good things my Father sent me to do. Which one are you going to stone me for?"

[33]They answered, "We are not stoning you because of any good thing you did. We are stoning you because you did a terrible thing. You are just a man, and here you are claiming to be God!"

[34]Jesus replied:

In your Scriptures doesn't God say, "You are gods"? [35]You can't argue with the Scriptures, and God spoke to those people and called them gods. [36]So why do you accuse me of a terrible sin for saying that I am the Son of God? After all, it is the Father who prepared me for this work. He is also the one who sent me into the world. [37]If I don't do as my Father does, you should not believe me. [38]But if I do what my Father does, you should believe because of that, even if you don't have faith in me. Then you will know for certain that the Father is one with me, and I am one with the Father.

[39]Again they wanted to arrest Jesus. But he escaped [40]and crossed the Jordan to the place where John had earlier been baptizing. While Jesus was there, [41]many people came to him. They were saying, "John didn't work any miracles, but everything he said about Jesus is true." [42]A lot of those people also put their faith in Jesus.

The Death of Lazarus

11 [1-2]A man by the name of Lazarus was sick in the village of Bethany. He had two sisters, Mary and Martha. This was the same Mary who later poured perfume on the Lord's head and wiped his feet with her hair. [3]The sisters sent a message to the Lord and told him that his good friend Lazarus was sick.

[4]When Jesus heard this, he said, "His sickness won't end in death. It will bring glory to God and his Son."

[5]Jesus loved Martha and her sister and brother. [6]But he stayed where he was for two more days. [7]Then he said to his disciples, "Now we will go back to Judea."

[8]"Teacher," they said, "the people there want to stone you to death! Why do you want to go back?"

[9]Jesus answered, "Aren't there twelve hours in each day? If you walk during the day, you will have light from the sun, and you won't stumble. [10]But

if you walk during the night, you will stumble, because you don't have any light." [11]Then he told them, "Our friend Lazarus is asleep, and I am going there to wake him up."

[12]They replied, "Lord, if he is asleep, he will get better." [13]Jesus really meant that Lazarus was dead, but they thought he was talking only about sleep.

[14]Then Jesus told them plainly, "Lazarus is dead! [15]I am glad I wasn't there, because now you will have a chance to put your faith in me. Let's go to him."

[16]Thomas, whose nickname was "Twin," said to the other disciples, "Come on. Let's go, so we can die with him."

Jesus Brings Lazarus to Life

[17]When Jesus got to Bethany, he found that Lazarus had already been in the tomb four days. [18]Bethany was only about two miles from Jerusalem, [19]and many people had come from the city to comfort Martha and Mary because their brother had died.

[20]When Martha heard that Jesus had arrived, she went out to meet him, but Mary stayed in the house. [21]Martha said to Jesus, "Lord, if you had been here, my brother would not have died. [22]Yet even now I know that God will do anything you ask."

[23]Jesus told her, "Your brother will live again!"

[24]Martha answered, "I know he will be raised to life on the last day,[x] when all the dead are raised."

[25]Jesus then said, "I am the one who raises the dead to life! Everyone who has faith in me will live, even if they die. [26]And everyone who lives because of faith in me will never really die. Do you believe this?"

[27]"Yes, Lord!" she replied. "I believe you are the Christ, the Son of God. You are the one we hoped would come into the world."

[28]After Martha said this, she went and privately said to her sister Mary, "The Teacher is here, and he wants to see you." [29]As soon as Mary heard this, she got up and went out to Jesus. [30]He was still outside the village where Martha had gone to meet him. [31]Many people had come to comfort Mary, and when they saw her quickly leave the house, they thought she was going out to the tomb to cry. So they followed her.

[32]Mary went to where Jesus was. Then as soon as she saw him, she knelt

x11.24 *the last day:* When God will judge all people.

at his feet and said, "Lord, if you had been here, my brother would not have died."

³³When Jesus saw that Mary and the people with her were crying, he was terribly upset ³⁴and asked, "Where have you put his body?"

They replied, "Lord, come and you will see."

³⁵Jesus started crying, ³⁶and the people said, "See how much he loved Lazarus."

³⁷Some of them said, "He gives sight to the blind. Why couldn't he have kept Lazarus from dying?"

³⁸Jesus was still terribly upset. So he went to the tomb, which was a cave with a stone rolled against the entrance. ³⁹Then he told the people to roll the stone away. But Martha said, "Lord, you know that Lazarus has been dead four days, and there will be a bad smell."

⁴⁰Jesus replied, "Didn't I tell you that if you had faith, you would see the glory of God?"

⁴¹After the stone had been rolled aside, Jesus looked up toward heaven and prayed, "Father, I thank you for answering my prayer. ⁴²I know that you always answer my prayers. But I said this, so the people here would believe you sent me."

⁴³When Jesus had finished praying, he shouted, "Lazarus, come out!" ⁴⁴The man who had been dead came out. His hands and feet were wrapped with strips of burial cloth, and a cloth covered his face.

Jesus then told the people, "Untie him and let him go."

The Plot to Kill Jesus
(Matthew 26.1-5; Mark 14.1, 2; Luke 22.1, 2)

⁴⁵Many of the people who had come to visit Mary saw the things Jesus did, and they put their faith in him. ⁴⁶Others went to the Pharisees and told what Jesus had done. ⁴⁷Then the chief priests and the Pharisees called the council together and said, "What should we do? This man is working a lot of miracles.ʸ ⁴⁸If we don't stop him now, everyone will put their faith in him. Then the Romans will come and destroy our temple and our nation."ᶻ

⁴⁹One of the council members was Caiaphas, who was also high priest that

y11.47 miracles: See the note at 2.11.   z11.48 destroy our temple and our nation: The Jewish leaders were afraid that Jesus would lead his followers to rebel against Rome and that the Roman army would then destroy their nation.

year. He spoke up and said, "You people don't have any sense at all! ⁵⁰Don't you know it is better for one person to die for the people than for the whole nation to be destroyed?" ⁵¹Caiaphas did not say this on his own. As high priest that year, he was prophesying that Jesus would die for the nation. ⁵²Yet Jesus would not die just for the Jewish nation. He would die to bring together all of God's scattered people. ⁵³From that day on, the council started making plans to put Jesus to death.

⁵⁴Because of this plot against him, Jesus stopped going around in public. He went to the town of Ephraim, which was near the desert, and he stayed there with his disciples.

⁵⁵It was almost time for Passover. Many of the Jewish people who lived out in the country had come to Jerusalem to get themselves ready[a] for the festival. ⁵⁶They looked around for Jesus. Then when they were in the temple, they asked each other, "You don't think he will come here for Passover, do you?"

⁵⁷The chief priests and the Pharisees told the people to let them know if any of them saw Jesus. This is how they hoped to arrest him.

At Bethany
(Matthew 26.6-13; Mark 14.3-9)

12 Six days before Passover Jesus went back to Bethany, where he had raised Lazarus from death. ²A meal had been prepared for Jesus. Martha was doing the serving, and Lazarus himself was there.

³Mary took a very expensive bottle of perfume[b] and poured it on Jesus' feet. She wiped them with her hair, and the sweet smell of the perfume filled the house.

⁴A disciple named Judas Iscariot[c] was there. He was the one who was going to betray Jesus, and he asked, ⁵"Why wasn't this perfume sold for 300 silver coins and the money given to the poor?" ⁶Judas did not really care about the poor. He asked this because he carried the moneybag and sometimes would steal from it.

⁷Jesus replied, "Leave her alone! She has kept this perfume for the day of my burial. ⁸You will always have the poor with you, but you won't always have me."

---

a11.55 get themselves ready: The Jewish people had to do certain things to prepare themselves to worship God.   b12.3 very expensive bottle of perfume: The Greek text has "expensive perfume made of pure spikenard," a plant used to make perfume.   c12.4 Iscariot: See the note at 6.71.

A Plot to Kill Lazarus

[9]A lot of people came when they heard that Jesus was there. They also wanted to see Lazarus, because Jesus had raised him from death. [10]So the chief priests made plans to kill Lazarus. [11]He was the reason that many of the people were turning from them and putting their faith in Jesus.

Jesus Enters Jerusalem
(Matthew 21.1-11; Mark 11.1-11; Luke 19.28-40)

[12]The next day a large crowd was in Jerusalem for Passover. When they heard that Jesus was coming for the festival, [13]they took palm branches and went out to greet him.[d] They shouted,
  "Hooray![e]
God bless the one who comes
    in the name of the Lord!
God bless the King
    of Israel!"

[14]Jesus found a donkey and rode on it, just as the Scriptures say,
[15]"People of Jerusalem,
    don't be afraid!
Your King is now coming,
and he is riding
    on a donkey."

[16]At first, Jesus' disciples did not understand. But after he had been given his glory,[f] they remembered all this. Everything had happened exactly as the Scriptures said it would.

[17-18]A crowd had come to meet Jesus because they had seen him call Lazarus out of the tomb. They kept talking about him and this miracle.[g] [19]But the Pharisees said to each other, "There is nothing we can do! Everyone in the world is following Jesus."

---

d12.13 took palm branches and went out to greet him: This was one way the people welcomed a famous person.   e12.13 Hooray: This translates a word that can mean "please save us." But it is most often used as a shout of praise to God.   f12.16 had been given his glory: See the note at 7.39.   g12.17,18 miracle: See the note at 2.11.

Some Greeks Want to Meet Jesus

[20]Some Greeks[h] had gone to Jerusalem to worship during Passover. [21]Philip from Bethsaida in Galilee was there too. So they went to him and said, "Sir, we would like to meet Jesus." [22]Philip told Andrew. Then the two of them went to Jesus and told him.

The Son of Man Must Be Lifted Up

[23]Jesus said:

The time has come for the Son of Man to be given his glory.[i] [24]I tell you for certain that a grain of wheat that falls on the ground will never be more than one grain unless it dies. But if it dies, it will produce lots of wheat. [25]If you love your life, you will lose it. If you give it up in this world, you will be given eternal life. [26]If you serve me, you must go with me. My servants will be with me wherever I am. If you serve me, my Father will honor you.

[27]Now I am deeply troubled, and I don't know what to say. But I must not ask my Father to keep me from this time of suffering. In fact, I came into the world to suffer. [28]So Father, bring glory to yourself.

A voice from heaven then said, "I have already brought glory to myself, and I will do it again!" [29]When the crowd heard the voice, some of them thought it was thunder. Others thought an angel had spoken to Jesus.

[30]Then Jesus told the crowd, "That voice spoke to help you, not me. [31]This world's people are now being judged, and the ruler of this world[j] is already being thrown out! [32]If I am lifted up above the earth, I will make everyone want to come to me." [33]Jesus was talking about the way he would be put to death.

[34]The crowd said to Jesus, "The Scriptures teach that the Messiah will live forever. How can you say that the Son of Man must be lifted up? Who is this Son of Man?"

[35]Jesus answered, "The light will be with you for only a little longer. Walk in the light while you can. Then you won't be caught walking blindly in the dark. [36]Have faith in the light while it is with you, and you will be children of the light."

h12.20 Greeks: Perhaps Gentiles who worshiped with the Jews. See the note at 7.35.   i12.23 be given his glory: See the note at 7.39.   j12.31 world: In the Gospel of John "world" sometimes refers to the people who live in this world and to the evil forces that control their lives.

The People Refuse to Have Faith in Jesus

After Jesus had said these things, he left and went into hiding. ³⁷He had worked a lot of miracles[k] among the people, but they were still not willing to have faith in him. ³⁸This happened so that what the prophet Isaiah had said would come true,

"Lord, who has believed
our message?
And who has seen
your mighty strength?"

³⁹The people could not have faith in Jesus, because Isaiah had also said,
⁴⁰"The Lord has blinded
the eyes of the people,
and he has made
the people stubborn.
He did this so that they
could not see
or understand,
and so that they
would not turn to the Lord
and be healed."

⁴¹Isaiah said this, because he saw the glory of Jesus and spoke about him.[l] ⁴²Even then, many of the leaders put their faith in Jesus, but they did not tell anyone about it. The Pharisees had already given orders for the people not to have anything to do with anyone who had faith in Jesus. ⁴³And besides, the leaders liked praise from others more than they liked praise from God.

Jesus Came to Save the World

⁴⁴In a loud voice Jesus said:
Everyone who has faith in me also has faith in the one who sent me. ⁴⁵And everyone who has seen me has seen the one who sent me.

---

k12.37 miracles: See the note at 2.11.   l12.41 he saw the glory of Jesus and spoke about him: Or "he saw the glory of God and spoke about Jesus."

⁴⁶I am the light that has come into the world. No one who has faith in me will stay in the dark.

⁴⁷I am not the one who will judge those who refuse to obey my teachings. I came to save the people of this world, not to be their judge. ⁴⁸But everyone who rejects me and my teachings will be judged on the last day[m] by what I have said. ⁴⁹I don't speak on my own. I say only what the Father who sent me has told me to say. ⁵⁰I know that his commands will bring eternal life. This is why I tell you exactly what the Father has told me.

Jesus Washes the Feet of His Disciples

13 It was before Passover, and Jesus knew that the time had come for him to leave this world and to return to the Father. He had always loved his followers in this world, and he loved them to the very end.

²Even before the evening meal started, the devil had made Judas, the son of Simon Iscariot,[n] decide to betray Jesus.

³Jesus knew he had come from God and would go back to God. He also knew that the Father had given him complete power. ⁴So during the meal Jesus got up, removed his outer garment, and wrapped a towel around his waist. ⁵He put some water into a large bowl. Then he began washing his disciples' feet and drying them with the towel he was wearing.

⁶But when he came to Simon Peter, this disciple asked, "Lord, are you going to wash my feet?"

⁷Jesus answered, "You don't really know what I am doing, but later you will understand."

⁸"You will never wash my feet!" Peter replied.

"If I don't wash you," Jesus told him, "you don't really belong to me."

⁹Peter said, "Lord, don't wash just my feet. Wash my hands and my head."

¹⁰Jesus answered, "People who have bathed and are clean all over need to wash just their feet. And you, my disciples, are clean, except for one of you." ¹¹Jesus knew who would betray him. That is why he said, "except for one of you."

m12.48 the last day: See the note at 6.39.   n13.2 Iscariot: See the note at 6.71.

[12]After Jesus had washed his disciples' feet and had put his outer garment back on, he sat down again.[o] Then he said:

> Do you understand what I have done? [13]You call me your teacher and Lord, and you should, because that is who I am. [14]And if your Lord and teacher has washed your feet, you should do the same for each other. [15]I have set the example, and you should do for each other exactly what I have done for you. [16]I tell you for certain that servants are not greater than their master, and messengers are not greater than the one who sent them. [17]You know these things, and God will bless you, if you do them.
>
> [18]I am not talking about all of you. I know the ones I have chosen. But what the Scriptures say must come true. And they say, "The man who ate with me has turned against me!" [19]I am telling you this before it all happens. Then when it does happen, you will believe who I am.[p] [20]I tell you for certain that anyone who welcomes my messengers also welcomes me, and anyone who welcomes me welcomes the one who sent me.

Jesus Tells What Will Happen to Him

(Matthew 26.20-25; Mark 14.17-21; Luke 22.21-23)

[21]After Jesus had said these things, he was deeply troubled and told his disciples, "I tell you for certain that one of you will betray me." [22]They were confused about what he meant. And they just stared at each other.

[23]Jesus' favorite disciple was sitting next to him at the meal, [24]and Simon motioned for this disciple to find out which one Jesus meant. [25]So the disciple leaned toward Jesus and asked, "Lord, which one of us are you talking about?"

[26]Jesus answered, "I will dip this piece of bread in the sauce and give it to the one I was talking about."

Then Jesus dipped the bread and gave it to Judas, the son of Simon Iscariot.[q] [27]Right then Satan took control of Judas.

Jesus said, "Judas, go quickly and do what you have to do." [28]No one at the meal understood what Jesus meant. [29]But because Judas was in charge of

o13.12 sat down again: On special occasions the Jewish people followed the Greek and Roman custom of lying down on their left side and leaning on their left elbow, while eating with their right hand. p13.19 I am: See the note at 8.24. q13.26 Iscariot: See the note at 6.71.

the money, some of them thought that Jesus had told him to buy something they needed for the festival. Others thought that Jesus had told him to give some money to the poor. ³⁰Judas took the piece of bread and went out.

It was already night.

The New Command

³¹After Judas had gone, Jesus said:

Now the Son of Man will be given glory, and he will bring glory to God. ³²Then, after God is given glory because of him, God will bring glory to him, and God will do it very soon.

³³My children, I will be with you for only a little while longer. Then you will look for me, but you won't find me. I tell you just as I told the people, "You cannot go where I am going." ³⁴But I am giving you a new command. You must love each other, just as I have loved you. ³⁵If you love each other, everyone will know that you are my disciples.

Peter's Promise
(Matthew 26.31-35; Mark 14.27-31; Luke 22.31-34)

³⁶Simon Peter asked, "Lord, where are you going?"

Jesus answered, "You can't go with me now, but later on you will."

³⁷Peter asked, "Lord, why can't I go with you now? I would die for you!"

³⁸"Would you really die for me?" Jesus asked. "I tell you for certain before a rooster crows, you will say three times that you don't even know me."

Jesus Is the Way to the Father

14 Jesus said to his disciples, "Don't be worried! Have faith in God and have faith in me.ʳ ²There are many rooms in my Father's house. I wouldn't tell you this, unless it was true. I am going there to prepare a place for each of you. ³After I have done this, I will come back and take you with me. Then we will be together. ⁴You know the way to where I am going."

⁵Thomas said, "Lord, we don't even know where you are going! How can we know the way?"

r14.1 Have faith in God and have faith in me: Or "You have faith in God, so have faith in me."

⁶"I am the way, the truth, and the life!" Jesus answered. "Without me, no one can go to the Father. ⁷If you had really known me, you would have known the Father. But from now on, you do know him, and you have seen him."

⁸Philip said, "Lord, show us the Father. That is all we need."

⁹Jesus replied:

Philip, I have been with you for a long time. Don't you know who I am? If you have seen me, you have seen the Father. How can you ask me to show you the Father? ¹⁰Don't you believe that I am one with the Father and that the Father is one with me? What I say isn't said on my own. The Father who lives in me does these things.

¹¹Have faith in me when I say that the Father is one with me and that I am one with the Father. Or else have faith in me simply because of the things I do. ¹²I tell you for certain that if you have faith in me, you will do the same things I am doing. You will do even greater things, now that I am going back to the Father. ¹³Ask me, and I will do whatever you ask. This way the Son will bring honor to the Father. ¹⁴I will do whatever you ask me to do.

The Holy Spirit Is Promised

¹⁵Jesus said to his disciples:

If you love me, you will do as I command. ¹⁶Then I will ask the Father to send you the Holy Spirit who will help* you and always be with you. ¹⁷The Spirit will show you what is true. The people of this world cannot accept the Spirit, because they don't see or know him. But you know the Spirit, who is with you and will keep on living in you.

¹⁸I won't leave you like orphans. I will come back to you. ¹⁹In a little while the people of this world won't be able to see me, but you will see me. And because I live, you will live. ²⁰Then you will know I am one with the Father. You will know you are one with me, and I am one with you. ²¹If you love me, you will do what I have said, and my Father will love you. I will also love you and show you what I am like.

²²The other Judas, not Judas Iscariot,ᵗ then spoke up and asked, "Lord,

---

s14.16 help: The Greek word may mean "comfort," "encourage," or "defend."   t14.22 Iscariot: See the note at 6.71.

what do you mean by saying that you will show us what you are like, but you will not show the people of this world?"

²³Jesus replied:

If anyone loves me, they will obey me. Then my Father will love them, and we will come to them and live in them. ²⁴But anyone who doesn't love me, won't obey me. What they have heard me say doesn't really come from me, but from the Father who sent me.

²⁵I have told you these things while I am still with you. ²⁶But the Holy Spirit will come and help[u] you, because the Father will send the Spirit to take my place. The Spirit will teach you everything and will remind you of what I said while I was with you.

²⁷I give you peace, the kind of peace only I can give. It isn't like the peace this world can give. So don't be worried or afraid.

²⁸You have already heard me say I am going and I will also come back to you. If you really love me, you should be glad I am going back to the Father, because he is greater than I am.

²⁹I am telling you this before I leave, so when it does happen, you will have faith in me. ³⁰I cannot speak with you much longer, because the ruler of this world is coming. But he has no power over me. ³¹I obey my Father, so everyone in the world might know that I love him.

It is time for us to go now.

Jesus Is the True Vine

15 Jesus said to his disciples:

I am the true vine, and my Father is the gardener. ²He cuts away every branch of mine that doesn't produce fruit. But he trims clean every branch that does produce fruit, so that it will produce even more fruit. ³You are already clean because of what I have said to you.

⁴Stay joined to me, and I will stay joined to you. Just as a branch cannot produce fruit unless it stays joined to the vine, you cannot produce fruit unless you stay joined to me. ⁵I am the vine, and you are the branches. If you stay joined to me, and I stay joined to you, then you will produce lots of fruit. But you cannot do anything without me. ⁶If you don't stay joined to me, you will be thrown away. You will be like dry branches that are gathered up and burned in a fire.

u14.26 help: See the note at 14.16.

[7]Stay joined to me and let my teachings become part of you. Then you can pray for whatever you want, and your prayer will be answered. [8]When you become fruitful disciples of mine, my Father will be honored. [9]I have loved you, just as my Father has loved me. So remain faithful to my love for you. [10]If you obey me, I will keep loving you, just as my Father keeps loving me, because I have obeyed him.

[11]I have told you this to make you as completely happy as I am. [12]Now I tell you to love each other, as I have loved you. [13]The greatest way to show love for friends is to die for them. [14]And you are my friends, if you obey me. [15]Servants don't know what their master is doing, and so I don't speak to you as my servants. I speak to you as my friends, and I have told you everything my Father has told me.

[16]You did not choose me. I chose you and sent you out to produce fruit, the kind of fruit that will last. Then my Father will give you whatever you ask for in my name.[v] [17]So I command you to love each other.

The World's Hatred

[18]If the people of this world[w] hate you, just remember that they hated me first. [19]If you belonged to the world, its people would love you. But you don't belong to the world. I have chosen you to leave the world behind, and this is why its people hate you. [20]Remember how I told you that servants are not greater than their master. So if people mistreat me, they will mistreat you. If they do what I say, they will do what you say.

[21]People will do to you exactly what they did to me. They will do it because you belong to me, and they don't know the one who sent me. [22]If I had not come and spoken to them, they would not be guilty of sin. But now they have no excuse for their sin.

[23]Everyone who hates me also hates my Father. [24]I have done things no one else has ever done. If they had not seen me do these things, they would not be guilty. But they did see me do these things, and they still hate me and my Father too. [25]This is why the Scriptures are true when they say, "People hated me for no reason."

v15.16 in my name: Or "because you are my followers."   w15.18 world: See the note at 12.31.

²⁶I will send you the Spirit who comes from the Father and shows what is true. The Spirit will help[x] you and will tell you about me. ²⁷Then you will also tell others about me, because you have been with me from the beginning.

16 I am telling you these things, so that you will not turn away. ²You will be chased out of the synagogues. And the time will come when people will kill you and think they are doing God a favor. ³They will do these things because they don't know either the Father or me. ⁴I am saying this to you now, so that when the time comes, you will remember what I have said.

The Work of the Holy Spirit

I was with you at the first, and so I didn't tell you these things. ⁵But now I am going back to the Father who sent me, and none of you asks me where I am going. ⁶You are very sad from hearing all of this. ⁷But I tell you I am going to do what is best for you. This is why I am going away. The Holy Spirit cannot come to help[x] you until I leave. But after I am gone, I will send the Spirit to you.

⁸The Spirit will come and show the people of this world the truth about sin and God's justice and the judgment. ⁹The Spirit will show them that they are wrong about sin, because they didn't have faith in me. ¹⁰They are wrong about God's justice, because I am going to the Father, and you won't see me again. ¹¹And they are wrong about the judgment, because God has already judged the ruler of this world.

¹²I have much more to say to you, but right now it would be more than you could understand. ¹³The Spirit shows what is true and will come and guide you into the full truth. The Spirit doesn't speak on his own. He will tell you only what he has heard from me, and he will let you know what is going to happen. ¹⁴The Spirit will bring glory to me by taking my message and telling it to you. ¹⁵Everything the Father has is mine. This is why I have said that the Spirit takes my message and tells it to you.

x15.26; 16.7 help: See the note at 14.16.

Sorrow Will Turn into Joy

[16]Jesus told his disciples, "For a little while you won't see me, but after a while you will see me."

[17]They said to each other, "What does Jesus mean by saying that for a little while we won't see him, but after a while we will see him? What does he mean by saying he is going to the Father? [18]What is this 'little while' that he is talking about? We don't know what he means."

[19]Jesus knew they had some questions, so he said:

You are wondering what I meant when I said that for a little while you won't see me, but after a while you will see me. [20]I tell you for certain that you will cry and be sad, but the world will be happy. You will be sad, but later you will be happy.

[21]When a woman is about to give birth, she is in great pain. But after it is all over, she forgets the pain and is happy, because she has brought a child into the world. [22]You are now very sad. But later I will see you, and you will be so happy that no one will be able to change the way you feel. [23]When that time comes, you won't have to ask me about anything. I tell you for certain the Father will give you whatever you ask for in my name. [24]You have not asked for anything in this way before, but now you must ask in my name.[y] Then it will be given to you, so you will be completely happy.

[25]I have used examples to explain to you what I have been talking about. But the time will come when I will speak to you plainly about the Father and will no longer use examples like these. [26]You will ask the Father in my name,[z] and I won't have to ask him for you. [27]God the Father loves you because you love me, and you believe I have come from him. [28]I came from the Father into the world, but I am leaving the world and returning to the Father.

[29]The disciples said, "Now you are speaking plainly to us! You are not using examples. [30]At last we know that you understand everything, and we don't have any more questions. Now we believe you truly have come from God."

[31]Jesus replied:

Do you really believe me? [32]The time will come and is already here when all of you will be scattered. Each of you will go back home and

y16.23,24 *in my name . . . in my name:* Or "as my disciples . . . as my disciples."   z16.26 *in my name:* Or "because you are my followers."

leave me by myself. But the Father will be with me, and I won't be alone. ³³I have told you this, so that you might have peace in your hearts because of me. While you are in the world, you will have to suffer. But cheer up! I have defeated the world.ᵃ

Jesus Prays

17 After Jesus had finished speaking to his disciples, he looked up toward heaven and prayed:

Father, the time has come for you to bring glory to your Son, in order that he may bring glory to you. ²And you gave him power over all people, so he would give eternal life to everyone you give him. ³Eternal life is to know you, the only true God, and to know Jesus Christ, the one you sent. ⁴I have brought glory to you here on earth by doing everything you gave me to do. ⁵Now, Father, give me back the glory I had with you before the world was created.

⁶You have given me some followers from this world, and I have shown them what you are like. They were yours, but you gave them to me, and they have obeyed you. ⁷They know that you gave me everything I have. ⁸I told my followers what you told me, and they accepted it. They know I came from you, and they believe you are the one who sent me. ⁹I am praying for them, but not for those who belong to this world.ᵇ My followers belong to you, and I am praying for them. ¹⁰All I have is yours, and all you have is mine, and they will bring glory to me.

¹¹Holy Father, I am no longer in the world. I am coming to you, but my followers are still in the world. So keep them safe by the power of the name you have given me. Then they will be one with each other, just as you and I are one. ¹²While I was with them, I kept them safe by the power you have given me. I guarded them, and not one of them was lost, except the one who had to be lost. This happened so that what the Scriptures say would come true.

¹³I am on my way to you. But I say these things while I am still in the world, so my followers will have the same complete joy that I do. ¹⁴I have told them your message. But the people of this world hate them, because they don't belong to this world, just as I don't.

a16.33 world: See the note at 12.31.   b17.9 world: See the note at 12.31.

¹⁵Father, I don't ask you to take my followers out of the world, but keep them safe from the evil one. ¹⁶They don't belong to this world, and neither do I. ¹⁷Your word is the truth. So let this truth make them completely yours. ¹⁸I am sending them into the world, just as you sent me. ¹⁹I have given myself completely for their sake, so they may belong completely to the truth.

²⁰I am not praying just for these followers. I am also praying for everyone else who will have faith because of what my followers will say about me. ²¹I want all of them to be one with each other, just as I am one with you and you are one with me. I also want them to be one with us. Then the people of this world will believe that you sent me.

²²I have honored my followers in the same way you honored me, in order that they may be one with each other, just as we are one. ²³I am one with them, and you are one with me, so they may become completely one. Then this world's people will know that you sent me. They will know that you love my followers as much as you love me.

²⁴Father, I want everyone you have given me to be with me, wherever I am. Then they will see the glory you have given me, because you loved me before the world was created. ²⁵Good Father, the people of this world don't know you. But I know you, and my followers know that you sent me. ²⁶I told them what you are like, and I will tell them even more. Then the love you have for me will become part of them, and I will be one with them.

Jesus Is Betrayed and Arrested
(Matthew 26.47-56; Mark 14.43-50; Luke 22.47-53)

18 When Jesus had finished praying, he and his disciples crossed the Kidron Valley and went into a garden.ᶜ ²Jesus had often met there with his disciples, and Judas knew where the place was.

³⁻⁵Judas had promised to betray Jesus. So he went to the garden with some Roman soldiers and temple police, who had been sent by the chief priests and the Pharisees. They carried torches, lanterns, and weapons. Jesus already knew everything that was going to happen, but he asked, "Who are you looking for?"

---

c18.1 garden: The Greek word is usually translated "garden," but probably referred to an olive orchard.

They answered, "We are looking for Jesus from Nazareth!"

Jesus told them, "I am Jesus!"[d] [6]At once they all backed away and fell to the ground.

[7]Jesus again asked, "Who are you looking for?"

"We are looking for Jesus from Nazareth," they answered.

[8]This time Jesus replied, "I have already told you that I am Jesus. If I am the one you are looking for, let these others go. [9]Then everything will happen, just as I said, 'I did not lose anyone you gave me.' "

[10]Simon Peter had brought along a sword. He pulled it out and struck at Malchus, the servant of the high priest, cutting off his right ear. [11]Jesus told Peter, "Put your sword away. I must drink from the cup[e] that the Father has given me."

Jesus Is Brought to Annas
(Matthew 26.57, 58; Mark 14.53, 54; Luke 22.54)

[12]The Roman officer and his men, together with the temple police, arrested Jesus and tied him up. [13]They took him first to Annas, who was the father-in-law of Caiaphas, the high priest that year. [14]This was the same Caiaphas who had told the Jewish leaders, "It is better if one person dies for the people."

Peter Says He Doesn't Know Jesus
(Matthew 26.69, 70; Mark 14.66-68; Luke 22.55-57)

[15]Simon Peter and another disciple followed Jesus. That disciple knew the high priest, and he followed Jesus into the courtyard of the high priest's house. [16]Peter stayed outside near the gate. But the other disciple came back out and spoke to the girl at the gate. She let Peter go in, [17]but asked him, "Aren't you one of that man's followers?"

"No, I am not!" Peter answered.

[18]It was cold, and the servants and temple police had made a charcoal fire. They were warming themselves around it, when Peter went over and stood near the fire to warm himself.

---

d18.3-5 *I am Jesus:* The Greek text has "I am" (see the note at 8.24).   e18.11 *drink from the cup:* In the Scriptures a cup is sometimes used as a symbol of suffering. To "drink from the cup" is to suffer.

Jesus Is Questioned by the High Priest
(Matthew 26.59-66; Mark 14.55-64; Luke 22.66-71)

¹⁹The high priest questioned Jesus about his followers and his teaching. ²⁰But Jesus told him, "I have spoken freely in front of everyone. And I have always taught in our synagogues and in the temple, where all of our people come together. I have not said anything in secret. ²¹Why are you questioning me? Why don't you ask the people who heard me? They know what I have said."

²²As soon as Jesus said this, one of the temple police hit him and said, "That's no way to talk to the high priest!"

²³Jesus answered, "If I have done something wrong, say so. But if not, why did you hit me?" ²⁴Jesus was still tied up, and Annas sent him to Caiaphas the high priest.

Peter Again Denies that He Knows Jesus
(Matthew 26.71-75; Mark 14.69-72; Luke 22.58-62)

²⁵While Simon Peter was standing there warming himself, someone asked him, "Aren't you one of Jesus' followers?"

Again Peter denied it and said, "No, I am not!"

²⁶One of the high priest's servants was there. He was a relative of the servant whose ear Peter had cut off, and he asked, "Didn't I see you in the garden with that man?"

²⁷Once more Peter denied it, and right then a rooster crowed.

Jesus Is Tried by Pilate
(Matthew 27.1, 2, 11-14; Mark 15.1-5; Luke 23.1-5)

²⁸It was early in the morning when Jesus was taken from Caiaphas to the building where the Roman governor stayed. But the crowd waited outside. Any of them who had gone inside would have become unclean and would not be allowed to eat the Passover meal.ᶠ

²⁹Pilate came out and asked, "What charges are you bringing against this man?"

ᶠ18.28 *would have become unclean and would not be allowed to eat the Passover meal:* Jewish people who came in close contact with foreigners right before Passover were not allowed to eat the Passover meal.

[30]They answered, "He is a criminal! That's why we brought him to you."

[31]Pilate told them, "Take him and judge him by your own laws."

The crowd replied, "We are not allowed to put anyone to death." [32]And so what Jesus said about his death[g] would soon come true.

[33]Pilate then went back inside. He called Jesus over and asked, "Are you the king of the Jews?"

[34]Jesus answered, "Are you asking this on your own or did someone tell you about me?"

[35]"You know I'm not a Jew!" Pilate said. "Your own people and the chief priests brought you to me. What have you done?"

[36]Jesus answered, "My kingdom doesn't belong to this world. If it did, my followers would have fought to keep me from being handed over to our leaders. No, my kingdom doesn't belong to this world."

[37]"So you are a king," Pilate replied.

"You are saying that I am a king," Jesus told him. "I was born into this world to tell about the truth. And everyone who belongs to the truth knows my voice."

[38]Pilate asked Jesus, "What is truth?"

Jesus Is Sentenced to Death
(Matthew 27.15-31; Mark 15.6-20; Luke 23.13-25)

Pilate went back out and said, "I don't find this man guilty of anything! [39]And since I usually set a prisoner free for you at Passover, would you like for me to set free the king of the Jews?"

[40]They shouted, "No, not him! We want Barabbas." Now Barabbas was a terrorist.[h]

19 Pilate gave orders for Jesus to be beaten with a whip. [2]The soldiers made a crown out of thorn branches and put it on Jesus. Then they put a purple robe on him. [3]They came up to him and said, "Hey, you king of the Jews!" They also hit him with their fists.

[4]Once again Pilate went out. This time he said, "I will have Jesus brought out to you again. Then you can see for yourselves that I have not found him guilty."

g18.32 *about his death:* Jesus had said that he would die by being "lifted up," which meant that he would die on a cross. The Romans killed criminals by nailing them on a cross, but they did not let the Jews kill anyone in this way.   h18.40 *terrorist:* Someone who stirred up trouble against the Romans in the hope of gaining freedom for the Jewish people.

⁵Jesus came out, wearing the crown of thorns and the purple robe. Pilate said, "Here is the man!"ⁱ

⁶When the chief priests and the temple police saw him, they yelled, "Nail him to a cross! Nail him to a cross!"

Pilate told them, "You take him and nail him to a cross! I don't find him guilty of anything."

⁷The crowd replied, "He claimed to be the Son of God! Our law says that he must be put to death."

⁸When Pilate heard this, he was terrified. ⁹He went back inside and asked Jesus, "Where are you from?" But Jesus did not answer.

¹⁰"Why won't you answer my question?" Pilate asked. "Don't you know I have the power to let you go free or to nail you to a cross?"

¹¹Jesus replied, "If God had not given you the power, you couldn't do anything at all to me. But the one who handed me over to you did something even worse."

¹²Then Pilate wanted to set Jesus free. But the crowd again yelled, "If you set this man free, you are no friend of the Emperor! Anyone who claims to be a king is an enemy of the Emperor."

¹³When Pilate heard this, he brought Jesus out. Then he sat down on the judge's bench at the place known as "The Stone Pavement." In Aramaic this pavement is called "Gabbatha." ¹⁴It was about noon on the day before Passover, and Pilate said to the crowd, "Look at your king!"

¹⁵"Kill him! Kill him!" they yelled. "Nail him to a cross!"

"So you want me to nail your king to a cross?" Pilate asked.

The chief priests replied, "The Emperor is our king!" ¹⁶Then Pilate handed Jesus over to be nailed to a cross.

Jesus Is Nailed to a Cross
(Matthew 27.32-44; Mark 15.21-32; Luke 23.26-43)

Jesus was taken away, ¹⁷and he carried his cross to a place known as "The Skull."ʲ In Aramaic this place is called "Golgotha." ¹⁸There Jesus was nailed to the cross, and on each side of him a man was also nailed to a cross.

¹⁹Pilate ordered the charge against Jesus to be written on a board and put

i19.5 "Here is the man!": Or "Look at the man!"   j19.17 The Skull: The place was probably given this name because it was near a large rock in the shape of a human skull.

above the cross. It read, "Jesus of Nazareth, King of the Jews." [20]The words were written in Hebrew, Latin, and Greek.

The place where Jesus was taken wasn't far from the city, and many of the people read the charge against him. [21]So the chief priests went to Pilate and said, "Why did you write that he is King of the Jews? You should have written, 'He claimed to be King of the Jews.'"

[22]But Pilate told them, "What is written will not be changed!"

[23]After the soldiers had nailed Jesus to the cross, they divided up his clothes into four parts, one for each of them. But his outer garment was made from a single piece of cloth, and it did not have any seams. [24]The soldiers said to each other, "Let's not rip it apart. We will gamble to see who gets it." This happened so the Scriptures would come true, which say,

"They divided up my clothes

and gambled

for my garments."

The soldiers then did what they had decided.

[25]Jesus' mother stood beside his cross with her sister and Mary the wife of Clopas. Mary Magdalene was standing there too.[k] [26]When Jesus saw his mother and his favorite disciple with her, he said to his mother, "This man is now your son." [27]Then he said to the disciple, "She is now your mother." From then on, that disciple took her into his own home.

The Death of Jesus
(Matthew 27.45-56; Mark 15.33-41; Luke 23.44-49)

[28]Jesus knew that he had now finished his work. And in order to make the Scriptures come true, he said, "I am thirsty!" [29]A jar of cheap wine was there. Someone then soaked a sponge with the wine and held it up to Jesus' mouth on the stem of a hyssop plant. [30]After Jesus drank the wine, he said, "Everything is done!" He bowed his head and died.

k19.25 Jesus' mother stood beside his cross with her sister and Mary the wife of Clopas. Mary Magdalene was standing there too: The Greek text may also be understood to include only three women ("Jesus' mother stood beside the cross with her sister, Mary the mother of Clopas. Mary Magdalene was standing there too.") or merely two women ("Jesus' mother was standing there with her sister Mary of Clopas, that is, Mary Magdalene."). "Of Clopas" may mean "daughter of" or "mother of."

A Spear Is Stuck in Jesus' Side

[31]The next day would be both a Sabbath and the Passover. It was a special day for the Jewish people,[l] and they did not want the bodies to stay on the crosses during this day. So they asked Pilate to break the men's legs[m] and take their bodies down. [32]The soldiers first broke the legs of the other two men who were nailed there. [33]But when they came to Jesus, they saw he was already dead, and they did not break his legs.

[34]One of the soldiers stuck his spear into Jesus' side, and blood and water came out. [35]We know this is true, because it was told by someone who saw it happen. Now you can have faith too. [36]All this happened so that the Scriptures would come true, which say, "No bone of his body will be broken" [37]and "They will see the one in whose side they stuck a spear."

Jesus Is Buried
(Matthew 27.57-61; Mark 15.42-47; Luke 23.50-56)

[38]Joseph from Arimathea was one of Jesus' disciples. He had kept it secret though, because he was afraid of the Jewish leaders. But now he asked Pilate to let him have Jesus' body. Pilate gave him permission, and Joseph took it down from the cross.

[39]Nicodemus also came with about 75 pounds of spices made from myrrh and aloes. This was the same Nicodemus who had visited Jesus one night.[n] [40]The two men wrapped the body in a linen cloth, together with the spices, which was how the Jewish people buried their dead. [41]In the place where Jesus had been nailed to a cross, there was a garden with a tomb that had never been used. [42]The tomb was nearby, and since it was the time to prepare for the Sabbath, they were in a hurry to put Jesus' body there.

---

l19.31 *a special day for the Jewish people:* Passover could be any day of the week. But according to the Gospel of John, Passover was on a Sabbath in the year that Jesus was nailed to a cross. m19.31 *break the men's legs:* This was the way that the Romans sometimes speeded up the death of a person who had been nailed to a cross. n19.39 *Nicodemus who had visited Jesus one night:* See 3.1-21.

Jesus Is Alive
(Matthew 28.1-10; Mark 16.1-8; Luke 24.1-12)

20 On Sunday morning while it was still dark, Mary Magdalene went to the tomb and saw that the stone had been rolled away from the entrance. ²She ran to Simon Peter and to Jesus' favorite disciple and said, "They have taken the Lord from the tomb! We don't know where they have put him."

³Peter and the other disciple started for the tomb. ⁴They ran side by side, until the other disciple ran faster than Peter and got there first. ⁵He bent over and saw the strips of linen cloth lying inside the tomb, but he did not go in.

⁶When Simon Peter got there, he went into the tomb and saw the strips of cloth. ⁷He also saw the piece of cloth that had been used to cover Jesus' face. It was rolled up and in a place by itself. ⁸The disciple who got there first then went into the tomb, and when he saw it, he believed. ⁹At that time Peter and the other disciple did not know that the Scriptures said Jesus would rise to life. ¹⁰So the two of them went back to the other disciples.

Jesus Appears to Mary Magdalene
(Mark 16.9-11)

¹¹Mary Magdalene stood crying outside the tomb. She was still weeping, when she stooped down ¹²and saw two angels inside. They were dressed in white and were sitting where Jesus' body had been. One was at the head and the other was at the foot. ¹³The angels asked Mary, "Why are you crying?"

She answered, "They have taken away my Lord's body! I don't know where they have put him."

¹⁴As soon as Mary said this, she turned around and saw Jesus standing there. But she did not know who he was. ¹⁵Jesus asked her, "Why are you crying? Who are you looking for?"

She thought he was the gardener and said, "Sir, if you have taken his body away, please tell me, so I can go and get him."

¹⁶Then Jesus said to her, "Mary!"

She turned and said to him, "Rabboni." The Aramaic word "Rabboni" means "Teacher."

¹⁷Jesus told her, "Don't hold on to me! I have not yet gone to the Father. But tell my disciples I am going to the one who is my Father and my God, as well as your Father and your God." ¹⁸Mary Magdalene then went and told the disciples she had seen the Lord. She also told them what he had said to her.

Jesus Appears to His Disciples
(Matthew 28.16-20; Mark 16.14-18; Luke 24.36-49)

¹⁹The disciples were afraid of the Jewish leaders, and on the evening of that same Sunday they locked themselves in a room. Suddenly, Jesus appeared in the middle of the group. He greeted them ²⁰and showed them his hands and his side. When the disciples saw the Lord, they became very happy.

²¹After Jesus had greeted them again, he said, "I am sending you, just as the Father has sent me." ²²Then he breathed on them and said, "Receive the Holy Spirit. ²³If you forgive anyone's sins, they will be forgiven. But if you don't forgive their sins, they will not be forgiven."

Jesus and Thomas

²⁴Although Thomas the Twin was one of the twelve disciples, he wasn't with the others when Jesus appeared to them. ²⁵So they told him, "We have seen the Lord!"

But Thomas said, "First, I must see the nail scars in his hands and touch them with my finger. I must put my hand where the spear went into his side. I won't believe unless I do this!"

²⁶A week later the disciples were together again. This time, Thomas was with them. Jesus came in while the doors were still locked and stood in the middle of the group. He greeted his disciples ²⁷and said to Thomas, "Put your finger here and look at my hands! Put your hand into my side. Stop doubting and have faith!"

²⁸Thomas replied, "You are my Lord and my God!"

²⁹Jesus said, "Thomas, do you have faith because you have seen me? The people who have faith in me without seeing me are the ones who are really blessed!"

Why John Wrote His Book

³⁰Jesus worked many other miracles° for his disciples, and not all of them are written in this book. ³¹But these are written so that you will put your faith in Jesus as the Messiah and the Son of God. If you have faith inᵖ him, you will have true life.

o20.30 miracles: See the note at 2.11.   p20.31 put your faith in . . . have faith in: Some manuscripts have "keep on having faith in . . . keep on having faith in."

Jesus Appears to Seven Disciples

21 Jesus later appeared to his disciples along the shore of Lake Tiberias. [2]Simon Peter, Thomas the Twin, Nathanael from Cana in Galilee, and the brothers James and John,[q] were there, together with two other disciples. [3]Simon Peter said, "I'm going fishing!"

The others said, "We will go with you." They went out in their boat. But they didn't catch a thing that night.

[4]Early the next morning Jesus stood on the shore, but the disciples did not realize who he was. [5]Jesus shouted, "Friends, have you caught anything?"

"No!" they answered.

[6]So he told them, "Let your net down on the right side of your boat, and you will catch some fish."

They did, and the net was so full of fish that they could not drag it up into the boat.

[7]Jesus' favorite disciple told Peter, "It's the Lord!" When Simon heard it was the Lord, he put on the clothes he had taken off while he was working. Then he jumped into the water. [8]The boat was only about 100 yards from shore. So the other disciples stayed in the boat and dragged in the net full of fish.

[9]When the disciples got out of the boat, they saw some bread and a charcoal fire with fish on it. [10]Jesus told his disciples, "Bring some of the fish you just caught." [11]Simon Peter got back into the boat and dragged the net to shore. In it were 153 large fish, but still the net did not rip.

[12]Jesus said, "Come and eat!" But none of the disciples dared ask who he was. They knew he was the Lord. [13]Jesus took the bread in his hands and gave some of it to his disciples. He did the same with the fish. [14]This was the third time Jesus appeared to his disciples after he was raised from death.

Jesus and Peter

[15]When Jesus and his disciples had finished eating, he asked, "Simon son of John, do you love me more than the others do?"[r]

Simon Peter answered, "Yes, Lord, you know I do!"

"Then feed my lambs," Jesus said.

---

q21.2 the brothers James and John: Greek "the two sons of Zebedee." r21.15 more than the others do?: Or "more than you love these things?"

¹⁶Jesus asked a second time, "Simon son of John, do you love me?"
Peter answered, "Yes, Lord, you know I love you!"

"Then take care of my sheep," Jesus told him.

¹⁷Jesus asked a third time, "Simon son of John, do you love me?"

Peter was hurt because Jesus had asked him three times if he loved him.
So he told Jesus, "Lord, you know everything. You know I love you."

Jesus replied, "Feed my sheep. ¹⁸I tell you for certain that when you were
a young man, you dressed yourself and went wherever you wanted to go. But
when you are old, you will hold out your hands. Then others will wrap your
belt around you and lead you where you don't want to go."

¹⁹Jesus said this to tell how Peter would die and bring honor to God. Then
he said to Peter, "Follow me!"

Jesus and His Favorite Disciple

²⁰Peter turned and saw Jesus' favorite disciple following them. He was the same
one who had sat next to Jesus at the meal and had asked, "Lord, who is going
to betray you?" ²¹When Peter saw this disciple, he asked Jesus, "Lord, what
about him?"

²²Jesus answered, "What is it to you, if I want him to live until I return?
You must follow me." ²³So the rumor spread among the other disciples that
this disciple would not die. But Jesus did not say he would not die. He simply said, "What is it to you, if I want him to live until I return?"

²⁴This disciple is the one who told all of this. He wrote it, and we know
he is telling the truth.

²⁵Jesus did many other things. If they were all written in books, I don't
suppose there would be room enough in the whole world for all the books.

Note on Language

anguages are spoken before they are written. And far more communication is done through the spoken word than through the written word. In fact, more people *hear* the Bible read than read it for themselves. Traditional translations of the Bible count on the *reader's* ability to understand a *written* text. But the *Contemporary English Version* differs from most other English Bibles in that it takes into consideration the needs of the *hearer*, as well as those of the reader, who may not be familiar with traditional biblical language.

The *Contemporary English Version* has been described as a "user-friendly" and a "mission-driven" translation that can be *read aloud* without stumbling, *heard* without misunderstanding, and *listened to* with enjoyment and appreciation, because the language is contemporary and the style is lucid and lyrical.

A Word About the
Contemporary English Version

*T*ranslation *it is that opens the window, to let in the light;
*that breaks the shell, that we may eat the kernel; that puts
aside the curtain, that we may look into the most holy place; that re-
moves the cover of the well, that we may come by the water.* ("The
Translators to the Reader," King James Version, 1611).

The most important document in the history of the English language is the *King James Version* of the Bible. To measure its spiritual impact on the English speaking world would be more
impossible than counting the grains of sand along the ocean
shores. Historically, many Bible translators have attempted in
some measure to *retain the form* of the *King James Version*. But the
translators of the *Contemporary English Version* of the Bible have
diligently sought to *capture the spirit* of the *King James Version* by
following certain principles set forth by its translators in the document "The Translators to the Reader," which was printed in the
earliest editions.

This is the Word of God, which we translate

Accuracy, beauty, clarity, and dignity—all of these can and must be achieved in the translation of the Bible. After all, as the translators of the *King James Version* stated, "This is the Word of God, which we translate."

Every attempt has been made to produce a text that is faithful to the *meaning* of the original. In order to assure the *accuracy* of the *Contemporary English Version,* the Old Testament was translated directly from the Hebrew and Aramaic texts published by the United Bible Societies (*Biblia Hebraica Stuttgartensia,* fourth edition corrected). And the New Testament was translated directly from the Greek text published by the United Bible Societies (third edition corrected and compared with the fourth revised edition).

The drafts in their earliest stages were sent for review and comment to a number of biblical scholars, theologians, and educators representing a wide variety of church traditions. In addition, drafts were sent for review and comment to all English-speaking Bible Societies and to more than forty United Bible Societies translation consultants around the world. Final approval of the text was given by the American Bible Society Board of Trustees on the recommendation of its Translations Subcommittee.

We desire that the Scripture . . . may be understood

That the Scripture may be understood even by ordinary people was a primary goal of the translators of the *King James Ver-*

sion. And they raised the question, "What can be more available thereto than to deliver God's book unto God's people in a tongue which they understand?" Martin Luther also did his translation for the common people, and he established the following guidelines:

> We do not have to inquire of the literal Latin, how we are to speak German . . . Rather we must inquire about this of the mother in the home, the children on the street, the common man in the marketplace. *We must be guided by their language, the way they speak, and do our translating accordingly.*

Today more people hear the Bible read aloud than read it for themselves! And statistics released by the National Center for Education indicate that "almost half of U.S. adults have very limited reading and writing skills." If this is the case, a contemporary translation must be a text that an inexperienced reader can *read aloud* without stumbling, that someone unfamiliar with traditional biblical terminology can *hear without misunderstanding*, and that everyone can *listen to with enjoyment* because the style is lucid and lyrical.

In order to attain these goals of clarity, beauty, and dignity, the translators of the *Contemporary English Version* carefully studied every word, phrase, clause, and paragraph of the original. Then, with equal care, they struggled to discover the best way to translate the text, so that it would be suitable both for *private* and *public* reading, and for *memorizing.* The result is an English text that is enjoyable and easily understood by the vast majority of English speakers, regardless of their religious or educational background.

In the *hearing* of a translation, even the inclusion of a simple word like "and" can make a significant difference. Matthew 2.9 of the *Contemporary English Version* reads as follows: "The wise men listened to what the king said and then left. And the star they had seen in the east went on ahead of them until it stopped over the place where the child was."

"And" at the beginning of the second sentence assists both the person who reads the text aloud and those who must depend upon hearing it read. Like all other punctuation marks, the period after "left" is silent, and so the text without "And" could possibly be *heard* as, "The wise men listened to what the king said and then left the star they had seen in the east." However, as the text now stands, the oral reader must pause briefly for a breath before "And," which will signal the hearer that a new sentence has begun.

As another example, try reading the following two sentences aloud: "You yourselves admit, then, that you agree with what your ancestors did" and "for it was better with me then than now." Both suffer from potential tongue twisters ("admit, then, that" and "then than"). But the first is doubly difficult because it consists of a lengthy series of unaccented syllables that do not allow the reader to take a breath. In the *Contemporary English Version* every attempt has been made to avoid these and other kinds of constructions that could possibly prove problematic for oral reading.

According to the rules of English grammar, the pronoun *he*

must refer back to *God* in the following sentence: "The other, however, rebuked him saying, "Don't you fear *God*? You received the same sentence *he* did.' " But the reference is actually to Jesus, who is mentioned earlier in the passage. Traditional translations assume that the reader can study the printed text and finally figure out the meaning, but the *Contemporary English Version* is concerned equally with the reader and the hearer. And in many situations, the *hearer* may have only *one* chance to understand what is read aloud.

In poetry, the *appearance of the text on the page* is important, since in oral reading there is a tendency to stress the last word on a line and to pause momentarily before going to the next line, especially if the second line is indented. Compare the three following examples, where the lines of the same text have been broken improperly (left column) and properly (right column):

He brought me out into a broad place.	He brought me out into a broad place.
With the loyal you show yourself loyal.	With the loyal you show yourself loyal.
The Lord my God lights up my darkness.	the Lord my God lights up my darkness.

No fault is to be found with the translation itself. Yet there is a significant difference in the *appearance* of the text on the page, because the lines on the right have been *measured*, in order to prevent unfortunate runovers. In this form, the text not only looks better on the page, but it is easier to read and memorize, and it avoids such disastrous combination as "He brought me out into a broad" or "With the loyal you show yourself" or "The Lord my God lights up." Moreover, both formats require exactly the same amount of lines.

The first translation in the history of the English Bible to develop a text with measured poetry lines is the *Contemporary English Version,* in which the translators have consciously created a text that will not suffer from unfortunate line breaks when published in double columns. *Accuracy* is the main concern of translators, but it must be realized that in the translation of biblical poetry, what the reader *sees* is what will be *said,* and what others will *hear.* This means that lines improperly broken can easily lead to a misunderstanding of the text, especially for those who must depend upon *hearing* the Scriptures read.

Hebrew poetry has its own systems of sound, rhyme, and rhythm, as well as a *form* that involves much repetition. It is impossible in English to retain the sounds, rhymes, and rhythms of the Hebrew text, but traditional translations have attempted to reproduce the frequent repetition, in which a second line will repeat or expand, either negatively or positively, the thoughts of the previous line. However, this repetition is often ineffective for those English speakers who are unaccustomed to the poetic style of the biblical authors. And so, the translators of the *Contemporary English Version* have followed the example of Martin Luther in the translation of poetry:

Whoever would speak German *must not use Hebrew style.* Rather he must see to it—once he understands the Hebrew author—that he concentrates on the *sense* of the text, asking himself, "Pray tell, what do the Germans say in such a situation?" Once he has the German words to serve his purpose, let him drop the Hebrew words and *express the meaning freely* in the best German he knows.

The qualities that many critics value most in modern poetry are effortless *economy* and *exactness* of language. It is hoped that readers will discover similar features in the poetry of the *Contemporary English Version*, which strives for beauty and dignity, as much as for accuracy and clarity. In this translation, the poetry often requires fewer lines than do traditional translations, but the *integrity, intent,* and *impact* of the original are consistently maintained. Note, for example, the rendering of Job 38.14,15:

> Early dawn outlines the hills
> like stitches on clothing
>   or sketches on clay.
> But its light is too much
> for those who are evil,
>   and their power is broken.

Whenever the contents of two or more verses have been joined together and rearranged in the poetic sections of the *Contemporary English Version*, this is signaled by an asterisk (*) before the first verse number in the series.

In everyday speech, "gender generic" or "inclusive" language is used, because it sounds most natural to people today. This means that where the biblical languages require masculine nouns or pronouns when both men and women are intended, this intention must be reflected in translation, though the English *form* may be very different from that of the original. The Greek text of Matthew 16.24 is literally, "If anyone wants to follow me, *he* must deny *himself* and take up *his cross* and follow me." The *Contemporary English Version* shifts to a form which is still accurate, and at the same time more effective in English: "If any of *you* want to be my followers, *you* must forget about *yourself. You* must take up *your* cross and follow me."

Since its publication, diverse groups of people around the world have read and enjoyed the *Contemporary English Version*. To better meet the needs of these global audiences, the *Contemporary English Version* has undergone a revision that addressed issues raised in reviews and feedback from readers. This revision has led to an edition that replaces many of the American idioms used in the first edition with others that communicate more meaningfully to all the English-speaking audiences around the world.

Variety of translations is profitable

The translators of the *King James Version* said, ". . . [a] variety of translations is profitable for the finding out of the sense of the Scriptures" and "we affirm and avow that the very meanest translation of the Bible in English, set forth by men of our profession . . . contains the Word of God, nay is the Word of God." They even stated. "No cause therefore why the Word translated should be denied to be the Word, or forbidden to be current, notwithstanding that some imperfections and blemishes may be noted in the setting forth of it."

Each English translation is, in its own right, the Word of God, yet each translation serves to meet the needs of a different audience. In this regard, the *Contemporary English Version* should be considered a *companion*—the *mission* and—of traditional translations, because it takes seriously the words of the apostle Paul that "faith comes by hearing."

It has pleased God in his divine providence

Translating the Bible may be compared to living the life of faith. God has not given us all the answers for our pilgrim journey, but we have been provided with all that we need to know in order to be saved. As the translators of the *King James Version* observed:

It has pleased God in His divine providence here and there to scatter those words and sentences of that difficulty and doubtfulness, not in doctrinal points that concern salvation (for in such it has been vouched that the Scriptures are plain), but in matters of less moment, that fearfulness would better beseem us than confidence . . .

For as it is a fault of incredulity, to doubt of those things that are evident; so to determine of such things that the Spirit of God has left (even in the mind of the judicious) questionable, can be no less than presumption.

Bible translators do not have the privilege and luxury of working from the original manuscripts of either the Old or New Testament. Indeed, there are numerous difficult passages where decisions must be made concerning what word or words actually belong in the text, and what these words may, in fact, mean. At such places, the best a translator can do is to give what seems to be one possible meaning for the difficult text and to indicate this by a note, which was also what the King James translators did: "so diversity of signification and sense in the margin, where the text is not clear, must needs be good; yea, is necessary, as we are persuaded." Fortunately, these "words and sentences of that difficulty and doubtfulness" do not in any way leave unclear the central message of the Bible or any of its major doctrines.

Editorial specialists, translators, clergy, and lay readers provided invaluable feedback and suggestions on the first edition of the *Contemporary English Version.* The input over the years since the first edition appeared has prompted the translators to revisit a small number of places where rewording was thought necessary to emend matters that might cause confusion or were deemed inaccuracies. This revised edition also addressed matters of stylistic consistency, smoother language for reading and hearing, and words or phrases that were perceived as dated or less used in general readership.

Having and using as great helps as were needful
The translators of the *Contemporary English Version* have not created new or novel interpretations of the text. Rather, it was their

goal to express mainstream interpretations of the text in current, everyday English. To do so required *listening* carefully to each word of the biblical text, to the way in which English is spoken today, to the remarks of their reviewers, and especially to the Spirit of God. Once again the comments of the translators of the *King James Version* are appropriate:

Neither did we think much to consult the translators or commentators . . . but neither did we disdain to revise that which we had done, and to bring to the anvil that which we had hammered; but having and using as great helps as were needful, and fearing no reproach for slowness, nor coveting praise for expedition, we have at the length, through the good hand of the Lord upon us, brought forth the work to that pass that you see.

The translators of the Contemporary English Version are indebted to all translators and biblical scholars who have gone before them and have mad it possible to understand something of the languages, cultures, and history of biblical times. And, together with the apostle Paul, they confess: *We don't have the right to claim that we have done anything on our own. God gives us what it takes to do all that we do.* (2 Corinthians 3.5)

Offer praise to God our Savior because of our Lord Jesus Christ! (Jude 24,25)

About *Phyllis Tickle*

Phyllis Tickle, founding editor of the religion department at *Publishers Weekly,* is one of the most highly respected authorities and popular speakers on religion in America today. She is the author of more than two dozen books, including the recently published *The Words of Jesus: A Gospel of the Sayings of Our Lord.* A lector and lay Eucharistic minister in the Episcopal Church, Tickle is a senior fellow of the Cathedral College of Washington National Cathedral. For more information, go to www.phyllistickle.com and www.allthewordsofjesus.com.

AMERICAN BIBLE SOCIETY
Sharing God's Word with the World

For more information about the American Bible Society, please go to www.americanbible.org.

FIND YOURSELF IN TARCHER
CORNERSTONE EDITIONS . . .

*a powerful new line of keepsake trade paperbacks that highlight the
foundational works of ancient and modern spiritual literature.*

Tao Te Ching
The New Translation from *Tao Te Ching: The Definitive Edition*
Lao Tzu, translated by Jonathan Star

*"It would be hard to find a fresh approach to a
text that ranks only behind the Bible as the most
widely translated book in the world, but Star
achieves that goal."*

—NAPRA ReVIEW

ISBN 978-1-58542-618-8

The Essential Marcus Aurelius
Newly translated and introduced by Jacob Needleman and John P. Piazza

*A stunningly relevant and reliable translation of
the thoughts and aphorisms of the Stoic philosopher
and Roman emperor Marcus Aurelius.*

ISBN 978-1-58542-617-1

Accept This Gift
Selections from *A Course in Miracles*
Edited by Frances Vaughan, Ph.D., and Roger Walsh, M.D., Ph.D.
Foreword by Marianne Williamson

"An invaluable collection from one of the great sources of the perennial wisdom—a gold mine of psychological and spiritual insights."
—KEN WILBER

ISBN 978-1-58542-619-5

The Kybalion
Three Initiates

Who wrote this mysterious guide to the principles of esoteric psychology and worldly success? History has kept readers guessing. . . . Experience for yourself the intriguing ideas of an underground classic.

ISBN 978-1-58542-643-0

The Spiritual Emerson
Ralph Waldo Emerson, introduction by Jacob Needleman

This concise volume collects the core writings that have made Ralph Waldo Emerson a key source of insight for spiritual seekers of every faith—with an introduction by the bestselling philosopher Jacob Needleman.

ISBN 978-1-58542-642-3

The Four Gospels
The Contemporary English Version
Foreword by Phyllis Tickle

Discover and understand the beauty and richness of the Gospels of Matthew, Mark, Luke, and John as never before. Here are the life and teachings of Jesus, as found in the four Gospels of the New Testament—now available in this important new collection from the Contemporary English Version translation with a foreword by bestselling author Phyllis Tickle.

ISBN 978-1-58542-677-5

The Hermetica: The Lost Wisdom of the Pharaohs
Timothy Freke and Peter Gandy

The singularly accessible collection of late-antique esoteric writings historically attributed to the legendary Hermes Trismegistus, venerated as a great and mythical sage in the Greco-Egyptian world and rediscovered during the Renaissance.

November 2008   ISBN 978-1-58542-692-8

Rumi: In the Arms of the Beloved
Translations by Jonathan Star

A remarkable new sounding of the poetry of Rumi and "an experience of the Divine that you will treasure for a lifetime."

—JOAN BORYSENKO, PH.D.

December 2008   ISBN 978-1-58542-693-5